THE FOUNDATIONS OF ECONOMICS

WALTER EUCKEN

THE FOUNDATIONS OF ECONOMICS

History and Theory in the Analysis of Economic Reality

Translated by
T. W. HUTCHISON

Springer-Verlag
Berlin Heidelberg New York London Paris Tokyo
Hong Kong Barcelona Budapest

Prof. Dr. Walter Eucken

Reprint of the lst English edition published 1950 by William Hodge and Company Limited, London. With kind permission of T & T Clark LTD Publishers, Edinburgh.

ISBN-13:978-3-642-77320-4 e-ISBN-13:978-3-642-77318-1
DOI: 10.1007/978-3-642-77318-1

2142/7130-543210 – Printed on acid-free paper

PREFACE FOR THE REPRINT EDITION

I CANNOT ESTIMATE what kind of impact Walter Eucken's *Grundlagen der Nationalökonomie* made on German academic economists in the decade following its original publication in 1940. Whatever this impact was, however, it must have begun to fade away somewhat in the ensuing decade of the fifties. For Eucken's work, though fiercely critical of some of the leading figures in the German Historical School, was steeped in the traditional ideas, interests, and aims of German political economy, including its historical ideas and interests, which were, to a large extent, eliminated and replaced in the fifties - (under the leadership of Erich Schneider and others) - by the Anglo-American 'Neoclassical Synthesis'. In the United States especially, then taking over a leading role, more extreme abstraction combined with the more and more extensive use of mathematics, became, from about 1950 onwards, a prominent, *avant-garde* feature of the subject. (In Eucken's *Grundlagen,* as the reader may easily confirm, there is hardly a single mathematical formula or geometrical diagram.)

Insofar, however, as in the concluding chapters Eucken turns to a study of the different types of economic order or economic system, he was preparing the way for his treatment of the basic principles of economic policy. In this respect, certainly, the historical importance of Eucken's *Grundlagen* is unquestionable. For he was probably the most influential academic economist in laying the intellectual foundations for Germany's Social Market Economy - (and so it might perhaps be claimed, for Germany's dominant economic position in Europe today).

In Britain and the United States at that time, Eucken's ideas were very little known and quite out of fashion; and the English translation of the *Grundlagen* - (undertaken by this writer on the suggestion of Friedrich Hayek, and published in 1950) - aroused very little interest. In method, theory, and policy, Eucken's ideas could hardly have been more remote from the then prevailing combination of Keynesian doctrines, with the increasingly abstract, mathematical analysis then gaining markedly in prestige.

Moreover, some of the main Keynesian policies were apparently enjoying considerable, not undeserved, practical success.

A rather piquant reaction to Eucken's ideas, particularly to those concerned with policy, may be found in a review of the English translation of the *Grundlagen* which appeared in the *Times Literary Supplement.* Though hardly an important publication for specialists in economics, the 'T.L.S.' may be regarded as representative of British *bien pensant* intelligentsia. Eucken was accused by the Oxford reviewer of responsibility for mass unemployment and social inequality 'unparalleled even under the Nazis'. Moreover, in other writings at this time, the reviewer was predicting that the experiment with a market economy in West Germany was about to collapse in political and economic chaos, while the Soviet zone, with its centrally planned system, would further and further surpass the western zone in economic growth.

Today, over forty years later, the countries of Eastern Europe are faced with politico-economic problems which have some broad similarities – (though also, of course, profound differences) – with those of West Germany around 1950. Eucken's *Grundlagen,* therefore, has a new interest and a new relevance for those concerned with laying the foundations for free market economies, following the total collapse of centrally planned systems.

The *Grundlagen* also possesses today a second, rather different kind of interest and relevance. In the last few years, among a growing number of American and British economists, sharp and fundamental questioning and criticism has been mounting of the kind of extremely abstract mathematical analysis for which the exponents of such exercises, over several decades, have been claiming, more or less successfully, such high significance and prestige. The empirical and predictive content of these abstract exercises, and their relevance for real-world problems and policies – (which was the traditional aim and interest of almost all economists, from Petty to Keynes, down to about 1950) – is increasingly being called in question. At the same time, even some of the leading abstract or 'theoretical' economists such as, for example, the late Sir John Hicks, have increasingly been emphasizing the historical dimension of economics and political economy. The methodological problems, therefore, of 'History and Theory in the Analysis of Economic Reality' – (to quote the subtitle of Eucken's book) - are appearing to some economists of increasing interest and importance.

A new edition of the *Grundlagen,* therefore, may be especially timely, both as a profound contribution to the discussion of the principles of economic policy, with special reference to today's fundamental issues in Eastern Europe in the nineties, and also with regard to some of the basic methodological questions now being raised by some American and British economists about the role of history. For those increasingly numerous students in some American graduate schools who now believe that no more than a handful of the more recent journal articles or conference papers, need be regarded as *'lesenswert'* by academic economists, the republication of such a non-mathematical work as Eucken's can hardly be of interest. By such economists, however, who still believe that major masterpieces of economic literature from all ages and countries should have a place on their reading-lists or their shelves, a new edition of Eucken's *Grundlagen* - quite apart from its topical interest and relevance - may be regarded as a notable event.

Woodbridge, C.T., USA
and
Birmingham, England
November 1991

T. W. Hutchison

CONTENTS

INTRODUCTION

THE FIRST GERMAN edition of this book appeared in 1940. Since then the book has gone through five more editions and has been translated into Spanish and Italian. The present English translation is based on the sixth German edition.

The author was Professor of Economics at the University of Freiburg, Germany. Professor Eucken was a student at a time when the Historical School dominated the teaching of economics at the German universities. Although, at the beginning of his career, he did some work along the lines of the Historical School, neither the aims nor the methods of historical research in the field of economics as practised by the representatives of the Historical School satisfied him; and the fact that the members of this school were unable to explain the causes of economic events such as the German inflation after World War I was an added reason for him to turn to economic theory. He became, among German economists, the foremost opponent of the Historical School, which he criticised in several publications. Through his writings and his teaching he contributed his share to the revival of interest in economic theory which was noticeable in the 'twenties. And he was one of the few economists left in Germany who helped to keep this interest alive during the 'thirties and during World War II. During this time he published *Kapitaltheoretische Untersuchungen* (1936), and the present volume, which immediately gave rise to an extensive discussion in German economic journals. Some of Professor Eucken's articles should be mentioned as supplementary material to the present volume: in particular "Die Überwindung des Historismus" (in *Schmoller's Jahrbuch*, 1938) and "Wissenschaft im Stile Schmoller's" (*Weltwirtschaftliches Archiv*, 1940).

The success which the book had in German-speaking countries was undoubtedly due partly to the fact that it filled a gap in the literature which was perhaps more acutely felt there than in other countries. The central theme of the book, the dual aspect of economic problems which has led to a dual approach to them, one historical, the other theoretical, is, of course, an old one. It was extensively discussed in the latter part of the nineteenth century, the main protagonists in the controversy being Schmoller on the one hand and Menger on the other. Both had weighty arguments on their side. The historians could rightly claim that the economic development of a country in any given period is part of the general historical development, can therefore only be understood against the background of a knowledge of the political, social, and intellectual history of the time, and consequently must be treated by the methods characteristic of historical research. Their opponents could claim with equal right that these methods do not enable us to explain the interrelationships within an economic system, i.e. do not allow us to trace observed economic facts to their economic causes. The issue was never settled satisfactorily. Menger was unable to convince the followers of the Historical School and Schmoller unable to convince the followers of the Theoretical School; and the study of economics after the controversy had died down proceeded as before along two entirely different lines.

The events of the last twenty years in Germany and the world were bound to give rise to a new discussion and a new approach to the problem. They seemed to offer ample proof that nothing could be further from the truth than Sombart's statement that political events do not decisively influence economic developments. The impact of political revolutions on the economy became so obvious that many of the younger generation in Germany drew the conclusion that abstract economic theory could contribute next to nothing to an understanding of economic reality. It seemed much more realistic to trace the economic development of a country in a given period directly to the great historical (social, political, and intellectual) forces which characterised the period. Economic theory, never as firmly established in Germany as in Anglo-Saxon countries, seemed again destined to take to the defensive.

The author took up the challenge which this situation

presented. What is required for a full understanding of economic reality anywhere and at any time? This is the main question which the book attempts to answer. At a time when many theorists seem to conceive of theory as an exercise in logic rather than as a tool the ultimate purpose of which is to help explain economic reality and when many historians consider economic theory as an unnecessary tool in their workshop, a book should be welcome which starts out from the observation of simple economic facts purposely taken from everyday economic life; develops out of them a general conceptual apparatus; returns to the facts by indicating how this apparatus can be applied to, and is indispensable for, an understanding of economic reality; and in the process gives an answer to the problem of the respective roles of the economic historian and the economic theorist.

Although this book deals with a methodological problem, the reader will find it very different from the standard type of treatise on methodology. He will not find abstract discussions of the "inductive" or "deductive" method in economics, or of the relationship of the social sciences to the natural sciences and the like, topics which are usually treated at length in methodological literature. The strong feeling for economic reality, the wide knowledge of economic history, the conviction that the appropriate procedure in economics cannot be found by abstract reasoning about methodology but is dictated by the character of the economic problems themselves, the author's approach to his problem and his results give the book a characteristic stamp of its own.

F. A. Lutz

PREFACE

OVER THE LAST hundred years numerous different efforts have been made by economists to achieve a better understanding of the economic world. The classical economists built up a system of remarkable logical consistency, and developed the methods indispensable in economic analysis. But they were unable to attain to a complete understanding of the modern economic world, this world of industrialism, new kinds of social problem, cyclical fluctuations, and of the modern struggles for economic power. The more pressing the contemporary problems became, the more intolerable became the gulf between economic science and the real world.

The two most powerful developments in economics in the nineteenth century both arose from an effort to understand the real economic world better: these were the Historical School, and the modern system of economic theory. Menger, Walras, and Jevons and the other masters, who planned and began to build the modern structure of economic theory, were aiming at a better grasp of economic reality by thinking afresh over the basic conditions of economic life. The approach of the Historical School was entirely different. Rejecting theory, they engaged in extensive descriptions of particular branches of industry, of the social conditions of different countries, of agriculture, and of much else besides. These were all seen as part of a process of historical development and constructed into "stages" and "styles" of economic development. However different the two movements may have been in their methods and results the impulse behind them was the same: the desire for a greater understanding of the real economic world. "Both followed the spirit of the time in rejecting speculative theories and seeking their results in the realm of observation", as Friedrich von Wieser pointed out in 1891.

The theories of economic development and of economic

fluctuations both have the same objective. By understanding the course of economic development they aim to approach nearer to economic reality and bridge the gulf between analysis and the real world. The theory of full employment is also seeking to introduce more realism into economic science. In this it proceeds very far. Its propounders believe that economic analysis should abandon proportions, *relative* prices, and marginal quantities of goods, and conduct their analysis in terms of *aggregates* of consumption, production, investment, and savings. In this respect they follow in the way of the Mercantilists. We are not concerned here to criticise; we only want to emphasise that the theory of full employment too is aiming at a better understanding of the real economic world.

This book is in the service of the same cause. Centralised planning, full employment policies, new forms of economic crises, and an unusually rapid change in the daily facts of economic life are compelling economists once again to put to themselves the question of how a grasp of the real economic world can be obtained. The modern economic world is continually facing the economist with new claims, and it is these claims that we are trying here to answer.

Our conclusion is that the analytical apparatus of economics must and can be extended to include a morphological study of economic phenomena. This morphological study of economic history reveals a limited number of pure forms out of which all actual economic systems past and present are made up. To work out these pure forms, and at the same time provide a basis for theoretical analysis which will explain the course of the economic process, are our two tasks. In spite of all the changes which economic development brings, a certain constancy of form is observable. We should no longer concentrate in our scientific theories on trying to keep up with the rapid day-to-day development of the economy. Such attempts serve only to remind one of Tantalus, always grasping too late at the fruit as it moved further and further away from him. We are aiming rather at constructing a morphological and theoretical system which is able to comprehend *all* economic life, however it may develop, and which is able to catch, as in a net, the changing shape of economic reality. Along with this morphological system it may also be possible to make full use of earlier theoretical achievements for our modern problems.

The development of economics in the Anglo-Saxon countries was quite different from what it was in Germany. In the 1870's English political economy underwent no such profound impact as that of the Historical School in Germany, and the transition from classical to modern economic theory was not by "revolution", but proceeded gradually under the sure leadership of Marshall. Continuity was, then, the characteristic of economics in the Anglo-Saxon world. But recently it has been entirely different. A sudden crisis has arisen. Keynesian theories start from different problems and work with different methods and categories from those which were previously dominant. Much that seemed secure has now become questionable; and this crisis has spread to the economic thought of all countries.

In such periods of uncertainty it may be of value to turn back to the elementary facts of the economic world and put all ideologies firmly on one side. Previously the aims of this book would not have been so understandable to the English or American reader as they may be in the present situation. As we penetrate into the actual conditions of economic life it becomes clear that a precise grasp of the real economic world demands an understanding of the different forms in which economic activity takes place, and therefore that a morphological analysis must precede a theoretical analysis. So I believe that it is just the morphological suggestions in this book which may be of interest to English and American readers, particularly from the point of view of the fundamentals of economic policy.

It is a specially pleasant duty for me to thank Mr. T. W. Hutchison, who has undertaken with so much understanding the work of translation.

Freiburg, im Breisgau, March, 1950 WALTER EUCKEN

TRANSLATOR'S NOTE

I SHOULD LIKE to offer a short explanation about my translation of two of the most important terms used by Professor Eucken in this book: *Wirtschaftsordnung* and *Wirtschaftssystem.* It seemed safe to start by translating these as "economic order" and "economic system" respectively, and there would be obvious advantages in choosing such near equivalents. It soon becomes clear, however, that "economic system" by itself is not adequate as a translation of *Wirtschaftssystem.* In Professor Eucken's terminology this word is applied to a strictly limited range of limiting cases, abstract models, or types of economic system (or "order"), which the common English term "economic system" would quite fail to indicate.

Much awkwardness also follows by keeping to "economic order" as a translation of *Wirtschaftsordnung.* It is, perhaps, a rather minor objection that the term "economic order" is comparatively uncommon in English, except in a more abstract sense (as in Professor Hayek's title *Individualism and Economic Order*). More important is the awkwardness that arises in trying to translate a passage like the following (5th Ed., p. 84):

"In Landwirtschaft, Gewerbe, Handel und im Verkehr gab und gibt es in allen Ländern stets Teilordnungen; . . . Alle diese Teilordnungen greifen jeweils ineinander und sind lediglich Glieder der Gesamtordnung, d.h. der jeweiligen Wirtschaftsordnung . . . Im 20. Jahrhundert wechseln die Wirtschaftsordnungen in den einzelnen Staaten . . . sehr rasch, und es besteht ebenfalls ein Nebeneinander sehr verschieden gearteter Ordnungen; man vergleiche etwa die Wirtschaftsordnungen von England und Russland und Japan wie sie 1935 waren. . . ."

It seems very ungainly to write extensively in the plural about "economic orders" and "partial orders." It occurred that the plural (*ordnungen*) might be translated as "kinds, or sorts, of order" (or of partial order), which is more involved if not so awkward-sounding. After much hesitation I decided against this solution, scrapped "economic order" altogether, and translated *Wirtschaftsordnung* as "economic system" and *Wirtschaftssystem* as "(abstract) type of economic system", which brings out that this applies simply, as in Professor Eucken's terminology it does, to a limited range of "pure" or abstract types. It still remains that the balance of advantage in favour of this (or any other) solution seems very fine.

I am very grateful for their suggestions and assistance to the late Professor Eucken himself, Professor F. A. Lutz, and Mr. M. A. Michael, who have done much to render this English version a less inadequate counterpart of its German original than it otherwise would have been.

T. W. HUTCHISON

Part I

THE FIRST MAIN PROBLEM OF ECONOMICS

Chapter I

THE MAIN PROBLEM OF ECONOMICS AND ITS ORIGIN IN EVERYDAY LIFE

I. FACTS AND QUESTIONS

1. *The First Approach*

"For three hundred years", Hippolyte Taine once said, "we have been losing more and more the ability to look at things directly. Weighed down by tedious miscellaneous book-learning we find ourselves studying not the objects themselves, but mere representations of them, maps rather than the actual landscape." It is certainly true that every science and every culture, as it develops, comes in danger of losing its direct grasp. When this happens, it is time to put verbal arguments on one side, to forget about empty conceptual systems, and really to study the field itself. Economics is now in this position. It can only find a firm foundation by looking squarely at the facts and by putting simple decisive questions about them.

Like Descartes nearly three hundred years ago, I am standing in front of the stove which is heating my room. It is quite an ordinary stove, but to look at it prompts me to ask the most fundamental questions. Descartes, seeing the stove in front of him, looked at his coat and felt the writing paper with his hands, and asked: "Is this real? Or is it an illusion? Do I exist myself? What is truth?" This radical kind of questioning and doubt is the business of the philosopher, not of the student of any particular science, and so not of the economist. We do not doubt, as Descartes did, that the stove in front of us is there, as are the table, the coat, and the paper, We start from everyday experience and do not enquire how this comes to exist. For us to pose the philosopher's questions would only lead to a dangerous and inexcusable confusion of problems, though this is certainly a confusion that often occurs.

Although the scientist starts from everyday experience his questions go much deeper than do those of the naïve man in the street, and he can never take everyday experience for granted in the same unconcerned way. What is the material out of which the stove is constructed, asks the scientist. This question alone gives rise to a host of others which lead back to atomic physics. Why does the stove give out a particular quantity of warmth? This leads us on to the theory of heat. *Our* questions are different. Why was the stove produced at all? Why was it set up in this particular room? These seem fairly simple questions. Because it is cold in winter is obviously a correct answer. But we know from everyday experience that many different kinds of specialised services co-operated in the making of this stove, from those of the man who installed it, back to those of the miners of the coal and ore, and to those of the metal worker who helped make the mining machinery. The number of those co-operating is incalculable. The ore was brought in ships to Germany, so the workers who fixed the rivets in the ships indirectly contributed to the production of the stove. How was the co-operation of all these services arranged so that they all contributed finally to the making of this stove?

The same sort of question arises if one looks at the table in front of one, the window, or writing paper. The production of everything I see in my room has come about through this huge process of division of labour. Here is a problem which concerns us all. How is this process with its far-reaching division of labour controlled in its entirety, so that everyone comes by the goods on which his existence depends? To understand even how the stove that heats my room was produced we have to know how this whole process hangs together.

2. *The Five Aspects of the Main Problem*

This is the problem we have to deal with. It is an important one, although its importance was not fully realised before the eighteenth century. How does it confront us in everyday life? In the course of the day I have eaten particular quantities of bread, meat, and vegetables. I have had my stove burning and have had the electric light on for several hours in my room. Some of my needs for to-day have thus been met. I have not been able to satisfy other needs because I have not had the means. Other people's experience has been just the same. How is this whole process of social production so directed that people have to-day been able to meet some of their needs and not others? To put the same question from another point of view: Why is this field sown with wheat and that with tobacco and a third with sugar-beet? Looking down from an aeroplane, we would see the earth's surface divided up between different crops, and land of similar quality being used for different products. How and why does this come about? It does not seem that this distribution of the land between different uses happens at random. On what do the decisions about these uses depend? This is obviously a question of fundamental importance. The provision of the people with bread, tobacco, sugar, and other consumers' goods, depends on the way in which the land is used. How are supplies of labour directed to different particular uses? Why will the iron on which a worker is working to-day later be used partly for shipbuilding, partly for a bridge, and partly in the ironware industry? In short, why and how are the available resources in land, labour, and finished and half-finished goods directed to different uses? That is our first question.

Secondly: the skilled worker B who works in a machine-tool factory is paid 400 marks a month. For his contribution to the making of many other goods in the production of which these machine-tools are used the firm pays him 400 marks in money, and he uses this sum to purchase a certain quantity of consumers' goods. Why do this man and his family get this particular share of the goods produced in Germany this year? Why no more and no less? For many millions of people the same question can be asked, and their shares will be found to be entirely different. Some get only a quarter or a half of the pay B gets, others more or very much more. C has an account at a Savings Bank and gets 40 marks interest each month.

Why is that so? How is the huge stream of consumers' goods divided up along different channels, and how does it finally disappear in differing quantities and compositions into the individual households?

This second question, the question of distribution, can be approached from another angle. Countless men have contributed to the production of the stove we have been talking about above, and they did not do this for nothing. The shopkeeper got 80 marks for it. Is there any relation between these 80 marks and the income of those contributing to the production of the stove? If so, what? What share does each individual get, beginning with the dealer and the workers in the factory? This, too, leads us much farther afield to such questions as the income of the mine-owner, the blast-furnace man, and others.

Thirdly: the production of a stove takes time, while the services it renders last over many years. Even if there is some kind of relationship between the 80 marks I paid for the stove and the wages of the miner, the transport worker, and all the others who contributed to its production, most of these workers received their incomes long before I bought the stove and began very gradually to consume its services. Many of the workers who worked directly or indirectly on the stove used their incomes for buying food and consumers' goods long before it began to yield consumption services. How was it that consumers' goods were available for those who worked on the stove many months and years before it began to satisfy a need? Exactly the same question is to be asked about the income of B, the skilled worker. Perhaps many years will pass before consumers' goods, like shoes or clothes, are finished with the aid of the machine-tools he has helped to make. How was it that the production of the clothes and shoes which B needs this week was begun months and years previously, and how is production set going to-day so that there are no interruptions in the provision of consumers' goods in the future?

In whatever direction we look we come across the time structure of production. The peasant A gets to-day 60 litres of milk from his cows. He may sell it to a dairy and thus help to provide milk for to-day and to-morrow. If the milk goes to his calves it is helping to provide milk in the more distant future. In the one case production is directed to meeting needs that are nearer in time, in the other case to more distant needs expected in the future. How does this temporal direction of production come about? A ton of wrought iron ready and available to-day can be used for shoe-making machinery. The shoes are consumers' goods, and if a shoe-making machine is worn out after fifteen years, then all the inputs of wrought iron have ripened into consumption goods, or approximately so. But if the wrought iron is used for constructing a blast-furnace it will take much longer, perhaps many decades, before its services can be ripe for consumption.

Needs in the present, and in the near and distant future, are thus competing for satisfaction. How is the competition decided? This is where all the problems of investing and saving come in.

Our *fourth* question is related to the third one. As to the machinery a shoe factory should use, or the methods of production which could be used for constructing a stove, there will always be alternative possibilities. Many such technical possibilities exist and they have especially increased in recent times. The industrialist, farmer, transporter, and even each household, have continually to decide and choose the technical methods to be applied, even if the question is only one of deciding whether to use one's feet, a bicycle, a motor-bicycle, or a car. This problem of choosing which process to adopt out of a number of possibilities is an economic one. What are the reasons behind any particular solution to it? Economic history makes it clear how momentous such decisions may be, and how many men's destinies they may determine. The social changes brought about simply by the introduction of the power loom were in many ways revolutionary.

Fifthly and lastly is the question of *where* the stove was constructed, where the metal was obtained and the ore. Why did the trader buy the stove from a factory in the Rhineland? Why was a factory for stoves located there? Why was the iron produced in Essen and the ore bought in Sweden? Why is the production of coal, cement, corn, and beer distributed over the country in a particular way? And why are the retail shops and hotels in a city located as they are? A bird's-eye view of the earth would show streams of different goods, large and small, moving by land and sea to particular points. Between one country and another, for example between Germany and Sweden, goods are daily moving to and fro. At the same time there is a constant exchange of goods between one part of a country and another, between town and countryside, between one village and another, or within single towns. Every factory gets raw materials and half-finished goods from particular places and delivers its products to particular places. All production takes place in a certain spatial setting, and from the places of production countless streams and counter-streams of goods move to and fro. How is production directed *spatially*?

These five questions, arising as they do from the direct contemplation of our immediate surroundings, are not independent. They simply express different aspects of one and the same problem, looked at from five different viewpoints. That this is so can be seen from the economic actions of a single peasant, who sells in November a particular percentage of his wheat crop, and sows another. He then decides not simply how he is going to use his land, but also the time-structure of his production. As he sows he chooses a particular location and particular technical methods. As a result of all these choices a certain income accrues to him. In every factory certain goods will be produced in certain quantities year by year, and also certain incomes will be received by those taking part: the factory is located in a particular place, sends goods to particular destinations, uses particular technical methods, and by its purchases directs streams of goods *temporally* in a particular way. All these choices and activities are, of course, indissolubly bound up with one another.

The whole economic process, of which every firm and every household is simply a part, is a unified process. The direction of production to satisfy different kinds of needs, the time-structure of production, the nature of distribution, the use of particular technical methods and particular locations are all decided together. They are all concerned with meeting the existing scarcity of goods. We want to ask how this process hangs together *as a whole*, in order thereby to understand the individual events of everyday economic life.

3. *An Addition*

A skilled worker earning 400 marks a month in 1929, in 1930, after the introduction of short time, got only 300 marks. At the same time the prices of important consumers' goods fell, so that he could still buy per year rather more than three-quarters of what he could previously. A rolling mill in Westphalia in 1930 cut down its production of medium plate as compared with 1929, but produced just as much fine plate as in the previous year. The building firms C, D, and E in Berlin lacked contracts and dismissed a large number of workers, who lived on unemployment relief, some cultivating their private allotments more intensively. The exports of the chemical firm H in Leipzig to the countries of western Europe fell off, as did the turnover of Hamburg and Bremen importers. Other firms, for example the thread factory G, kept up their activity in 1930.

These movements are what constitute the fluctuations of the trade cycle. Recently there have been successful attempts to describe them statistically for single countries or for the world as a whole. Such statistical accounts are certainly useful, but it remains particularly important to keep in mind the original facts of economic life as they occur daily in factories, workshops, offices, farms, and households. While investigating relationships in the economy as a whole we want also to find out the causes of its fluctuations.

The vital importance of the whole problem should now be evident. It is changes in their conditions of life which rouse men to an understanding of scientific problems. Most people take the functions of the body for granted as long as they remain normal, and only when illness comes will they sometimes ask about, or at least feel the significance of, problems of physiology and biology. In tranquil periods few people ask questions about history, but in times of revolution many wish to discover the formative factors in history, its forces and its laws. In the same way it is in times of change and fluctuation in everyday economic life that the questions about how it hangs together come to the forefront. The worker in a machinery factory does not worry much about how it is possible that he uses consumers' goods day by day, while the products of his daily labour first become ripe for consumption many years later. If he is unemployed because his factory has closed from lack of orders, he perhaps begins to ponder over the chain of economic events which brought this about. Perhaps it was owing to an interruption in the process of investment. Then it begins to emerge that the seemingly academic question of the time-structure of production is of the greatest practical importance.

The question about the technical methods used in the production of the stove may not at first seem so important. But if owing to a new process being adopted production is greatly increased, while many workers are dismissed and older factories are condemned, then people will want to know how the effects of adopting a new technical method work themselves out through the whole economy. Economic difficulties will dissipate popular indifference to this problem.

4. *Criticism and Counter-Criticism*

(1) The first main problem of economics arises out of everyday experience. Experience, however, even everyday experience, cannot be grasped without *concepts*. We have been making use of concepts like "economy", "production", "income", "wages", "distribution", "work", and others. We did this without explaining or defining them. Was it not a mistake not to have defined the concepts first? In economics the primacy of definitions is seldom insisted on *à outrance*, but many economists act as though it were. They often start with questions such as "What is economising?" or "What is output?"—quite different questions from those we are asking. They give first place to questions about concepts and not to those about facts and their connections.

Questions of this kind lead the student astray from the start. Definitions and questions about definitions can have no place at the outset of the study of economics, and they are usually no longer put at the beginning of other sciences. A science is quite unable at the beginning of its investigations to provide scientific definitions. There is no basis on which to define the concept "economising" before investigating the facts. A definition which is attempted without such investigation can only be founded on popular usage and this leads to hazy and uncertain constructions being built up on terms defined in this way. It is hardly surprising that different students of the subject, according to their preferences, have different definitions of the basic concepts to offer, and thus start controversies as to what "economising" is—controversies as violent as they are valueless from the point of view of advancing our knowledge of economic reality.

Because everyday concepts cannot be defined immediately in a scientifically satisfactory way, economists must use them as they are used in ordinary life, that is, without definitions. In this way they get on with a direct analysis of their subject-matter. The results of their investigations are then summarised in definitions and these definitions can be used in further study. Even if concepts like "economising", "production", and "wages", taken over from everyday experience, are incomplete and indefinite when first used, they have to suffice provisionally like crutches which can be discarded later. We are only in a position to make scientific definitions when we have penetrated some way into the problems of our subject. Only then can it be decided which concepts can be of any use and which new and purely scientific concepts must be introduced. The view that science must begin with definitions because it has from the start to work with concepts is untenable and harmful. (At this early stage I can only put up this warning notice. The dangers of disregarding it will become apparent later.) We can no more begin with questions about definitions than we can with questions about the essence of "economising" or "capitalism" or the "crisis of capitalism", which will only get us bogged down in speculative profundities, and cause us to lose sight of economic reality.

Finally another false approach is to start not from one's own problems but with an account of earlier doctrines, in the hope that an advance may be made by commenting on them critically or favourably. But a science and its earlier doctrines can only remain alive by formulating direct questions about the real world.[1]

(2) Even when this central problem of economics is perceived and its importance recognised, it is often inadequately formulated. Its unity is often overlooked, particularly when a threefold or fourfold division of the subject is made, as was formerly customary, into production, distribution, and consumption or exchange. Each of these divisions had its separate theories. Such a division leads very easily to the marking off of separate spheres of production, exchange, distribution, and consumption, to one or other of which each separate economic problem is allotted. For many decades these divisions persisted, especially under the influence of their particular exponent J. B. Say, and they dominated the textbooks for a long period. They do not, however, correspond with economic reality and so must disappear. Such division of the subject causes us to lose sight of the unity of economic life, and how great this unity is can clearly be seen wherever one looks at economic life. A worker earns his wages for his contribution to "production" and thus gets his share in "distribution". He thereby receives money which comes under the heading of "exchange" and this is then used by the worker for purposes of "consumption". A weaving mill depends on bank credits, that is, on the "medium of exchange", for starting and carrying on "production", and in the course of "production" carries out the process of "distribution" to the workers and management. Being a producer of textiles, and not simply a final consumer of thread, it has to regulate its production programme according to the expected "consumption". Every change in the provision of credit, that is, in "the medium of exchange", impinges on production, distribution, and consumption, and *vice versa.* Therefore, there are no independent spheres in the economy and there should be no separate theories, only one problem and one theory.[2]

Another unsatisfactory approach to the problem is to grasp its unity but to overlook some of its different aspects, or to underestimate their importance. Here, too, economists have often failed. Ricardo, as is well known, described the task of political economy as "to determine the laws which regulate distribution". Certainly, not as much weight should be attributed to this sentence of Ricardo's as is usually done. Ricardo himself went much further. He dealt with the question of the guidance of production in trying to show how it followed from the oscillation of market prices around the costs of production. He dealt also in a limited way with our fourth question, that of the technical methods applied, when he raised the problem of the influence of machinery, and with the problem of location in his chapter on international trade. But these two latter important questions are treated by Ricardo as independent, and not as parts of the one total problem. In particular it is a defect of his system that he makes no mention, except incidentally, of the problem of the time-structure of production. Subsequently Ricardo had to agree that the time element has an important influence in the control of the economic process, which was not sufficiently recognised in his theory.

Modern theories are often far less comprehensive in the formulation of their problems than there is any need for them to be. Economic location is not considered, the problem of the technical methods to be applied is too often regarded as a special problem on its own, while the importance of the time structure of production is underestimated or even overlooked. Writers of such influence as Walras and Pareto thought that the time element should largely be excluded. They start in their systems from the fiction that the labour force and the sellers of raw materials use up the consumption goods at the same moment as they produce them. Obviously such an assumption is quite unrealistic and excludes all questions about investment and savings. Walras' system was once correctly described as resembling a palace of no relevance to the housing problem. This judgment is a correct one, mainly because the architect of the system did not clearly realise that all economic plans and actions have always to be seen in their temporal order, and that our daily economic life cannot be understood without a knowledge of its structure through time. Nor is the element of time one which can well be introduced subsequently. The main problem cannot be tackled if the time factor is left out. Most workers, as we have seen, receive as their wages not products created simultaneously with the services for which the wages are paid, but the fruits of productive processes that have been initiated much earlier. This fact has a decisive influence on the level of wages. Therefore an explanation of wages and of the whole theory of distribution, and, indeed, of any other economic question, will be inadequate if the temporal order of the economic process is not considered from the start. This underestimation, or complete neglect, of the time element has done much to widen the gulf between theoretical studies and the real economic world.

Problems must be formulated in terms of things and not of words, and must be unified and complete if justice is to be done to economic reality.[3]

II. EVERYDAY EXPERIENCE

The main problem of economics is not all that emerges from our everyday economic experience. We also find there a teeming confusion of opinions and ideologies on economic problems. This everyday economic experience in which we all share may thus be regarded in two ways. It provides the initial impulse for asking significant questions, but at the same time puts a considerable obstacle in the way of our finding really serviceable answers.

(1) Because everybody takes some part in economic life everyone has an opinion about the economic questions directly affecting him. The baker is concerned with the prices of bread and flour, with his guild or association, and with the wages of his employees. The industrialist is interested in tariff policies, railway freights, the price policies and regulations of the cartels from which he buys, and the worker with rents, prices, and wages. It is not that everyone thinks out an independent opinion as to how prices and wages are formed. Most people only repeat the views they hear around them. "Few men think, but all want to have opinions" (Berkeley).

Men do not confine their opinions simply to what is in their immediate surroundings. They range further afield and pronounce on the larger relations of the whole economic process from the standpoint of their own personal interests.

An industrialist, the price of whose raw materials is kept up by a cartel, but who does not sell his own products through one, will take a generally unfavourable view of cartels, unlike the industrialist who belongs to one. An official who benefits from a rise in pay is scarcely able to consider the effects on government expenditure as other than favourable. The artisan threatened by the competition of large-scale mechanised plants believes that the introduction of machinery is economically harmful and is ready to subscribe to any reasoning which appears to him to prove this.

It is not that the individual always weighs up correctly what is in his interest. For example, most retail traders at first welcomed the appearance of branded goods with fixed prices as adding to their security. Only later was it realised that branded goods and price maintenance were undermining the status of the independent retailer. Again, in 1922 and 1923 many German entrepreneurs demanded, supported, and approved an easy credit policy by the Reichsbank and took no account of the heavy damage inflation inflicted on their own positions. Everyone's opinions on the economic causes and effects of their actions are formed on the basis of their own actual or assumed interests.

What is convenient to these interests seems at once proper, correct, and reasonable, and what runs counter to them seems in all seriousness unfair and unnatural, or unsuitable and absurd. Every day our intellect is fooled and corrupted by the trickery of our passions. Many men are genuine experts in their own economic environment, but they are unable to weigh up dispassionately the wider interrelationships. Everyone, even the director of a great modern business, sees things from the point of view of his own interests, and can survey only a small section of the whole huge process of the social economy.

(2) Along with the individual opinions of single people an effective part in everyday economic life and economic policy is played by the ideologies of groups. These arise wherever powerful economic bodies exist, and they tend much more than the multifarious opinions of individuals to be weapons deliberately created for the economic struggle.

Not all such ideologies are purely economic in character. Often religious, philosophical, or political ideas are used in economic ideologies. The religious and philosophical notion of world citizenship was used by free-trade interests, and nationalism by those interested in protective tariffs. The old German notion of the guild was used in support of the cartel. There are few religious or political notions which have not been made use of ideologically by economic interests, not only in the so-called capitalist age, but at all periods and places. In the struggle between merchants and hand-workers in the medieval towns during the thirteenth, fourteenth, and fifteenth centuries, the interested parties built their economic ideologies out of the dominant religious and political ideas of the time. This has also happened in the economic conflicts of the twentieth century. The purpose of such ideologies is either to conceal the true motives for the claims which are being advanced or to give these claims added force. In England in the middle of the eighteenth century it was widely held that high prices for food and low wages were economically desirable. An economist, Foster, in attacking this view remarked: "This is a doctrine which greed eagerly seizes upon. Men believe nothing more easily than an untruth that brings them advantage."

Pressure groups gain significantly in power and influence if there are intellectuals at their disposal to work out their ideologies for them. The whole intellectual history of mankind is full of attempts to secure and support claims to power by means of ideologies. He who pays the piper calls the tune. How often theologians try, and have tried, to use the great historical force of religion in the interest of the ruling class. Historians, too, consciously or not, serve the interest of groups in power or struggling for it. How much legal subtlety has been available throughout history to prove that the interests of pressure groups are in harmony with the law—positive or natural. Take, for example, the writings of Peutinger, the legal adviser of Augsburg high finance at the beginning of the sixteenth century, which were so skilful and influential in the struggle over the legal treatment of monopolies. A history of monopolist ideology from that time down to our contemporary cartels would be as interesting as it is badly needed. It would be found how these ideologies fitted themselves into the intellectual and political spirit of the times by appealing to natural law and to the freedom of economic activity for the individual (including the making of cartel agreements). Alternatively, with socialism in the ascendancy, it is urged that monopolies and cartel agreements prepare the way for socialisation. The argument always proves that the interests of the pressure groups harmonise with the common good. Such ideologies often have a significant effect, particularly on legal judgments and administrative practice.

Scientific theories, too, are sometimes used as ideological weapons, as, for example, the natural law theory which was used by the princes against the estates during the seventeenth and eighteenth centuries. Similarly, the economic theory of free trade became a weapon of vested interests in the nineteenth century. In the course of every serious depression the old long-discredited notion that too much of everything is being produced, in one country or in the world, is spread by interested writers in order to move opinion in favour of a planned restriction of production. The reverse may also happen in that an ideological weapon is accepted as part of economic science. The balance of payments theory was accepted by many economists as an explanation of the collapse of the mark in the years after 1919. It was not realised that the explanation of the falling value of the mark as the result of a passive balance of payments originated with business circles interested in cheap and ample credit, whose interests prejudiced them against the true explanation, that is, inflation. A tendency to romantic, even mystical, speculation is often associated with the interests of pressure groups. Adam Müller's enthusiastic reverence for the traditional economic order was taken and made to serve the interests of the influential landlords at the time of the Stein-Hardenberg reforms. Profundity is often a characteristic of the ideological weapon. To lay down a smoke-screen behind which the ideologies and activities of economic groups can develop is the service such writers render by their nebulous speculations.

Those looking more deeply into the struggles for power of economic groups—and economic life is full of such struggles—are apt to wax indignant at the way in which opinions and ideologies are shaped by economic interests. A distinction should be made between the opinions of economic individuals which may be of value in their own fields and those of group ideologies. Further, it would be more important, instead of growing indignant, to investigate calmly the play of interests in everyday economic life and think out a way of rising above these illusions and prejudices.

(3) This play of interests has been stressed not in any spirit of pessimism, but because it is of the greatest importance. We must now ask how it is possible in spite of all the "interested" opinions and ideologies in the world to attain to scientific knowledge of economic reality. Is it possible to get beyond everyday economic experience, or is the intellect always to be simply a tool of the will, at any rate in the field of economics? Can economics ever escape from the domain of interested opinions and ideologies, and if so, how? All genuine empirical sciences and scientific theories since the Greeks have seen the main task of science as that of rising to a scientific truth above the level of everyday debate. Is such a solution for our problem possible, and if so, how? Can there be a scientific economics free from the clash of interests?

It is not that what we learn from our everyday experience must be wrong because of its subservience to our interests. It may be either right or wrong, and what has to be found is a strict criterion and a scientific method for deciding that. For example, it is often the view of the workers that increases in wages, by adding to the purchasing power of the people, stimulate demand and economic activity. The employers, looking at the rise in cost brought about by wage increases, expect smaller profits, dismissals of workers, and thus a deterioration of the economic situation. Who is right in any actual case, or how far is one or the other right? That has to be answered scientifically. The popular idea that the truth must be found somewhere in the middle has no proper foundation. There is no reason why it should be just midway between the views of the trade unions and of the employers' associations. In economics the solutions to problems are not found as easily as that.

Many economists have not recognised the decisive importance of their task for everyday economic life. Even in writings on methodology this is usually overlooked, or only touched upon incidentally, without its basic importance being made clear. Often, biased ideologies are not seen for what they are, in spite of the ponderous concentrations of power operating behind them. This is due to a lack of realism of a specially dangerous kind. Alternatively, some reference may be made to the opinions of interested parties, and here or there traces of such opinions may be uncovered. But it is never noticed that they are present everywhere and that even economists themselves may be in constant danger of being captured by them. When science and ideological bias are combined, science surrenders its whole value, while the ideological weapon gains an enhanced effectiveness. Finally, it may be that, following Marx or modern existentialist philosophy, intellectual activity is seen simply as a reflection of the current conditions of life. Such philosophies recognise that doctrines and ideologies are tied up with the interests and power of those who express them. But the decisive question whether it is possible to shake off this servitude is negatived from the start. If this answer is correct economics like every other science would lose its right to exist. It would be merely one more biased doctrine and ideology of which there are quite enough already. How can the interrelationships of everyday economic life be genuinely explained free of all bias and subjectivism?[4]

Chapter II

THE DOUBLE NATURE OF THE PROBLEM—THE GREAT ANTINOMY

I. *The Individual-Historical Approach*
II. *The General-Theoretical Approach*
III. *The Great Antinomy*

I. THE INDIVIDUAL-HISTORICAL APPROACH

(1) THE FIRST MAIN problem of economics which we pose arises simply from looking directly at the facts now around us, at the stove, for example, as it is *to-day*, or at the wages of the workers *this week*, or the buying of food *to-day*. From this we are led to ask about the interrelationships of everyday economic life. If we think back a few years or decades, everyday economic life looked quite different and proceeded in many respects in quite a different way from that in which it does now and did then elsewhere in other parts of our own country and abroad. Henry Ford in the centre of American motor-car production at Detroit had an American village built in the style of the mid-nineteenth century. From all over the country buildings and workshops belonging to that period were brought together. Churches, schools, a town hall, blacksmiths' forges, windmills, and bakeries were erected, and there was a coach and horses to provide transport. Everyday economic life went on there in quite a different social, political, intellectual, and technical environment from that of contemporary Detroit; the difference being as great as that between the customs and ideas of Tibet and those of Poland, or those of Brazil and those of the eastern parts of the United States.

Further scientific study amply confirms these first impressions. For example, the profound political and social changes in Prussia at the beginning of the nineteenth century, by freeing the peasants from their bonds with the soil, giving them liberty of movement and of property, and by abolishing feudal dues and compulsory labour, completely altered everyday economic life both for the Prussian landlords and for the peasants. The course of the economic process in a south German village of the twelfth century can only be understood when seen as part of the political and social structure of the country, at the centre of which was the manor. The way in which everyday economic life proceeds depends on the nature of the country, the race, culture, and beliefs of the inhabitants, on the political institutions and structure of the state, in fact on the entire historical environment.

Furthermore, current everyday economic life is itself history. Most historical writings and the monumental works of history lay the emphasis on a special aspect. They select from events what seems particularly weighty and significant, stirring political events, impressive political, religious, or cultural personalities and their deeds, or important institutions, or the rise and fall of states and cultures. Usually the historian focuses on certain well-illumined aspects of history, and turns less often to the routine everyday economic life of the millions. But this everyday economic routine, as it was in the past, or as it is now, in England or Germany or elsewhere, in thousands or millions of farms, workshops, factories, and households, as it takes its monotonous and apparently uninteresting everyday course, is a real part of history. All human action belongs to history. The work of the miner or shopkeeper, and even what the reader of these lines does to-day, belongs to the history of this year, and thus to history. Whether the future historian will take any notice, we do not know and it is not of immediate relevance. It is this anonymous everyday side of history which ordinary men themselves live through, and of which their lives are a part, which is for most people of the most importance. Its importance, even from the point of view of the usual "large-scale" histories, stands out particularly in certain moments and epochs, as in the decline of the Roman empire, which was closely connected with the economic deterioration of its final centuries. Here the gradual change in the everyday economic life of the masses made itself felt with immense effect. Furthermore, no one can understand the political history, domestic or international, of the third and fourth decades of the twentieth century, unless it is viewed alongside the economic crisis of 1929–33 and the rapid change in the everyday economic life of the greater part of mankind which that brought. Apart from such special historical situations everyday economic life always forms one side of history even in times dominated by the most momentous and far-reaching political events, as in Cromwell's time in England, or Napoleon's in Europe. Even in periods such as these it remains the important side of history for those who live through it.[5]

(2) If contemporary everyday economic life is a part of contemporary universal history, questions about its interrelationships must be treated as questions of history. Economic life is to be understood against the background of the current historical situation: that is, for the economy of Sparta, against the background of the Spartan state; the English economy of the seventeenth century in the context of that century, and the economy of to-day in the context of to-day.

Earlier on we asked why tobacco grows in one field, wheat in another, and sugar-beet in a third. Owing to the completely different organisation of agriculture in different times and places, this is one question in, say, Germany in 1941 and quite another in 1925 or 1913, or in contemporary Russia, Britain, or America. Similarly, too, in the United States the problem was different in 1939 after the new Agricultural Act, to what it was in 1937 before the introduction of the new method of allocating the areas for cultivation to farmers.

It is the same with income, and with our question as to why a particular skilled worker got 400 marks a month, and why this income had a certain purchasing power. Such a question in the Germany of 1939, with the then existing wage and monetary policy, required quite a different sort of answer from what it did in the Germany of 1929 or 1870, and a quite different one again if it concerned a skilled worker in France, England, or the U.S.A. Whether wages are fixed by the state, whether trade unions or employers' associations exist and what power they exercise, are decisive factors in the answer to our question. For long periods of human history the level of income of the worker depended on whether he was a slave or free.

The time structure of production is also dependent on the historical situation. The saving of 1000 marks in 1939 had quite other effects than in 1890 or 1840, monetary and banking organisation being quite different at the two dates. There are still greater contrasts if we take longer intervals of time and different civilisations. The Roman who saved did so by buying a slave, the fellah of the nineteenth century by buying gold, and the Indian by buying jewellery.

Finally the choice of technical methods and of location is historically determined. In most contemporary states the military plans of the central authority influence location. Forty years ago they played no part, the decisions about location resulting from the plans of individual business men.

The actual circumstances always force us to treat our first main problem, however we turn it or interpret it, as a historical problem, in the same way that historians treat other historical problems; that is, with reference to the current historical situation not separated from its historical environment, but as part of the process of universal history.

II. THE GENERAL-THEORETICAL APPROACH

(1) Economic reality compels the economist to formulate his first main problem as a historical one, but it also forces him in quite another direction.

The individual's economic existence often depends on the activities of countless other people. Similarly, everyone in his economic activities affects the economic life of very many others. To understand economic reality is to understand all of this economic activity in its entirety, and how it fits together. The economic life of a single German is to-day only a part of the whole economic life of *all* Germans along with its relations with other countries.

It is not possible to understand economic life with all its interrelations simply by looking directly at contemporary economic reality. From whichever side we approach the first main problem of economics the simple direct contemplation of the facts of economic history will be inadequate for solving it.

We were asking just now why a skilled worker earned 400 marks a month, and why he can buy a particular quantity of goods with this sum. We saw that the answer to this question differed according to whether it related to the Germany of 1939, or that of 1925, or to other social and economic systems. The question had to be regarded as a historical one about a particular historical situation. If, however, we try to answer the question simply by looking at a particular historical economic situation, that of Germany in 1939 or 1925, we shall fail. Even if we disregard how the money wage was arrived at, we are unable to explain, simply by looking at the economic system in 1939 or 1929, why the prices of all the dozens of goods purchased then were at the level they were, and therefore why the skilled worker obtained a particular quantity of goods. Certainly we can find out by observation that he had to pay particular prices for bread, meat, and other goods, but we have to discover *why.* We would soon find ourselves in a mental maze if, using direct observation, we sought to answer a question about the level even of a single actual price—say, that of coal—merely by following back the process by which it was formed. It is clear that the price of coal depends on the prices of materials, wages, and freights, and on countless other prices. Thus dozens of new questions arise, and we soon find ourselves caught up in a network of economic relationships impossible to survey as a whole.

We might also ask how it comes about that last year my capital of 10,000 marks was bringing me 300 marks interest, with which I was able to buy a certain quantity of goods. Where does the stream of goods come from which continues to reach me, as a receiver of interest, year after year? What determines the size of this stream? Relying simply on direct observation we look to my debtor, a farmer, and from him to those who buy from and sell to him. After that we get lost in a confusion of facts and have to give up the attempt at an answer.

Again, let us enquire how the introduction of new spinning machinery affects the situation of the worker. Certainly it can be ascertained that if these machines are adopted in factories A, B, C, etc., a particular number of textile workers will be dismissed, and the production of thread will increase. But direct observation again fails us when we put the essential question as to why the workers dismissed find employment again, whether it is connected with the introduction of our new spinning machines, or as a result of some other factor, for example, a good harvest. Nor can the effects of this new machine on the provision of consumers' goods, on the machine industry, and on the cotton producer be discovered in this way. In any actual economic system so many factors are at work simultaneously that the effect of a single factor by itself can never be known, for its traces are soon lost sight of.

Finally, in everyday experience we find a number of facts side by side. For example, in Germany in 1931, there were: mounting unemployment, bank moratoria, falling prices, sharp reduction of imports, a slighter falling-off of exports, rising interest rates, the withdrawal of foreign credits, and many other facts besides. How did these facts fit together with one another? Did they occur together by coincidence? This would seem improbable, but *how* were they connected? We cannot find an answer to this question, which is so important for understanding the economic process at that time, simply by looking at the facts, those, for example, of the labour market or money market.

Our conclusion is that the actual sequence of economic events at any place or time cannot be understood in the same way as other historical facts. The activities of a statesman, the course of a war, diplomatic negotiations, or internal political reforms can be examined and understood by the historian. He may himself experience them, hear the reports of eyewitnesses, or by reading the sources get a picture of the events and the connection between them. An understanding of economic reality is not to be obtained in these ways, even when the economist has himself experience of it. Before this main problem of economics the usual historical methods fail. They have, in fact, failed, as the history of economics and of the so-called historical school in particular has clearly shown.

(2) There is only one way out of this situation. We must try to break down and analyse the complex phenomenon into its different components. We may perhaps build imaginary models, and by varying single factors attempt to find out the relationships we are looking for which are not immediately apparent. By using a model of an exchange economy we may investigate all the changes as they occur on the introduction of a new machine, assuming everything else remains the same. We may, too, through such a model, trace the real source of interest, or how a change in consumers' needs works out. It *may* also be possible to discover the data determining production, distribution, the time-structure of production, the technical methods applied, and the spatial distribution of economic activity. We do not yet know whether all this is attainable, but must form our judgment later.

We simply emphasise here that, as economic reality and its interrelationships cannot be directly understood through historical study alone, we must mobilise our full powers of analysis. This means putting our questions in a *general* form. By formulating the first main problem in a general form we can apply theoretical analysis to it, and perhaps in this way succeed in obtaining propositions of general validity about necessary relationships, that is, theoretical propositions which prepare the way for an understanding of concrete relationships. Theoretical analysis is thus simply the full use of our powers of thought. Even the pre- or unscientific man knows that thinking enables him to discover the relationships between things, for he is constantly, though unsystematically, using his powers of thought for this purpose. By thinking out his scientific theories man becomes able, as Lotze expressed it, "to transform what is given to us as *happening* together into what is *connected* together". He is enabled to arrive at generally valid propositions which are true and superior to his everyday judgments. We must make the attempt to formulate our first main problem as a *general-theoretical* problem.

We must proceed in this way *from the start*. The theoretical questions do not come at the end of our science, and the theoretical propositions which we have to seek are not simply a distillation of experience. The real source of genuine theoretical problems and analysis is quite different. We feel obliged to understand reality and its relationships. But we have no prospect of achieving this if we do not put the problem in a general form, and therefore make it accessible to theoretical investigation. It is not any doctrinaire spirit or love of philosophical speculation that leads us to study theoretical problems, but simply our striving after scientific experience.* There can only be such a thing as "scientific experience" in this field, as contrasted with "everyday" experience, which is quite a different thing, if it proves possible to treat the problems as general-theoretical problems. At this point we find ourselves directly confronted by what we may call the Great Antinomy.[6]

III. THE GREAT ANTINOMY

The first task of the economist is to get a grasp of economic reality. This may be a requirement which, however justified and necessary, may not be *possible.* The economist has to see economic events as part of a particular individual-historical situation if he is to do justice to the real world. He must see them also as presenting general-theoretical problems if the relationships of the real world are not to escape him. How can he combine these two views? If he does only the one or only the other, he is out of touch with the real world.

For example, we might put the question of the guidance of production purely historically, and ask why in England at the present time land and labour are distributed in a particular way between different uses. If we tried to solve this problem by direct observation we would get many single facts, but no relationships. We would fail to understand the real world, and would achieve only a chaos of details about individual firms, individual farms, and individual decisions. We would miss those essential relationships of which the real world is made up.

We might also put the question of the guidance of production as a general-theoretical question. Then the problem

* **Wissenschaftliche Erfahrung.**

would be separated from its historical setting. We would not be concerned then with contemporary England or Germany, or particular firms, but with analytical models. We may perhaps discover abstract relationships, but we would have lost contact with the real world. We would no longer see anything of the variety of actual historical phenomena and of individual facts.

Economists are confronted here by what we are calling the Great Antinomy of their subject, which they have to overcome if they are to understand the course of economic life.

The sudden and momentous political revolutions of recent decades have brought out forcefully the individual-historical nature of economic life. The tempo at which states have altered their constitutions, their market and labour organisation, their currencies, etc., has tremendously increased. The changes in everyday economic life have been accelerated. In so rapidly changing a world, any study of general problems and any theoretical investigation may seem pointless. One contemporary theoretical economist has been led to say that we have come to "the twilight of economic theory". If this were so, it would mean giving up scientific study of the economic process. Without general-theoretical study there can be no scientific experience in this field, just as there cannot be without individual-historical study.

The physical or chemical world has what has been called a certain "invariant general form".* The uniformity of chemical reactions, or the uniform movement of bodies or growth of plants, makes it possible to formulate theoretical questions and generally valid physical, chemical, or biological laws. No such uniformity exists in the economic world, which exhibits an immense variety of forms and historical processes. In Germany in A.D. 1300, or 1800, or 1949, in Italy in 200, in South America in 1500, or even in Egypt in 3000 B.C., physical and chemical reactions were the same, but economic life was not carried on in the same forms. A single order of Nature exists and has existed, but there is an unlimited and constantly changing variety of economic "orders" or systems.† Economic life appears to lack all uniformity. How, then, is our

* Invariante Gesamtstil. † Wirtschaftsordnungen.

main problem of economics to be posed in the theoretical form necessary if the real world is to be understood?[7]

The call to get at the facts and away from words has often been sounded among economists. This is as it should be, but it is not enough. The call has to be carried out in practice or it remains itself mere words. In carrying it out we are confronted at once with the Great Antinomy, without the elimination of which it is impossible to get a grasp of economic reality. All work on our subject must be directed to overcoming this antinomy. Another appeal that is often heard is that historians and theorists must work together in economics, and that nothing could be more harmful than conflict between them. This, too, is true and the appeal is a sign of the existence of this great antinomy and of a desire to overcome it. But this again is not nearly enough. What is required is a clear recognition of the full extent of the task, which can then be tackled fundamentally. A superficial compromise between theoretical and historical investigation or mere methodological reflections about their co-operation are pointless. The sharpness and tension of this antinomy must be fully understood. This historical aspect of the problem requires perception, intuition, synthesis, understanding, and a feeling for living individual experience. The general theoretical aspect calls for reasoning, analysis, and the elaboration of analytical models. How are these two faculties, lively perception and theoretical reasoning, to be harnessed together? How can the problem be grasped in all its historical variety, and at the same time be raised to a general level accessible to theoretical study?

We have described the first, but not the only, main problem of economics. Every day it faces mankind, but it is not to be solved simply by everyday experience. If economists try to work out a solution on the confused basis of everyday experience they will encounter grave difficulties. However pressing the solution of this problem may be—and everybody is calling for a solution—its mere formulation confronts one with the greatest difficulties. The antinomy has made itself felt more forcibly in recent decades than formerly. The course of universal history has not only brought about more rapid changes in institutions, and therefore shown up more emphatically the historically changing character of the problem. It has led, also, to the structure of our social economy becoming more and more complex, thus making theoretical analysis more and more clearly indispensable.

The economist resembles a traveller starting off on a journey from which he promises himself striking and spacious vistas. But already after the first step he finds himself surrounded by what seems to be an impenetrable jungle.

Part II

A CRITIQUE OF ECONOMICS: A SECOND MAIN PROBLEM

Chapter I

INTRODUCTION

HAVE ECONOMISTS SUCCEEDED, by a combination of history and theory, in understanding the economic process and its relationships in their entirety, thus overcoming what we are calling the Great Antinomy? To give a complete answer to this question we should have to undertake a comprehensive critical review of the history of economics, which is not possible here. We are concerned only with some salient points.

We must start with classical political economy. Its great and lasting service has been its discovery of the interdependence of the whole economic process, and its development of the method of economic theory. This was an essential step towards an understanding of economic reality. It was their lack of a clear perception of the Great Antinomy which was the main weakness of the classical economists.

It would be quite wrong to maintain that the classical economists understood nothing about history, and that the historical aspect of economic life was unknown to them. Such a criticism would only show a misunderstanding of the classical writers. Most of the physiocrats, Smith, Hume, Malthus, J. S. Mill, and many others, had a great knowledge of history. The *Wealth of Nations*, in fact, is a work of history giving the reader a social and historical survey of the world from England to China and South America. It has been repeatedly asserted that the classics had a considerable grasp of theory but none of history, and that in their ignorance of the variety of political and economic systems they succumbed to a kind of theoretical absolutism. This is a criticism which though constantly repeated gains nothing thereby in validity.

The relations between classical political economy and history must be examined more closely. The classics were the products of the Age of Reason of the seventeenth and eighteenth centuries, an age by no means ignorant of history, though it asked different questions of it than did the nineteenth century. Well aware of the peculiarities of individual men and peoples, its questions were clearly not basically concerned with individuals, but with the universal, God-given, rational, "natural" order and its "natural" laws. Montesquieu, for example, an important representative of the spirit of the eighteenth century, who strongly influenced Adam Smith, possessed an immense knowledge of individual states and peoples from antiquity down to his own day, but research into individual facts, states, and peoples was not for him an end in itself. By studying individual cases he wanted to get a general understanding of the lives of states and peoples, and of the effective forces of history, and in that way to lay the foundations on which to build a just and rational state. He wanted to discover a just political system by the study of actual political systems. He sought to arrive at generally valid and applicable knowledge by a universal study of historical facts and forces. "To revel in the wealth of centuries of historical material, or to give oneself up to the study of some single historical phenomenon, which was the attitude of mind of the nineteenth century, would have seemed to him simply amusing dilettantism" (Franz Schnabel).

The classical economists' attitude to history was similar. Many of them had a great understanding of it, but their aim was not to describe the economic life of a particular people at a particular moment in all its uniqueness, say, for example, the Chinese economy, which aroused such interest in the middle of the eighteenth century. The classical economists wanted rather to find in the peculiar characteristics of the Chinese or any other economy the rational and just structure for economic systems *generally*, or *generally* valid economic laws, and to understand in its entirety the behaviour of men in economic life. The classical economists looked among the variety of actual historical economic systems for the one natural system, and found it in the competitive one. The historical schools of the nineteenth and the beginning of the twentieth centuries, who concentrated on describing individual historical phenomena, were unable to understand this attitude towards history. Their criticism usually failed to see its importance and closeness to reality, and the very good knowledge that the classical economists had of the real economic world.

Nevertheless, classical political economy failed not simply because of defects in its theoretical system, but mainly because its theoretical solutions did not fit the existing historical variety of economic life. We can appreciate the efforts of the classics to discover a rational natural order by studying the diversity of economic institutions, but all the same they did not satisfactorily explain economic life as it actually was. Their analytical powers were applied essentially to the *one* case which they considered "natural", the system of free competition in all markets, while analysis of monopoly was kept well in the background. Yet free competition has never been completely general, not even at the time of the classical writers in the last third of the eighteenth century and the first half of the nineteenth. The historical school has criticised the classics for knowing only their own period, however well their theory may have fitted it. This criticism itself does not fit the historical facts. Even in the era of the classical economists there existed in Europe many closed guilds and monopoly rights, as well as centrally directed economic systems, so that a study of free competition alone does not cover the historical facts of that time. We know that the classical economists did not feel this divergence between theory and reality so strongly, because they were mainly concerned to look for the "natural", rational, and workable economic system, but we, if we wish to understand economic reality, cannot tolerate it.

Economists have to understand not only the economic process in America in 1941 with its powerful monopolies and the important controlling influence wielded by the central administration, but also, equally, everyday economic life in Germany at the beginning of the twentieth century, or the war economy of 1914–18, or the everyday economic life of a great manor of the early Middle Ages. A theory which puts in the foreground of the subject the formation of "natural" prices in a particular form of market in an exchange economy (that is, under perfect competition) must fail when confronted with other historical facts and economic forces. The classical economists in their theoretical analysis did not do justice to the variety of institutions, and thus failed to recognise the magnitude of the Great Antinomy. They built theories which could not justly account for the full range of economic reality and its historical development.[8]

A new start had to be made in the nineteenth century. The point of departure was the realisation that classical political economy did not account for the realities of economic history, and that it had become doctrinaire. All sorts of ways for rebuilding economics on a new basis were tried, but here we are concerned simply with the different types of approach adopted in the study of economics, disregarding the fact that a single economist makes use of different methods, and so is to be classified with different types.

(1) To many economists of the nineteenth and early twentieth centuries consideration of their subject meant the study of concepts and their content. "What is an economy?" "What is the economic principle?" Or more fundamentally, "What is society?" Questions of the definition of concepts were deliberately given first place with the intention of getting an understanding of the "essence" of economy and of economic events.

"Economic theory", says Spann, in a study of exchange and price, "is not merely concerned with the outward appearance of the fact, say, that A and B are exchanging (though there is already a theoretical interpretive element in the way this fact is ascertained), but with grasping the meaning of what is observed, that is, the *essence* of exchange. I shall show that the concept of price is deduced from the concept of exchange, and from that of price the concept of distribution, so I shall begin my study with the concept of exchange."

Such attempts to get at the "essence" of economics by analysing concepts, to formulate this "essence" in a definition, and then to build up systems of concepts called "theories" from which detailed conclusions are deduced, were frequently made by economists in the last century, as a glance at any of the stock textbooks will show. Economics carried on in this way might be called "conceptual" or "formalist" economics.*

* Begriffsnationalökonomie.

It proceeds not only by putting the analysis of certain basic concepts at the beginning, but also by approaching particular detailed problems by analysing concepts. In studying trade problems the first question asked is, "What is trade?" The intention is to understand what trade "essentially" is, before coming to a theory of trade. Only at that stage are the facts considered, and if a firm does not fit the definition it is not included among those engaged in "trading". Those students of the subject who may begin with definitions but do not go on to make deductions from these definitions, applying them to the subject-matter and problems of economics, should not be counted among the "formalist" economists. Only where the doctrine, or part of it, depends on definitions of concepts or "essences" can one really speak of the "conceptual" or "formalist" procedure in economics.

This procedure raises some important problems of intellectual history. It amounts to a resurrection in the nineteenth and early twentieth centuries of the medieval tendency to conceptual realism or reification,* in a secular non-theological and much altered form. It would be interesting to enquire how this came about, but more important here is the question what this procedure achieves in economics.

Logicians have sometimes maintained—J. S. Mill, for example—that every definition contains an axiom. A definition is a proposition that is neither capable of, nor requires verification because it is self-evident. This may be the case with mathematical definitions, but it is not so with definitions in an empirical science when they are properly arrived at. Here, definitions, as we showed in Part I, represent the results of factual investigation and are based on analysis of the subject-matter.

In an empirical science like economics, if definitions are actually made the starting point, then they *are* axioms, or pseudo-axioms. They may be claimed to be self-evident and not in need of verification, but in truth are neither of these. Such subjective definitions are adopted as the premises for deductions, and the validity of the conclusions conceals the fact that owing to the arbitrary fixing of the premises the

* Begriffsrealismus.

procedure is worthless. The term "economy", for example, is defined as "the regulating of human life so as to achieve a lasting harmony between needs and their satisfaction", or elsewhere as "the weighing up of the means to be devoted to ends". A list of such definitions could be prolonged indefinitely. It is held that the goal of the economist and the solution of his problems is to be reached by means of such definitions. This is to overlook the fact that deductions from definitions only yield the knowledge already contained in the definitions. Everyone from his everyday experience has some notion of "economy", and he may express this in a definition. But all the conclusions then drawn are not new scientific revelations, but simply explanations of the concepts previously formed without scientific study.

Spann describes the concept of "society" as the central concept of all social sciences and lays down quite unjustifiably, and without so much as a glance at the facts, that only two concepts of society are possible: an "individualist" or a "universalist". He then decides in favour of a "universalist" concept, and builds up a system for which great claims are made but which in truth only represents the elaboration of propositions already contained in the arbitrarily defined concept of "society". The concept here becomes a fetish. Many economists begin their studies of money with the question of what money "essentially" is, and whether it is to be defined as a "good" or a "claim". The lengthy debates held over this question are absolutely fruitless, for how can one arrive at the essence of money before one has a picture of the interdependence of the whole economic system? But the attempt is made by deductions from a definition of money as a "good" or as a "claim" to solve real monetary problems. In spite of an appearance of scientific rigour there is neither any proof nor verification whatever. Answers to real questions concerning the value of money and the functions of the gold standard are, however, actually attempted along these lines.

In attempting to make deductions from pseudo-axioms or definitions this sort of "conceptual" economist is misusing his powers of reasoning. (Everything that needs to be said about this procedure can be found in Kant. But the *Critique of Pure*

Reason was written in vain as far as "conceptual" economists are concerned.) From this fundamental error stem first, the lack of realism, and secondly the sectarianism, which are both connected with the "conceptual" procedure in economics.

On the subject of lack of realism many may know the story of the medieval monks who were discussing one winter the question whether milk froze. They never thought of finding the answer by putting a bowl of milk outside in the cold, but looked for one by analysing the concept or "essence" of "coldness" and of "milk"—naturally without success. Their procedure was precisely the same as that of the many "conceptual" economists of to-day, when they debate whether economics is or is not concerned with quantities, and start from some concept of "economy". If they would only look for a moment at economic facts, the question would quickly be answered, just like the question of the freezing of milk. But these economists are too distracted by their cogitations about concepts to perceive actual conditions. In the same way the purpose of theoretical analysis, the other aspect of scientific knowledge, is misunderstood. For such economists "theory" is a structure of concepts built up *before* the facts are scientifically established. It is not understood that all empirical sciences have to start work with the concepts of everyday life, and that the only way they can get beyond everyday experience is by penetrating into the facts of their subject-matter and by formulating the problems these facts present—*not* by laying down definitions. The economist cannot legitimately lay down scientific definitions at the start of an investigation. At the same time it is not realised that it is impossible to penetrate into the facts of economic reality without theoretical analysis. The "theory" of the "conceptual" economists has nothing in common with genuine theoretical investigation of real problems.

If the actual course of economic events is looked at in the wrong way, *and* the theoretical apparatus is defective, then any understanding is impossible. What we have called the Great Antinomy is not seen at all. The procedure is both unhistorical and untheoretical. There may be a desire to understand economic reality more profoundly than can be done simply by the ascertaining of individual facts, but as this sort of economist is busy with concepts rather than facts, his discoveries relate simply to his own schemes of concepts rather than to the structure of the real world, with which they have nothing to do. Instead of looking for and finding the order and interrelations in the seeming chaos of facts, they construct a chaos of concepts supplementary to the facts. This sort of economics ends in tiresome and useless debates about categories and concepts, as, for example, in that about Universalism and Individualism, while economic life in the real world, with its many formidable problems, passes it by. Because the "essences" of things are studied before the things themselves, the first result is merely vacuous verbiage, while the things themselves and their problems pass unnoticed.

Sectarianism: the arbitrariness of the definitions laid down by these economists at the start, makes it impossible to come to agreed conclusions. Of necessity their procedure leads to the creation of a number of hostile camps. What comes first is not the discovery of the facts and their problems, or their intellectual analysis, but the arbitrary definition and interpretation of words. Whether such definitions and "essentialist" explanations are accepted or not is a matter of individual sympathies rather than of objective perception. Acceptance of a particular view as to the "essence" of "society" or "the state", or of "a national economy" or "capitalism", is *personally* rather than *factually* conditioned. Sects are formed, with prophets at their head, with a single disciple or a multitude of disciples, one emphasising one word and one another, each having his own personal interpretations.

This history of economics, especially in recent decades, has been marked by the rise and decline of such sects. New prophets are constantly appearing with some seemingly radical point of view and asking energetically what economising essentially is, or what "a nation" or "science" is. They feel they are breaking fresh ground, failing to notice that they are simply following out one of the oldest of errors. If they suit the fashion of the moment their views may have some transient success. But new prophets soon push them into the background, just as they themselves succeeded the old.

Nomina sunt odiosa. Battles between such sects are carried on with all the bitterness of religious wars. Words and definitions become slogans. The scientific atmosphere is polluted, and non-economists are rightly suspicious of such a tumult of personalities and systems. This complaint has often been made. To do away with it we must understand how this sectarianism comes about. It arises, as we now recognise, in the fundamental error of "formalist" or "conceptual" economics. It will disappear only when this error in method disappears.[9]

(2) "The phenomenal world can be regarded from two essentially different points of view: *either* as made up of concrete phenomena in their positions in space and time and in their concrete relations with one another, *or* as forms regularly recurring amid the changes of the concrete phenomena, the understanding of these forms being the object of science. From the former viewpoint study is directed at understanding the concrete, or rather the *individual,* and from the latter the *general,* aspect of phenomena. Corresponding to these two main points of view we find two great classes of scientific knowledge, the former of which we may briefly call the individual, and the latter the general." With this sentence Carl Menger began his famous *Investigations of the Method of the Social Sciences* in 1883, and it summarises the main point made throughout the book. In his view the two intellectual objectives correspond to two completely different procedures, that is, to two different kinds of sciences. Historical economics has as its task the knowledge of concrete phenomena and their individual interrelationships, theoretical economics, on the other hand, has as its task their "laws" or "the general nature of exchange, price, rent, supply, and demand".

We are not discussing here how far this division of economics—and it does not only apply to economics—was already developing in the history of the subject before Menger, or its subsequent effects, or its relations with Rickert's and Windelband's methodological theories. One point only is important here: whether or not under the influence of Menger a division in economics between theoretical and historical studies has in fact taken place. Menger laid down the principle on which many economists carry on their work. A dualism has become widely established in economics. What the theoretical sciences aim at or seek to know is the *general* aspect of phenomena, and for the historical sciences it is the *individual* or particular aspects and characteristics of the empirical world. The two objectives are equally justified, particularly in economics. "These two kinds of sciences differ from one another fundamentally in their relationship to empirical reality. With every step they advance the theoretical sciences move further and further away from empirical reality, while the historical sciences are always trying to get nearer and nearer to given individual facts" (A. Amonn). To put it in another way: the theoretical scientist leaves the individual historical aspect to the historical economist, while the latter leaves the "general" aspect to the theorist. Each tries to reach his own particular goal by his own particular route.

This dualism can only be overcome when it is fully realised what serious damage it has done and is doing. As is well known, more recent developments in scientific method have not followed in the path of Menger, Rickert and Windelband. These divisions in the sciences are not admitted, nor are their allegedly different objectives. There is but one world the problems of which it is the aim of all sciences to understand. Menger's division is, so to speak, a "literary" one and has its place only in books, with no significance in the real world. So let us now drop this philosophical and methodological criticism of "dualism" and confine ourselves strictly to economic problems.

It is true to say that *in so far as this division between theoretical and historical economics is seriously carried out, the real problems of economics are left unsolved,* and the science completely loses its way. For example, during the economic crisis of 1929–33 the collapse of many monetary systems suggested important scientific problems: how did the heavy fall in prices, the unemployment, and the falling off of production come about? According to the "dualist" procedure the historical economist describes the facts in Germany, Britain, and other countries and the fate of the German mark, and finds out the quantity of unemployment and what happened in agriculture, in the iron and steel and coal industries, etc. He is to give an account of the concrete facts. The theoretical economist works out theories of money, wages, and production. He devotes himself to the "general" aspect. The result of all this is very small. No answers are forthcoming to the questions posed, for example, about the collapse in prices, the unemployment, and the fall in production in Germany, Britain, and the other countries during this period. The main objective is not reached. The actual course of the economic process is not understood because its interrelationships are not known. Menger speaks of the historical economist having to discover the concrete relationships, which is *for him* an impossible task. How can he with his historical method find out the relations between a fall in prices, unemployment, and falling production, and the real causes of these events? He sees a confusion of facts side by side, the relations between which cannot be discovered by his methods of investigation. On the other hand a theory of the labour market, money and production in their general aspects does not provide any knowledge of the real world. It is simply "art for art's sake". Both sciences, historical and theoretical, remain sterile and fail to cope with their vital problems.

Here is a second example. Since the end of the last century cartels and cartel policy have been of great importance for the course of economic life in Germany. Economists have tried to give an account of cartels, their formation, their fate, and their effects on outsiders and on consumers. They have tried to describe the concrete phenomena. At the same time we have a theory of monopoly which purports to explain "general" relationships. Both history and theory proceed independently, and only a few economists try to link them together. Just because of this lack of co-operation the scientific treatment of actual cartel problems is usually unsatisfactory. Only when history and theory are combined is it possible to build up a scientific picture of the concrete effects of cartels and of the factors which bring them into being, that is, of the real relationships concerned.

Besides these two examples we could mention all those cases and problems referred to in Part I which all pointed to the conclusion that there can be no knowledge of everyday economic life if history and theory are not harnessed together. Without the combination of the two not even the seemingly simplest of concrete questions can be answered, not even the question why this field is sown with corn.

The impossibility of doing this must be specially emphasised, because in recent decades the separation of historical from theoretical studies has become wider and wider, until now we see two types of economist standing side by side each speaking a language the other does not understand, and neither able by himself to understand the real course of economic life.

In particular there are many modern theoretical economists who in their efforts at the formal refinement of their theoretical apparatus widen this gap by losing contact with historical and other economic facts. Modern economic theory arose out of the effort to overcome the lack of realism of the older political economy. Wieser quite rightly observed that the rejection of speculative doctrines and a desire to get closer to the facts was common both to the historical school and to modern theoretical economics. The actual course of economic life was to be understood by a fresh analysis of the same basic facts. This was the decisive impulse behind the formation of modern economic theory. It has certainly persisted with some theoretical economists and has been responsible for new successes in recent decades. With many others, however, it is no longer effective, and by their theoretical methods they are withdrawing at every step further and further from the real world. Of Marshall, one of the creators of modern theory, Keynes once said: "He wanted to enter the vast laboratory of the world, to hear its roar and distinguish the several notes, to speak with the tongues of business men, and yet to observe all with the eyes of a highly intelligent angel. So 'he set himself', as is recorded in his own words, 'to get into closer contact with practical business and with the life of the working classes'." And Keynes unfortunately was right when he added: "Marshall felt all this with a vehemence which not all his pupils have shared."

The stimulus of concrete problems and the force of historical facts is no longer sensed by many theoretical economists. The increasingly mathematical formulation of economic theory has had the same effect, though there is no reason why it should have done so. The resulting propositions, in spite of their formal and logical correctness, have little or nothing to do with a deterioration of theoretical economic analysis itself which had been mastered by the classics more fully than by many modern economists. There is to-day a very noticeable tendency in the abstract reasoner to keep his distance from the concrete object, and the equanimity with which he ignores historical conditions or leaves them to the historian is often quite astounding. Here is one of the reasons why economic theory does not achieve what it should in explaining the problems of the real world and why the growth in the literature of economic theory is out of all proportion to its real contribution. A new approach must be made if there is not to be a reaction in the direction of an empiricism simply concerned with describing the maximum number of facts, a trend which is clearly observable in America. The new approach must not follow this type of empiricism, which is also incapable of understanding economic reality and its relationships. It must aim at grasping and overcoming the Great Antinomy.[10]

(3) The danger of the dualist separation of theoretical and historical economics leading to complete loss of touch with real economic problems was early realised, though not clearly explained. Early on, Schmoller criticised Menger's thesis of two separate scientific objectives, maintaining that though this separation may doubtless have had some justification, "this division must not be regarded as an unbridgeable gulf". Schmoller and many other economists of similar opinions wanted and want a unified economics, and to this extent we must completely agree with them.

The question remains as to how they want to bring this about, and whether they have shown themselves able to tackle the problems of economic reality and its relationships. Again we are concerned not with individuals but with a method of study and a kind of scientific thinking which has established itself well beyond the confines of economics alone. "Descriptive economics provides the material for general theory. This material is the more complete the more fully the phenomena are described in all their actual characteristics, changes, causes, and consequences," said Schmoller in his debate with Menger. Consequently it is necessarily of primary importance, "to increase, improve and make more accurate our empirical observation, so that with the aid of the better and more extensive descriptive material of every kind, classifications and definitions can be improved, and typical sequences and their connections, causes, and ramifications may be more clearly understood. If a science from time to time concentrates mainly on description it is by no means in neglect of theory, but to provide a necessary foundation for it."

Empirical economists in all countries have acted and are acting in accordance with these principles, whether in trying to describe past or present facts in words or, as statisticians, in figures. The huge quantity of works about different individual trades in the past or present, or different branches of industry or particular industrial firms, about agriculture or social conditions in particular countries, are inspired by the idea that by collecting and classifying facts and describing particular economic situations some final total picture called theory will be achieved. The empirical investigator hopes in this way, that is, by trying to be "realistic", to get an understanding of the real economic world.

This history of science—and not only of economics—teaches that the real world cannot be understood by purely empirical methods. It is only necessary to consider the fate of the German historical school between 1870 and 1930, which arose in the very justifiable effort to study exhaustively the real economic world, but which in fact produced generations of economists who may be accused of lack of realism with far more justice than can the classical economists. It was not faulty procedure in carrying out the programme of the empiricists that led to its failure, but the fact that an understanding of the real world was inevitably out of their reach. Why was this?

In the first place, knowledge of economic reality or of the real world can only come as an answer to a question. Material can only be collected and facts observed in a significant way if definite problems have first been formulated. The historian, say, of Germany in the era of Bismarck has to proceed by constantly asking questions and formulating problems. The mere massing together of material has little sense and fails to reveal the motives of those engaged and their relationships in history. The botanist reaches a proper understanding of a plant by asking questions: What is its structure? How does it get nourishment? How is it reproduced? Were he merely to describe the plant he would simply be putting a number of facts side by side. Similarly the economist. If he is studying the economy of a particular area he is not getting any nearer a real explanation by collecting material about the land and people, or gathering geological, technical, geographical, legal, political, and economic facts. He has to put questions: Why has cotton spinning and weaving been started here? Why are wages comparatively low? Why are the units in agriculture small? Why are the returns from forestry small? The questions are produced out of everyday experience. In looking for an answer to them he is justified in expecting to get a picture of the economy of that area. As his study proceeds new problems will keep arising.

The pure empiricist does not take this path, as may be seen from the many typical examples of his work. He wants passively to record reality as it is in its fullness and to observe and describe it simply by amassing material on climate, land, people, and the legal and economic systems. He does not start from a problem.

Secondly, the empiricist fails to realise that in order to be able to answer a question when it *has* been formulated the instrument of theory is needed. He assigns to theory quite a different function, and considers that the scientist should start by collecting facts, and once he understands the relations between them, he should *then* advance towards theory. Schmoller speaks of the tendency of all science "to become as it advances as deductive as possible", and attacks over-emphasis on the individual and special in the social sciences. A general picture of economic phenomena is possible and necessary, and it is theory that gives this picture. A passage in the preface to the hundredth volume of his *Investigations* is very characteristic: "Works on economic history and the history of administration predominate in this series, and there is not a single volume devoted to theoretical economics. My opponents will say that this is because I do not appreciate theory. My answer is that I rank it too high."

To hold that Schmoller and his followers are not opponents but supporters of theory is correct, only it must be kept clear that this empiricist theory is something quite different from the theory needed for scientific knowledge. The problems of the economic process must from the start be put in a "general" form and treated theoretically in order to discover the interrelationships in an economic system. Theoretical propositions must be formulated and applied if we are to explain, for example, the depreciation of the dollar during and after the American Civil War, or of the German mark between 1914 and 1923, or if the connections between the fall in foreign exchange rates, the rise in prices and wages, the changes in production and in foreign trade relations and in the quantity of money are to be understood. Empiricists believe that the connections between facts can be discovered simply by describing the facts, and that a theory can in the end be constructed out of numerous descriptions of particular cases of monetary depreciation. That such attempts fail is because no *connections* between the facts can be established out of all the material about prices, monetary circulation, foreign trade, the national debt, industrial and agricultural production in Germany and America during this period. Schmoller's demand that *before* a theory is worked out the phenomena shall be described with their causes and effects is completely impossible. The indispensable tools are lacking. So it comes about that empiricist economics collects together a mass of facts, but fails to understand economic reality and its relationships.

Thirdly, the "theory", which according to Schmoller, is to express "what is general and typical in the unlimited variety of daily events in history", exists only in myth. It is to be a description of the *concrete*, but at the same time is to be *general* in character. This "theoretical" picture is to comprise the most important political, economic, and technical facts of Germany, England, and America, at different periods, and yet be "'general". It is useless to ask what the significance is to be of so unhistorical and false a picture of the real world, a picture that has never been painted and never can be. To demand that a theory of this kind be created is to show a failure to recognise the Great Antinomy and to understand the purpose of genuine theoretical analysis. Empirical economics, in spite of its generous words about theory inevitably misunderstands theoretical study, and is incapable of undertaking it.

It is clear from what we have said why the purely empirical economist of any type, even the statistician, is bound to fail to understand concrete economic life and its interrelationships. All the representatives of this method, past or present, fail to perceive how the economic process, of which each individual economic fact is a part, hangs together as a whole. In this way it represents a decline from classical political economy. It has no way of advancing beyond a collection of unanalysed facts. Its vision and thinking is *pointilliste* and unrealistic, for it misses the significance of the interdependence of all economic activities. Because it cannot provide reliable answers to the questions posed, it has to fall back again and again on attempted explanation at the level of everyday experience. The result for empiricist economists is they are incapable of dealing with the biased opinions and ideologies of "interested" parties.[11]

The four ways of thinking in economics which we have sketched here are very different, and at very different scientific levels, but they all fail to understand fully what we call the Great Antinomy. There is, however, another procedure which takes the Great Antinomy as its starting point and thus has a special claim to our attention.

Chapter II

"STAGES" AND "STYLES" OF ECONOMIC DEVELOPMENT

I. THE PROCEDURE

THE BASIC IDEA is quite simple: one looks for phases, steps, or stages in the course of history, with the object of constructing a theory which will explain everyday economic life at each phase or stage, and which is only to be valid for this phase or stage. Karl Bücher, for example, asks for a separate theory for each of his three "stages" of development (household economy, city economy, and national economy*) through which he considers the peoples of central and western Europe to have passed. He maintains that "the working out of such stages of economic development is an indispensable aid, or even the only way in which the results of economic history can be made of service to economic theory".

The motives behind the creation of this complex of economic stages of development differed widely. The leading idea behind all sciences in the nineteenth century was that of *development.* List, Knies, Roscher, Hildebrand, Schönberg, Schmoller, Bücher, and Sombart are only a few names from the great host

* Hauswirtschaft, Stadtwirtschaft, Volkswirtschaft.

of those who saw economic reality as a process of development. Knies speaks of a law of relativity which pervades all studies of economics which follow the historical method. Everything changes in the course of development, man himself, legal and economic institutions, the applicability of economic ideas, and the justification for economic policies. The fact of development is always the fundamental fact and the study of economic development the fundamental task of economics. The task was conceived in a way which corresponded to the spirit of the time; that is, it was believed that what must be looked for were typical forms or regularities in development. "The laws by which the broad development of nations takes place are of the same form as those for individuals", said Roscher. This normal regular sequence of development, it was firmly believed, could be best mastered by working out "stages of development". Such schemes soon met with criticism. But the criticism was itself based on the notion of development. Knies, as early as 1852 wrote, "The general models of the stages of economic development of nations, as portrayed by Friedrich List and his successors, have been discredited. Their abstract basis, the *petitio principii* in which they are involved, and the general sterility of their formulæ must be granted. But", Knies continues warningly, "we must urgently beware of underestimating the significance of the task to be achieved. The study of historical development, the study of the laws of development of an economy, is certainly the only way by which we can attain to a full understanding of the economic situation of our time, and of the direction in which we are moving." Bücher was quite right when he held that a unified conception of the regular historical course of economic development is the foundation for a theory of stages of development.

In the twentieth century this line of investigation has entered a second and new phase. The idea of development now fades into the background, corresponding with the general intellectual tendencies of the time. "Attention is no longer concentrated on the sequence of the stages, or on their connections with one another, or on their development out of one another, but on capturing the different characteristics of the economic life of each stage" (Spiethoff). This new phase in the study of "stages" of development may, perhaps, be called the discovery of "styles" of economic development. An attempt is here made to determine the economic "style" of the classical, medieval, or modern age. These "styles" are to be put side by side rather than one after the other. Compared with the previous investigations of economic "stages" there has been a certain shift in objectives. Instead of attempting to investigate "stages" of development by ranging over the whole course of European history, it is now single periods and peoples that are studied, the procedure being to build up from below. These distinctions between "stages" and "styles" of development may be of interest from some points of view, but they are not important for the question on which we have to concentrate. Both "stages" and "styles" of development are cross-sections from economic history. As Spiethoff says: "Styles and stages are constructed for different purposes. But the results of the construction of stages of development largely serve the purposes for which the 'styles' of development are worked out. The means used are essentially the same, that is both are cross-sections of economic history." Thus the results of working out "styles" and "stages" of development are closely similar. The series of "styles" of development proposed by Spiethoff, household economy, city economy, regional economy, and national economy, are not significantly different from some of the older systems of "stages" of development.

All these cross-sections, whether stages or styles, are constructed for the purpose of overcoming the Great Antinomy. This is the clear aim of their creators. They are to provide a realistic basis for theoretical analysis. Each of these types is to be a picture of historical reality. They are to resemble pictures in which individual details are omitted in order to bring out more clearly the essential features of economic life. The details are left to the economic historian. Sombart's "economic systems" are not meant to be a series of abstract forms, but to capture concrete historical characteristics. His account of "Capitalism" as an economic system aims at describing actual economic life. Bücher was well aware that the "national economies" of to-day contained elements belonging to "city economies" or "household economies". But according to him a particular form of economy, the "national economy", actually predominated or was "normal" in the eyes of contemporaries, and this normality was described in the economic "stage" of the "national economy".

Broad and attractive prospects are here opened up. For every "stage" or "style" a theory is to be built, a historical theory, peculiar to and relevant to a particular period of time and limited in validity to a particular period of time. That is what the earlier historical school wanted. Knies explained that to each stage of economic development there was to be a corresponding stage of theory. The "absolutism" of the classical economists would in this way be overcome. The classics may have been right for their own period and its institutions, but beyond this their claims were unjustified. Contemporary historical economists have essentially the same aims. However the individual "stages" or "styles" of development may be labelled, whether the series consists of "primitive independent economies", "craft industries", "capitalism", or of "household economies", "city economies", "regional economies", "national economies", there will always be the task of constructing a theory for each "stage" or "style" of development. Each "stage" or "style" is intended to give a picture of reality, and so the theory to be based on them has been called by Salin, Spiethoff, and many others "intuitive" or descriptive theory. Sometimes a "timeless" economic theory or a purely formal theory is worked out first, which is to explain phenomena not subject to historical change. But most economic phenomena *are* subject to change, and these are what the "intuitive" or descriptive theories purport to deal with. Whatever the formal terminological details, there would seem here to be a sure way of overcoming the Antinomy, of eliminating the opposition between history and theory, and of coming to grips with economic reality.

This point of view is held by many well outside the circle of those actually working at the construction of "stages" and "styles" of development. Nor is it confined to representatives of the historical school, or to certain economic historians. That history in all its variety is capable of being studied theoretically by constructing cross-sections is widely taken for granted, whatever variations in emphasis there may be over points of detail. This view is held to be *the* solution of the Antinomy. Even theoretical economists when reflecting on economic history, regard their task as that of studying the contemporary "stage" or "style" of economic development. Even those theorists who take no account of the variety of historical development, if asked what it was they really studied, would answer that fundamentally it was the economic forms of the present day, or of the last decade, or of "capitalism". If contemporary circumstances alter, they would hold that the theory must alter, for the forms taken by contemporary events are always for them of particular importance. In a socialist economy, it might be added, economic theory would have to alter correspondingly, just as, for example, after the changes in the economic constitution caused by Fascism, Italian theoretical economists tried to build a new fascist theory corresponding to the political situation and the new economic "style". The only difference between these modern theoretical economists and the exponents of "stages" and "styles" of development is that the interest of the former is concentrated more on the present day, with the economics of the past kept comparatively in the background. The notion is generally held that each period must have its own theory and its own economics and that the economist's task is to adapt his work to the developments of economic history.[12]

A formidable question faces us at this point. Is it possible to overcome the Antinomy in this way and to get an understanding of economic reality? The path seems accessible, but does it lead to our objective? It is not a question of whether this or that conception of the theory of "stages" or "styles" of economic development is the better. We are not asking whether Sombart's, Schönberg's, Bücher's, or Spiethoff's economic "systems' or "stages" or "styles" are to be adopted. Our question is a more radical one: Is it possible *at all* to obtain scientific results by constructing cross-sections of development, and theories limited in application to a particular period? If it is, then we simply have to proceed with discussing the details of such cross-sections. If not, then we must turn back and look for a new path.

II. THE PROCEDURE CRITICISED—A SECOND MAIN PROBLEM

Before beginning our criticism it is necessary to say something about the habitual, but incorrect, application of the term "ideal types" to these "stages" or "styles". Being intended to give a picture of real economic life, the only suitable term for them would be "real types". Such a "real type" as that of "city economy" or "capitalism" is meant to portray the real condition of the economy of a country at a particular time. "Ideal types", as the term implies, do not represent real conditions. We shall be concerned later with how they are obtained, what they are, and what purpose they serve. They differ fundamentally from "real types". We shall show whether and how both "real" and "ideal" types can be used by the economist as instruments for increasing knowledge. But these questions cannot be cleared up if the two sorts of types are confused, and two logically quite different forms are given the same name. To-day *both* "real types" *and* the genuine "ideal types" are called "ideal types", as though both red and green were called "green". The two must be kept apart.

The contrast between ideal types and real types will be brought out clearly later on in this book. It is necessary to refer to it here, because it is impossible to work with an apparatus of concepts which would so soon prove to be faulty. But the content of the critical analysis that follows remains valid also for those who cannot bring themselves to abandon the former inadequate terminology.[13]

The nature of the subject determines the particular questions to be put about this procedure. The aim is to portray historical reality by constructing economic stages or styles of development, thereby creating a basis for theoretical analysis. Two questions suggest themselves. Can the economic reality of to-day and of the past be portrayed by types like these (*v.* Sections A and B below)? And, *secondly*, do they afford a foundation for theoretical analysis (*v.* Section C below)?

The first question, which is historical, subdivides further. We mentioned just now that the creators of these types had two main motives behind their work. Either they wanted to give a picture of the course of economic development; or, putting the notion of development in the background, they wanted simply to construct types representative of what is and has been realised in the economic world in the past and in the present. Can the actual course of economic events be represented by a succession of "stages" (*v.* Section A below)? Further there is the separate question as to whether economic reality at a particular time and place can ever be portrayed by means of that sort of "type" (*v.* Section B below). The latter question is obviously more important for our purpose.

A. STAGES OF DEVELOPMENT

The question whether economic history can be adequately represented as a series of economic stages of development has already been answered in the negative.

(1) All nineteenth-century exponents of "stages" of historical development started with a particular, limited conception of history. For them "history" covered roughly the last three thousand years, this picture being later extended by some thousands of years by the discoveries and decipherings in Mesopotamia and Egypt. There may certainly have been an interest in the conditions of human life in the so-called state of nature, the original conditions of human beings, and in its economy and economic forms, but the beginning of history proper was regarded as coming some few thousand years before the birth of Christ. In the opening decades of this century a revolutionary extension of the idea of history took place. As a result of the co-operation between students of pre-history, ethnology, and history, the horizon has been extended temporally by hundreds of thousands of years, and spatially over the whole earth. The last few thousands of years of European history have their place in the perspective of the whole of world history as a brief unique lightning-flash, the effects of which cannot yet be surveyed. What seemed to the nineteenth-century historian to be the whole, or the one essential phase—these last thousands of years in Europe—is now seen as simply a part of a much vaster whole. The decline of cultures and their regressions emerge much more clearly, so that an irreversible

series of "stages" of development has become completely inadequate. Furthermore, even though the economic organisation of cultures of which there are no written records cannot be at all precisely described, it is perfectly clear that with their different natural, social, and political environment it must have taken on quite different forms. Bücher and other economists wanted to apply their "stages" of development simply to the Hellenic-European area. The narrowness of these limits did not seem of importance to him and his contemporaries, and the whole course of history proper was regarded as having been explained. But as soon as the new and wider picture of history replaced the old one, this limitation to a few thousand years of economic life is seen to be a decisive defect.[14]

(2) However, such "stages" of economic history are inadequate even for the three thousand years of European economic history for which they were specially constructed. That even the limited validity claimed for them cannot be granted is a much weightier and more decisive objection. The very series of historical facts which they purport to explain cannot be compressed into such schemes of development.

For example, we know now that the economy of the ancient world, its economic institutions, the extent of its long-distance trade, and its productivity, reached their zenith in the third and second centuries B.C. An extremely productive economy with extensive division of labour had grown up, especially in the countries of the Eastern Mediterranean, in the empire of Alexander and his successors. From that time on these countries fell back, and as they gradually came under the Roman Empire, entered on a long process of decline which individual emperors' attempts at revival could not arrest. "The outstanding characteristic of the economic life of the later Roman Empire was gradual impoverishment" (Rostovtzeff). If we were to try to apply Hildebrand's well-known scheme of development ("natural economy", "monetary economy", "credit economy") to this long epoch in our culture, we would have to reverse its order if it were not to conflict with the actual historical sequence of events. In the third century B.C. in Egypt under the Ptolemi a banking system arose—that is, a "credit economy"—which decayed in the course of the following centuries. The Roman banking system of the second and 1st centuries B.C. disappeared under the Empire. The regression was not simply one from a credit economy to a monetary economy. Later, in the first century A.D., the monetary economy also collapsed. In the third century A.D. the circulation of coins was confined simply to a few sectors of the economy, and a barter or "natural" economy became again the normal form for economic life. Hildebrand held that the higher form always developed in a gradual transition out of the lower, the new gradually overcoming the old. In these five hundred years the opposite took place, the more primitive form supplanting the more advanced.

Bücher's scheme of development also fails and has to be reversed, if it is not to conflict radically with the facts. The Hellenistic states of the third century B.C. had reached the stage of a "national economy". During the following centuries a process of decline set in: trade fell off, the division of labour shrank, and the towns decayed. In the course of the third century A.D. the peasants in most areas of the great empire returned, so far as it was at all possible, to a "household" economy, almost every farm meeting its needs mainly by its own production. Economic decline, not development, is the basic characteristic of these three hundred years. This was no short interlude or rapidly reversed withdrawal, but a long-drawn-out process, as long as the period from 1400 till to-day. It was a decline of the greatest importance in world history, the effects of which have persisted into our day, and which by itself is sufficient to demonstrate the error of the theories of development and its stages.[15]

There is another case, nearer at hand, of a painful regression which lasted for centuries with after-effects persisting to the present day, which reduces *ad absurdum* the theory of stages of development. There is a widely held opinion that extensive national economies or "capitalism" developed directly out of the medieval city economy with its craft industries working for local requirements. However, in the middle and later phases of the medieval period, division of labour had been developed over a wide area extending to Asia and Africa. The burden of organisation and enterprise was borne by the long-distance traders, who often put out work to their dependent workers. The great cotton cloth producers in the south German towns of Regensburg, Augsburg, and above all Ulm, needed cotton, which came from Syria and Cyprus *via* Venice, and they found their markets as far distant as Spain, France, and northern and eastern Europe. In the medieval town the long-distance trader and wholesaler belonged economically to the leading aristocratic class, which was usually also politically dominant. His field of economic activity was not simply his town and the surrounding neighbourhood, but the whole of Europe. The great cultural achievements of the medieval towns did not take place within the narrow limits of a local "town" economy. Also in the many thousands of small towns there was no "town" economy. They were too small for all the necessary branches of manufacture to develop. There were, too, country towns which supplied agricultural products in exchange for many of the manufactured goods they needed. These came from long distances, and these towns were thus involved in what has, with some exaggeration, been described as "the medieval world economy". The picture as drawn by Bücher, Schmoller, Below, or Sombart of the medieval economy at its height and later stages has been proved wrong. "Towards the end of the fifteenth century a far-reaching unification of Europe took place. Most of the countries of Europe were in intensive economic exchange and communication, and within the total picture of the European economy, as it may justly be called, there were smaller areas of particularly active exchange and particularly close mutual dependence. These were complementary with one another in production and in needs, and formed regional economic units and markets." "Flanders became the market place for the goods of the world. The Mediterranean, North Sea, Baltic, and Central European systems were linked, or woven, together at this point. England, the lower Rhine, Northern France, South Germany, Saxony, Northern and Central Italy, became predominantly manufacturing areas, the seat of textile, metal, and arms production for export purposes" (Clemens Bauer).

This period came to an end towards the latter part of the

sixteenth century. The economic area of Europe was broken up, the former extensive division of labour, with so many branches of production dependent on it, shrank. It was the formation of the modern states which above all brought about this painful long-drawn-out process. The modern state with its new objectives in power politics saw the world market as a battle arena where import prohibitions, prohibitive tariffs, and the other weapons of mercantilist policy might be employed. In Western Europe, in England, France, and Spain, where already in the sixteenth century absolutist states had been built up, comparatively large economic areas remained and these were still further extended by colonial conquests. It was otherwise in Germany, where the old Empire fell apart into countless small states, as also did Italy. The process of decay was particularly marked and persistent in Germany, which dissolved into very small economic units. What took place, therefore, was not an advance from a "town" economy to a "regional" economy, but the break-up of European economic unity. This collapse of the European economy and its division of labour was particularly felt by its main supporters, the towns and cities. The importance of the former great centres of trade and manufacture like Bruges, Lübeck, Nuremberg, and Venice dwindled. The impressive achievement of Augsburg at the time of the Fuggers and Welsers was more a finale than an overture. The economic, intellectual, and political horizon of the "bourgeois" class narrowed. What is often called the "Early Capitalism" of the sixteenth century was in truth the later phase of an economic period. The regression was for no short interval, but was a long-lasting development of historical importance for the whole world, without which it is impossible to understand German political and economic history in the nineteenth century and German life to-day. "It is especially necessary in portraying German history in this period to be free from those false notions of development and progress which suggest that because the German economy of about 1700 seemed narrow in ideas and extent, it must before that time have been still narrower. In this respect the well-known theories of economic stages of development have had a specially harmful effect" (Rörig).[16]

All this schematising of historical development and progress, whatever its basis, leads nowhere. When Schmoller held that in the course of historical development the areas of economic co-operation get larger and larger in size and population, he overlooked the periods of regression. Sombart, too, was wrong when he sought to trace a gradual development from the self-sufficient economic units of the early Middle Ages, through the period of craft manufacture,* down to modern capitalism. The basic idea is wrong. These theories of development and economic "stages" distort our view of history and must be put on one side, if we are to see the historical landscape as it really is.

B. "ECONOMIC SYSTEMS", AS CONTRASTED WITH "STYLES" OF ECONOMIC DEVELOPMENT

Ranke once demanded that every period of history should be judged "not for what emerged from it, but independently as it existed itself". That is truly what we should want to do. To look in history only for lines of development is to run the risk of regarding earlier periods simply as the precursors of later ones, the fourteenth century simply as the precursor of the fifteenth, and the fifteenth of the nineteenth, and of failing to see the individual period or individual man or historical event as they independently existed. The theory of economic stages was intended not only to describe development, but to epitomise the economic life of a period, the economy of the ancient world as a "household" economy,† that of the Middle Ages at their height and in their later stages as a "town" or "city" economy.‡ The question arises as to whether this is possible. The theory of economic "styles" as conceived by Spiethoff leaves the element of "development" in the background. As to these "styles" the only question is whether such "real" types as the "independent" economy,§ the "household" economy,|| the "regional" economy,¶ or "capitalism" can represent the economic form and concrete historical detail of a period. This second question which we now have to answer

* Handwerksmässiger Wirtschaft.
† Oikenwirtschaft.
‡ Stadtwirtschaft.
§ Eigenwirtschaft.
|| Hauswirtschaft.
¶ Landschaftwirtschaft.

goes deeper than our previous one. For it asks whether a living and understanding account of history can ever be given by means of the "types" usually employed.

It would be pointless at this stage to answer in purely methodological terms. The procedure must be seen at work, and only the study of the actual history of economic life can decide the answer.

1. *The Historical Facts*

We shall begin with some cases from the ancient world and the Middle Ages and take as our first example the world-wide Roman empire of Augustus, and the two economically most important countries Egypt and Italy. In Egypt the primeval principle still held that the land belonged to the state, and that the peasants were tenants of the state. The fellaheen worked in compulsory organised groups under the orders and supervision of a state official. They might sell food only with the permission of the state, otherwise most of their produce had to be delivered to the state warehouses, from which it was sold. The earlier Roman emperors tried to create an additional class of independent private landowners, in this way continuing the policy of the Ptolemies. But the mass of the rural population continued in its old bonds to the state, as did many of the craftsmen, traders, shipping and transport workers. They too were often conscripted together in groups under the command of state officials. Side by side with this sector of the economy consisting of the tied fellaheen, was the other predominantly Greek sector with its centre at Alexandria. Here were large private manufacturing and commercial firms with extensive connections and shipping business. Numerically this commercial section of the economy was small compared with that of the older centralised state-controlled monopoly which embraced the mass of the population.

The economic "order" or system* in Italy at that time was entirely different. In Italian agriculture large and medium-sized estates had grown up alongside the older and smaller peasant farms, and occupied a greater part of the country's area. The farmers were linked with the market in differing

* Wirtschaftsordnung.

degrees. Those with the least connection were the older small peasant farmers who mostly wove at home their own cloth and obtained their tools and other consumers' goods from traders and craftsmen by the sale of oil and wine. The medium-sized and larger farms worked more for the market, and being more closely involved in an exchange economy, specialised more on agricultural production for the market. In manufacture in the towns the small and medium-sized firm was predominant, employing partly free and partly slave labour. Organisations such as guilds did not usually limit the independence of the individual firms.

In the course of the first century A.D. the independent peasant disappeared altogether in Italy. The medium-sized and large farm worked by slaves which had been typical of the previous epoch was also on the decline. Instead, the soil of Italy was now worked by small tenants on farms which partly belonged to the emperor, and partly to a small class of private owners. The agriculture of Italy, and therefore the whole economy, was now characterised by another form of land cultivation. A "tenant" economy* had established itself and another kind of economic system† arisen. It would be unhistorical to call something a "style" of economic development which was typical both of the Egyptian economy and of the Italian economy at the time of Augustus, as well as at the time of Hadrian.

Two hundred years later, at the time of Diocletian and Constantine, at the beginning of the fourth century, the economic system of the Roman empire had the following main characteristics. The control of the economy was now in the hands of the state, rather than in those of private individuals. Private property still existed, but the owner's rights were extensively restricted. The husbandman or tenant had declined into partial slavery, being now tied by heredity to his landlord and to his job and its location. Many craftsmen and traders in the towns were also tied from birth to their jobs, being enrolled in compulsory corporations and compelled to demand only the prices fixed by the state. As the farmers mostly produced for themselves the manufactured goods they needed, the

* **Kolonenwirtschaft.** † **Wirtschaftsordnung.**

craftsmen and traders sold little to them. The army, that is, the state, was the main market for manufactured goods. The larger workshops were usually managed by the state, which employed labour tied to the particular workshop, as in Egypt.

The fundamental difficulty in the economic history of the ancient world lies in the fact that it is only for the later centuries, and for certain countries, that the sources are sufficient for an understanding of the economic system of the time. Of fifth-century Athens, of the much discussed Spartan system of the same period, and of the Greek economic system of the time of Homer, we can only obtain a partial picture. It is quite clear, however, that a very great variety of different economic systems existed, and that it is impossible to epitomise this historical variety in a single "stage" or "style" of development.[17]

After the Middle Ages reached their climax, and to some extent already before that, not only can particular aspects of the various economic systems be established—for example, whether market exchange existed or not—but also the structure and framework of the systems. The thousand years of the Middle Ages were by no means without revolutionary changes in the economic system, and different systems often existed simultaneously in different areas. In general two main epochs in medieval economy may perhaps be distinguished: that in which the great manors dominated economic life, and that after about the twelfth century in which the towns were largely emancipated from the domination of the religious and secular landlords, and in which the long-distance merchants of the big cities became the most important organisers of economic life. The crusades and the colonisation of the German territories in the east were especially closely connected with this profound revolution. The first period cannot properly be called that of a barter or a "household" economy, nor the second that of a money economy or of a "town" economy. None of these terms fit the facts and they all fail in the decisive task of making comprehensible the structural elements of the medieval economy. The manors, common down to the eleventh century, belonged to a different economic system from that of the later rent-receiving landlords. Under this latter system the control of economic life passed more and more out of the hands of the manors. The rise of the rent-receiving landlords* was a sign of the dissolution of the old order, the eclipse of the independent economic unit of the manor, the passing of economic leadership to the farms with a consequent change in the conditions of labour, and a closer relation between the individual peasant farmer and the exchange economy. In northern Europe, and in parts of central Europe, the free peasant had maintained his existence, so that in these parts yet another system of agriculture obtained. At the same time we must realise that even in the first five hundred years of the Middle Ages extensive commercial relations existed, though they were confined, except for some particular types of goods, to certain sections of the European economy.

The second period, in which long-distance merchants came more and more to the forefront throughout the whole European economic system, brought the welding together of Europe into one great economic area. In this the single sections, as we have just mentioned, were closely linked together in the provision and marketing of important goods like food and clothing. Again it would be premature and mistaken to conclude, without qualification, that there was a uniform "style" of economic development in this period. Great differences in structure existed between the area south of the Alps, the Mediterranean area, and that north of the Alps. The guilds, for example, developed much earlier in the south than in the north. There were also important differences in economic organisation within the southern and within the northern areas. Lübeck in the fifteenth century, to take an example, aimed in its economic policy at the defence of the positions it had earlier conquered, and closed entry to the guilds, following what was, on the whole, a conservative policy—at the very time that Nüremberg was pursuing a policy of freedom of production, immigration, competition, and of general expansion. The economic system of the two cities was completely different, though both were governed by a commercial aristocracy. Where, as in Freiburg, the craftsmen had gained power in the city, economic policy was, of course, different, the monopoly

* **Rentengrundherrschaft.**

policy of the guilds being prosecuted much more vigorously, so that with imports from other cities being cut off long-distance trade markedly declined. A comparison of these three cities alone at this one period shows three different economic systems side by side, and the differences were certainly of fundamental importance. They affected continually the every-day economic life of the trader, the craftsman, the farmer, and the shopkeeper, and the whole city or area both in prosperity and in decline.[18]

2. *The Different Economic Systems*

These brief remarks on the economic systems of the ancient world and of the Middle Ages, must suffice for the present. If we add now a picture of economic reality in modern times, we may arrive at some conclusions about our problem, which will be essential for understanding economic reality at any period.

(1) Whether it is the economy of ancient Egypt or of Augustan Rome or of medieval France or modern Germany or anywhere else, every economic plan or economic action of every peasant, landlord, trader, or craftsman takes place within the framework of an economic order or system, and is only to be understood within this framework. The economic process goes on always and everywhere within the framework of an historically given economic system. The system may be a bad one, but without a system no economy is possible.

If we were looking down on the world and its amazing swarm of human beings, on the variety of employments, the different patterns of related activities, and on the streams of goods, the first question we would ask is, "What is the order or system underlying all this?" That would be the right question, for we could say nothing of significance about what was going on, if the system remained unknown. Many people who have looked at an ant-heap will have wondered about the system it represents. One of the great differences between an ant-heap and a human economic system is that the system of the ant-heap never changes, as man's economy does. Anyone taking a bird's-eye view of Germany in 1700 or of China to-day, and asking what the economic system was like, would get a different answer from that of someone asking about the economic system in Germany to-day.

Does one central authority direct everyday economic life, or do countless single individuals make their own decisions? Does this system consist of small independent economic bodies, such as family economies? Do the individual units have their own central directing authority? In that case the whole consists of a number of small centrally directed economic bodies, as in many parts of China around 1900. Or are there larger centralised administrative authorities extensively regulating everyday economic life, as did the early medieval manors? If many individual economic units, though they may make their plans independently, are dependent on and exchange with one another—as in Germany around 1900—then the question arises as to the *form* of the system of exchange relationships. What are the rules of the game? The bird's-eye view shows not only streams of goods, but the way in which the detailed day-by-day activities of men fit together. What is the system behind the daily application of labour? For example, in 1940 in Russia and the United States men were working both on the land and in the factories. How were the proportions between these arranged in the two countries? An investigation would have shown very different systems to be at work, in Russia the predominant characteristic of the labour supply being that of a centrally directed economy, while in America freedom of contract prevailed.

In agriculture, manufacture, trade, and communications, whatever the country, there is always a particular partial system: labour relations are ordered in a certain way, and there is always a certain monetary system. All these parts fit together as sections of a whole system, that of the particular economic system in question: for example, the economic system of contemporary France, or that of Byzantium in the eleventh century.

In the past an immense, almost unlimited, variety of economic systems have arisen and disappeared. If one was asked to describe the different sorts of economic system existing in 1700 in the countries of Europe, in India, China, South America, and Africa, a series of pictures would have to be presented as varied as they would be interesting. In the twentieth century the economic systems in the different countries have been changing very rapidly—and not only in industrialised countries. There is a wide variety of economic systems to be seen side by side, for example, those of England, Russia, and Japan, as they were in 1935. The economic system of a country is made up of the totality of forms in which the daily economic process takes its course.

(2) How did the different kinds of economic system, to-day and in the past, come into being?

Most of them grew up in the course of history, only a few being created on the basis of a comprehensive plan. In the ancient world, in the early and later Middle Ages, in the first century or two following the Renaissance, and in the regions outside European civilisation, the various economic systems were usually the result of historical growth and but seldom due to any significant extent to a will to create an entire economic system on certain fixed principles. They were shaped by their framework of physical environment, and by political and economic events at home and abroad, without any comprehensive systematic plan. Certainly, many states in the ancient world and in modern times, and many medieval cities, have influenced their economic system by their economic policies. Nevertheless these economic systems must be regarded as the products of growth, for intervention was mostly not the result of a total plan for ordering the whole economy, or parts of it, such as agriculture, manufacture, and industry or the monetary system. The motives for such measures were rather some passing political difficulties at home or abroad, and they proceeded piecemeal case by case. If medieval towns by measures of price policy, or by blocking immigration, or forbidding guilds, altered their previous economic system, they did so as moves in the struggles for power of their time, or in order to remove particular evils, but not with any fundamental intention of establishing a comprehensive *a priori* system, for, say, the whole trade of a city.

History can show only a few cases where an economic system was constructed on the basis of certain general, rationally thought out constitutional principles calculated to render it efficient. The great re-shaping of the economic system which took place at the turn of the eighteenth and nineteenth centuries and in the first half of the nineteenth century is a relevant example. Private property and freedom of contract and competition were the governing principles by which the economic system was to be shaped. Out of the understanding of the interdependence of the whole of everyday economic life, and from the discovery that competition is a highly effective regulating mechanism, the classical economists developed their governing principles, and proposed great reforms in order to realise these principles in practice. They believed and hoped that a simple system of natural freedom, as Smith put it, could bring into being a well-ordered competitive economy. In this case an economic system was to be built on the basis of an economic "constitution". By an "economic constitution" we mean the decision as to the general ordering of the economic life of a community. Of course, there are also partial constitutions: for example, for the monetary system, for agriculture, or for the conditions of labour.

It may be the case that an economic constitution is intended to shape an economy or part of it, but that in fact the economic system does not correspond, or not completely, with the constitution. This is a characteristic of the later part of the nineteenth and the beginning of the twentieth centuries. According to the basic principles of most modern economic constitutions there is supposed to be private property and freedom of contract and competition. The actual economic systems supposedly based on such an economic constitution in fact diverge more and more from these principles. To an increasing extent, for example, "freedom of contract" is used to abolish competition by means of cartel agreements. The governing principle of competition is thus contradicted by the actual development of important sectors of the economy, for example, in the coal and iron and steel industries. Freedom of contract is often used to alter the form of the market and build up concentrations of economic power. "The simple system of natural freedom", contrary to expectations, does not bring about a competitive order. To take another example, that of the English monetary system at the same period: Peel's Act of 1844 shaped the economic constitution of the country. Definite governing principles, precisely thought out in theory, were to be laid down for the creation of money. The creation of money was to be concentrated in a monopolist central bank, and in the main limited by the purchase of gold. On this constitutional basis the English monetary system was ordered and developed in a manner impossible without such a basis, although the result was different from what the makers of Peel's Act had intended. These men had been thinking of paper money, not of bank money. A system therefore developed in which money was created both by the bank of issue *and* by the private banks by way of credit expansion. The quantity of credit was regulated by the interacting instruments of the discount rate and open market policy, and the English money market was thereby controlled by the Bank of England in a way not foreseen in the monetary constitution.

To summarise: there are, then, two sorts of economic system, differing in their origin, those that "grow" and those that are "created". If the former were predominant in the past, the latter have come prominently to the fore in recent times. The modern industrialised world does not simply let an economic system grow, although the system usually seems to diverge from the governing principles of its corresponding economic constitution. This divergence of *economic* systems from the principles on which they are based applies analogously in many other fields of life, for example, to legal systems. Legal history and sociology have shown in detail how legal norms have either grown or been created by statute. The way cities have been built is another example. Most cities come into existence without any total plan, growing up around a nucleus, and developing in the course of generations through the many individual plans of countless architects. An economic system may grow up in a similar way. On the other hand, there are cities which have been built on a basic comprehensive plan, as were many of those founded in Europe in the eighteenth century. With these, too, the further development was not in accordance with the plan and its governing principles, but diverges from it in important respects—just as the actual conditions under a consciously created economic system often fail to realise in practice the governing ideas of the economic constitution.[19]

(3) The economic system is not determined by the legal system. It depends on the determining economic facts, and on the forms in which the everyday economic process takes its course.

For example, nothing conclusive about the structure of the economy can be deduced from the fact that private property may be established by law. It would be quite mistaken to conclude from the existence of private property that it will be combined necessarily with a predominantly exchange economy. Private property was the rule with the Romans and in the early Middle Ages in Europe, but at these periods many farms existed, both small and large, which were, in the main, centrally directed economic units with few outside relations of exchange. Even to-day in south-east Europe, in countries where there is private property, family economic units can be found which exchange very little with other units. These communities are small centrally directed economic bodies. Many countries in the east took over the fundamental civil law of central and western European countries, although their economic system was completely different, and continues to be so. One could take, similarly, the economic system of German agriculture as it developed after 1933, where the plans of the individual units were powerfully influenced by the central authorities, and where supplies were regulated by a central plan. There was here a strong element of central administration of the economy, but the right of private property remained.

On the other hand, the absence of private property does not necessarily imply central direction of the economy. In various of the empires in the ancient east all land belonged to the emperor, but he did not necessarily control production. He may have done so at certain periods in certain countries, but in other periods and countries the tenant farmers were free to exchange, and the incompleteness of their property rights was only apparent in their having to pay dues. This fact makes economic history much more difficult to interpret. For what is discovered about legal institutions allows but few and uncertain conclusions to be drawn about the structure of the economic system.

Economists two hundred years hence will not be able to form any real picture of the economic system of our day if their knowledge is limited to our more important legal norms. Since 1900 Germany has had one law of property, that of the Civil Code. But she has been through many different economic systems in the half-century since then. During the two great wars central direction of the economic system prevailed, replacing an exchange economy. After the first war, in the period when many cartels and combines were being formed, the economic system again changed its structure, different forms of economic organisation being developed in many branches of industry. After 1933 new elements of a centrally administered economy emerged. But the same law of property was in force the whole time. To conclude that the law of property is unimportant for the economic system would certainly be mistaken. But the form of an economic system is not determined by the law of property. If the Supreme Court of the Reich, for example, at the end of the last century had not confirmed the legality of cartel agreements, the development of cartels in Germany would not have followed the course it did. But that the cartel movement began at all, that cartels took on particular forms in certain industries, while in other industries little was done in the way of forming cartels, so that the industrial system was a mixed one, all this is only to be explained on other grounds. There is also the case of trade unions and the formation of employers' associations. A precondition for these is a suitable law relating to association, but the fact that such groups arise, how and when they arise, and the policy they pursue, cannot be deduced simply from the legal system of the society.

The economic system and the legal system are therefore not one and the same. This is not to deny or belittle the importance which the nature of the legal system often has for the economic system, which is illustrated by the examples we have just given. Correspondingly the reverse influence of the development of the economic system on the legal system is undeniable. The legal system, so far as it is of economic importance, is created mainly in order to deal with already existing facts of the economic system. The laws relating to the family, for example, have not created the family, which already existed of its own accord. The legislator simply gave it a legal form. It is the same with the economic system. The makers and administrators of the law try to modify the already existing shape of the economic system by laying down norms and delivering judgments. Moreover legal norms are often directly created by those engaged in economic activities under a particular economic system. In Germany in recent decades the general rules regulating conditions of delivery, merchandise, payment, etc.,* have been created by private firms or associations in industry, trade, banking, and transport, and have been inscribed into the firms' contracts. A considerable part of the civil law of the state has been supplanted in Germany by this kind of "self-made" economic legislation, to use Grossmann-Doerth's term.

The relationships between the economic system and the legal system change in the course of history. It is not possible to generalise about them here. They have to be studied in the individual context of each historical situation.

(4) Naïve pre-scientific observation cannot give an understanding of an actual economic system. It lacks the necessary analytical methods and its horizon is too narrow, not only because pre-scientific interest usually is confined simply to the existing economic system, but also because it does not even suffice for an understanding of *this* system. The individual German industrialist, craftsman, or peasant has a good knowledge of that part of the present German economic system in which he is himself active. The craftsman knows about his own raw materials and markets, how his firm gets its labour supplies, and he knows some of the relevant sections of the law and some of the regulations of his own guild or union. But he has, and can have, no knowledge of the German economic system as a whole. The individual lives in his own particular economic surroundings and has an outline picture of them. But his surroundings are only a small section of the huge structure of a modern economic system.

* Allgemeine Geschäftsbedingunge.

Only by scientific investigation can questions about the structure of the economic system be answered. Every economist and every economic historian has to answer such questions, because economic reality cannot be properly understood without an answer to them. But they are very difficult questions.

The first difficulty is with earlier periods where very careful and exhaustive study of the sources, and most precise hypotheses, are necessary for clarifying the structure of the economic system. Anyone, for example, who wants to study the economic system in South Germany in the fifteenth century will not learn much from the information available about the legal norms of the time, or from the economic condition of particular craftsmen, or prices, or the turnover of certain firms. He must use the sources with great care if he wants to find out how the "putting out"* system worked in the towns and the countryside, how there grew up a unique system of economic exchange with great power concentrated in the hands of bodies like the great Ravensburger Trade Association, and how many of the forms of a centrally directed economy were fused with many of those of an exchange economy. If he has a picture of the economic system, then information about prices and turnover or the income of the home-workers begins to make sense, and the apparently chaotic juxtaposition of facts and details takes on an order.

This is not, however, the decisive difficulty in the way of understanding the structure of an economic system. The meagreness of the sources about earlier periods is a serious difficulty, but not the greatest. Even the economic system under which we live to-day, and those of which we ourselves have had experience, are not easily understood. If we ask about the economic system in Germany at the time of William II we shall usually get the answer that "capitalism" was then predominant. But this tells us nothing about the structure of the economy. It might be added that "laissez-faire" was the rule, but this also tells us nothing, since it might apply to any sort of system so long as it was not one in which the state shaped the details of economic life. In any case there was not

* Verlagssystem.

at that period a system suitably described as "laissez-faire". "A free market economy" is also an unsatisfactory description. Certainly there was freedom of contract, but within this framework the most varying forms existed, from perfect competition to bilateral monopoly. The term "free market economy" tells us nothing about what these forms looked like. Furthermore, there existed at the same time household units and many agricultural units which did not belong at all to the free market economy. A term like "free market economy" is a crude simplification, and unsuitable as a description, since it tells us nothing about the formative elements in the German economic system of that time, or about the way they fitted together.

A scientific investigation has to describe precisely the individual parts of the system, and show how these partial systems fit together into the whole. No partial system exists on its own, but is linked up by the division of labour with the rest of the economy. For example, it is well known that the monetary system in Germany before 1914—as in most other civilised countries—was regulated by the gold standard, for which special rules of the game existed. Descriptions of the gold standard usually simply account for its technical functioning. But as Lutz says, "a particular kind of monetary system belongs to a particular kind of economic system". The monetary system at that period could only have arisen as part of a particular economic system, and could only have functioned within its framework. Above all, it was necessary for the functioning of the gold standard that German everyday economic life was not controlled by a central authority, but that an exchange economy prevailed in which competition and flexible prices existed, and that the trade policies of states tended to link national economies into a world economy. After 1924 the nature of the economic system changed in Germany and in other countries, an independent trade cycle policy was pursued, the price system grew rigid, and trade policy made the international exchange of goods more difficult. It was then impossible for the gold standard to be preserved as part of the economic system, and efforts to reintroduce it failed. This example is enough to show how the system in one sector of the economy has to be understood as a part of the whole system. This is only possible after scientific study. The same applies to the systems in the labour market or the markets for goods.

Briefly formulated the task of the scientific economist is to get a knowledge of the structure of actual economic systems, this being the second main problem of economics. As the course of everyday economic life proceeds differently according to the form of the economic system, the knowledge of the different kinds of systems is the first step towards a knowledge of economic reality.[20]

3. "*Styles*" *of Economic Development*

Is it possible by "styles" of economic development and similar systems of types to describe economic life, and thus, as Spiethoff put it, "portray the real world in all its essential variety"? The answer to that question is contained in what we have just said, and that answer is "no".

First: the constructors of "stages" and "styles" survey European history, or that of single peoples or centuries, seize upon some characteristics that strike them, and in this way build their "types". They do not start from the question which alone probes the economic reality of a period, that of the structure of the economy. Rather they enquire, far too vaguely, about what is "essential" or "normal" in economic reality.

If the different "styles" of development to some extent explain the structure of an economy, it is more or less accidental. Usually they do not do so at all, and certainly they do not deal with the basic question of the economic system. Let us take, for example, the "stage" or "style" of economic development known as the "city" economy.* We may disregard the fact that, as we have just pointed out, this sort of "city" economy did not exist in the Middle Ages. Even if economic life in the middle and later medieval periods had consisted of a number of such independent economic units, an economic "style" such as the "city" economy would be a useless construction, since it says almost nothing about the economic system concerned. Were these "city" economies

* Stadtwirtschaft.

centrally directed, or were they made up of a number of individual economic units linked together by exchange? What sort of relations of exchange were there? Who bore the main responsibility in the system? How far were monopolies prevalent, and what form did they take? How did all these different elements fit together to form a whole? "Styles" of economic development such as the "city" economy give no answer to such questions, nor do types like "craft industry",* "village economy" or "regional economy".† The concept "national economy" also tells us nothing about the economic system. Even when it is added that the "national economy" is either a "free market economy" or a "planned economy", this is far too vague a description of an economic system. There was an immense and striking difference between the Italian and North American economies of 1936, but to call one a "planned economy" and the other a "free market economy" is an entirely inadequate description of the difference between these two economic systems. The concept of a "household economy"‡ characterises best the system to which it refers, for this construction does point to a central direction of the economic unit, though it does not give any precise description or explanation of the form of the centrally directed economy actually therein realised.

Secondly, this construction of "stages" and "styles" of economic developments leads to over-simplification. The economies of the different periods are described "monistically", while in reality there is always a variety of forms. By simplifying in this way it is believed that one can penetrate below the surface to what is essential. But, in fact, the essential characteristics of economic history are lost, and these concepts are used, as Max Weber put it, "like a Procrustes bed into which history is forced".

When attempts are made to characterise the economic system of the ancient world as a "household" economy, the mistake is being made, quite apart from other historical inaccuracies, of trying to press an immense variety of economic forms into a single type. Such a term as "household" or

* Handwerk. † Landschaftswirtschaft.
‡ Oikenwirtschaft.

"house" economy seems to represent a uniform scheme of things, while in fact, as the short sketch above showed, economic life was multiform and changing. Let us take another example. During the French revolution the economic system changed very rapidly. The opening years between 1789 and 1793 brought the removal of the old order, particularly of the great manors and of the privileges they had held since medieval and mercantilist times, and the establishment of another system, in which the characteristics of an exchange economy predominated. From 1793 onwards, under the pressure of war and with the victory of the Jacobin clubs, economic policy was reversed in the direction of state control of prices, commandeering of supplies, compulsory deliveries, rationing, and in some places the conscription of labour at harvest time. With the overthrow of the Jacobins in 1794 the pendulum swung back from a centrally directed economy towards an exchange economy. These rapid changes in the economic system were of the greatest importance historically, for without them the movements of wages and prices, foreign trade, unemployment, and the shortage of capital, that is, the whole everyday economic life of France at that time, cannot be understood. Those concerned with constructing "stages" and "styles" of development take no account, and cannot take account, of such changes. For them the French revolution is the period of the "early national economy", or of "early capitalism". In this way important historical developments are lost behind a verbal screen.[21]

Thirdly, the construction of economic "stages" and "styles" has often led to economic phenomena being cut off much too sharply from their general historical environment. This is shown by the example we have just taken of the French Revolution. The economic system must not be treated in isolation but has to be seen for what it is, a part of the whole life of a people. By these "stages" and "styles" economic reality is separated for analysis from the other departments of life. Let us take another example. Economic history at the time of Diocletian can only be understood in the context of the totalitarian despotism of late Roman times. Those who work with "styles" of economy, from that of the "household" economy to that of "national economy", are not able to understand this relationship.

If we consider the economy of to-day we see it as one part of the life of the people, bound together with their intellectual and political life. We must get into the habit of treating the past in the same way. Stages of economic development and other systems of types are intended to give a picture of economic reality and facilitate an understanding of it, but in order to create them one has to split up the living historical whole.[22]

4. "*Capitalism*"

The European-American economy of the last hundred years differs essentially from any economy of the past, and it has been necessary to give it a label of its own. For this the concept of "capitalism" has been used and has won wide public acceptance. Many learned authorities have striven to define its characteristics and scope, but for our part we have to ask whether modern economic reality can properly be portrayed by this word "capitalism", in the way in which it is most often used?

There is the one great historical fact of industrialisation, which began one and a half centuries ago in England, and is still in full development. Though it has spread round the world this process is by no means completed and we are still in the midst of it to-day. At the beginning of the nineteenth century it took hold of the countries of western and central Europe, for example, Germany, France, Belgium, Switzerland, and the east coast of the United States. Since the end of the nineteenth century it has taken root in Japan. After 1928 the new rulers of Russia forced it forward in that country on a vast scale. At the present moment the tempo is increasing. China, India, Brazil, Turkey, several of the Balkan states, and Spain want to be, and are being, industrialised. The British in 1850, or Europe and the United States at the beginning of this century, may have believed that they would become in the long run the industrial workshops of the world. To-day we can see that the whole world, wherever the natural conditions are at hand, is beginning to become an industrial workshop. This industrial revolution, unprecedented in world history, not only spreads from country to country, but continues its development in the old industrial countries, such as England and Germany, and as it proceeds on its course new economic forms are constantly appearing. This huge process has brought about the most far-reaching and shattering changes in the whole of men's lives. If the economist is to understand its past and present course he must see it as a part of universal history, that is, he must see how it finds its place within the rest of the history of the different nations and of humanity as a whole. This great historical process has to be treated as a whole, and it must be shown how it arose out of the particular spiritual, political, and economic situation of Europe, how the old units of management in manufacture and agriculture were destroyed, how it was accompanied by social revolution and the new phenomenon of the masses, and what its influence was on politics and war and on the religious and spiritual life of the people. Then it can be understood why in Britain industrialisation took a different course from what it took in Japan or Russia, and why in some places it grew up within the old order and gradually transformed it, while elsewhere destroying it completely.

Furthermore, the economist has to explain clearly *the economic system* under which a country or continent began to be industrialised, and how industrialisation in turn transformed the economic system. The economic systems under which industrialisation originated were of very different forms. In England, Germany, and other European countries the forms of an exchange economy prevailed. In other countries such as Russia and Turkey it was the state which intervened with its centralised administrative and directive measures to set the transformation of industry going. "Civilisation is a mighty wave," said Kemal Ataturk, "and he who is not ready to swim with it will be drowned or swept aside." In these countries industrialisation would not have developed so rapidly from below, as no active independent forces existed, and the pressure of tradition was too strong. Industrialisation was thus started under centralised state leadership. It took on a completely different character from what it had in the west, and worked out with quite different effects on the life of the people. Also, the phenomenon called to-day the "crisis of capitalism" can only be explained in the perspective of world history, and by analysis of *the economic system.* The vast revolution in economic forms which we are experiencing cannot be understood *simply* economically.

Everything which obstructs one's perspective of world history, or one's analysis of the economic system, makes it more difficult to understand modern economic life and its processes. The concept "capitalism" does both of these, particularly when it is used in the way it is.

The concept of "capitalism" was intended to explain a great deal, more even than most other "cross-sectional" concepts. The aim was not only to capture with it the essential nature of economic history lying behind the detailed phenomena, which is the main task of the economist. That was also the purpose of such other concepts as the "town" or "city" economy, or the "household" economy. The concept of "capitalism" is meant to point to the effective responsible agent in modern economics. Such phenomena as the destruction of old handicrafts, the formation of cartels, the expansion of world trade, and the transformation of the social structure were looked upon as the actions of a real being, "capitalism", and our crisis was the decay of this "being". Marx and his pupils have been specially effective in spreading this way of thinking. Many Marxists and other writers regard capitalism as something personifiable, or even actually as a person. We are told what "capitalism" has "done" in Europe or elsewhere, or that it will continue "its" work of destruction, or that at its height "capitalism" lived in accordance with a rhythm of boom and depression, while with its increasing age "it" has become calmer, more settled and reasonable, though "it" continues to destroy stocks of goods and exploit workers. Sometimes this represents simply a peculiar mode of expression, but often something more is implied. Capitalism has often come to be conceived as an active formative being, real and alive. The mass of mankind are generally fond of thinking in such categories and of the particular emotional overtones that are added in.

In the first place it must be noted that a serious logical error is being committed, namely, that of hypostatising. A general concept is treated as a thing, an object, or a person. A general personified concept of "capitalism" is made use of as a substitute for the study of economic reality. The question is asked why wheat, coffee, and other foodstuffs are destroyed in Canada, Brazil, and elsewhere. It is explained that "capitalism" has done this. This is regarded as an answer—a most convenient procedure, but a completely valueless one. Why does this strange thing "capitalism" destroy supplies at these points and not at others? If the student investigated the actual market forms he would then discover that under certain monopolistic market conditions, supplies of goods will be destroyed, and in other conditions not. He would then be getting at reality itself, rather than relying on a scheme of concepts.

Those who like to describe the exploits of "capitalism" in this manner imagine they are being very advanced. In fact, they are falling back into the ways of thought of primitive magic. They provide us with another example of the old error of confusing concepts with realities. The use of the concept of "capitalism" has been harmful in two other respects.

One consequence is that it makes it difficult or impossible to understand history. There is a tendency to explain how capitalism *arose* as part of the whole development of history, but then to separate its further life, and death, and effects from the rest of history. In the eyes of these students capitalism, *after its birth,* leads an independent existence. They fail to perceive that economic life, and hence industrialism also, is always and at every moment a part of the whole process of history with which it is in constant interaction, and that it is the whole time affecting, and being affected by, every other department of human life. "Capitalism" developing from its "early" to its "later" phases becomes a *deus ex machina* apparently providing solutions to real economic problems. Obvious and important historical relationships are overlooked. It can easily be proved that the French Revolution and subsequent changes in foreign politics and the internal transformations which followed, also altered the economic structure of Europe. Also the war of 1914–18, the subsequent peace treaties and revolutions, and the war of 1939–45 decisively affected the economic life of the period. Someone who regards "capitalism" as a personified embodiment of modern economic life, reducing all economic events to the behaviour of this "being", will be blind to the interrelations within history as a whole. He will therefore be able to believe that "in general political events are not of decisive importance for the course of economic development, and, in particular, the history of capitalism has proceeded in complete independence of the great political revolutions of recent centuries" (Sombart).

The whole discussion of the crisis of capitalism is wrong in its historical perspective. The transformation of the economic system and of everyday life can only be understood if economic events are treated together with the whole movement of history at the present time, with the great process by which the modern state was formed at the time of the Renaissance and which in recent decades has taken on a new character and penetrated into all branches of life. The transformation must also be linked up with the advance of nationalism and other ideas. The question must be put as one of universal history. How did intellectual, religious, political, social, and economic events lead to such a profound transformation of economic reality? To enquire about the essence of "capitalism" is to frame the question unhistorically and far too narrowly, to get it out of focus. It is still more unhistorical to believe in some compelling process of development.

Secondly, because the concept of capitalism says nothing definite about the structure of the economy it cannot suitably be used for describing economic reality. Everybody reads into its meaning the structure that suits his personal views: "economic anarchy", or a competitive economy, or "laissez-faire", or the domination of monopolies, or the control of the economy by the anonymous machinery of the state. Worse still, since the beginning of the industrial revolution, that is, for about a hundred and fifty years, there has been a comparatively rapid succession of changes of many different kinds, and a unique variety of economic systems have actually been working side by side. The variety itself is of the greatest historical importance. It has been, and is still, the task of the economist to study it systematically. But the term "capitalism" slurs over this variety. How, for example, is one to understand the profound changes in the European-American economic system since 1920, if questions about them are to be put as questions of the crisis of capitalism, a concept which does not account for the structure of modern economic life? In their search for the essential characteristics of economic reality some investigators have lost the ability to recognise this reality when they see it.[23]

The dire weakness in this procedure of constructing cross-sections, "stages", and "styles" lies precisely at what seems its strongest point. It was and is believed that they equip one with a true understanding of history. But what was constructed was not only an unhistorical series of phases of development, but concepts which illegitimately divorced economic events from the rest of the historical process, and which hindered the understanding of history and of the different economic systems.[24]

C. CAN THERE BE THEORIES LIMITED IN APPLICABILITY TO A PARTICULAR PERIOD?*

Let us ignore the fact that stages and styles of development do not portray real economic life, and even assume that they did not suffer from these fatal defects. Can "historical" theories, or "intuitive" theories, or theories limited in applicability to particular periods, or indeed any sort of theories, be based on these concepts? Can a theory be worked out limited in its applications to capitalism, valid for this period, and losing its validity on its passing? To this question also, though it often gets an immediate and somewhat naïve affirmative answer, we must reply "No".

(1) *First*, reference must be made to a peculiar fact, which has not received the consideration it requires and which it ought to stimulate. For over a hundred years distinguished economists have urgently and almost uninterruptedly been demanding that theories should be constructed limited in

* Zeitgebundene Theorien.

applicability to single historical periods, "stages", or "styles". Down to the present day not a single theory of that kind has been created.

It has been held that the classical political economists worked out a theory for their time, and that classical economic theory was adequate for explaining the economic process in England at the end of the eighteenth and the beginning of the nineteenth centuries. The classical theory was, on this view, a theory applicable to a particular period, and such theories ought to be developed for other countries and cultures. But the logical character and the range of validity of classical theory is not rightly described in this way. Not only is the relation of classical economics to history misunderstood, but there is also a misconception regarding the actual economic system existing at the time of the classical economists, which was not by any means a purely competitive system.

Modern theory, also, does not, as some modern theorists hold, describe or explain everyday economic life under "capitalism". It does both less and more than this. *Less* because it does not describe any real economic world, and so not that of capitalism. It consists of analytical tools of thought which first have to be applied before concrete phenomena can be described. It does *more*, because theoretical propositions are tools of thought suitable for application when particular conditions obtain, and for explaining concrete relationships, at *any* historical period, and by no means solely in the epoch of capitalism or at the present time. Modern economic theory cannot be interpreted as limited in applicability to a particular period.[25]

The urgency with which whole generations of economists have striven after theories valid for a single period of time—that is, for theories limited in applicability to a particular period—contrasts sharply with their complete failure to construct them

(2) Why cannot this programme of theories limited in application to particular periods be carried out?

Let us take that much discussed "style" of economic development the "town" or "city" economy. Is it possible to build a particular theory applicable to it? The answer is "no";

because the concept tells us nothing about the structure of the "city" economy. There can be no doubt that the everyday economic life of a city proceeds differently according to the economic system existing. Have all the guilds in the city a monopoly position, or are they altogether forbidden, or controlled by the town administration, or does the town administration intervene directly in supplying the inhabitants with goods, and if so which goods? Without an answer to all these questions it is impossible to attack the problem of how the economic process of a city fits together. It is not simply an accident that no "theory" was worked out for the city economy, for this was an impossibility.

Corresponding objections hold good for the concept of "capitalism". Because "capitalism" does not describe the structure of the economy of to-day, it is unsuitable as a basis for theoretical analysis. The economic systems in the so-called "capitalist" countries are so various and changing that the preconditions for the construction of a single theory to explain everyday economic life under "capitalism" do not exist. If a theory is claimed as achieving this it must be over-simplified and remote from economic reality. For example, such a question as how investment proceeds under "capitalism" is inadequate in its very formulation. The process of investment differs according to the structure of the economy, and depends on what form of exchange economy, or centrally administered economy, or what sort of monetary system exists. All this is concealed by the concept of "capitalism". Theoretical deductions are of little use if they start by assuming conditions so obscure and so ambiguously described as those given by the concept of "capitalism", for the very foundation on which the theoretical structure is to be built up is uncertain. Ingenuity and carelessness are here curiously blended.

The "city economy", "capitalism", and other cross-sections, "stages", and "styles" of economic development do not provide any precise manageable set of characteristics. Every theory contains propositions which state necessary relationships valid under certain sets of conditions, and these propositions cannot be worked out if no clear set of conditions is provided as foundation. These concepts are useless as analytical tools for theoretical work. The demand for theories applicable to particular periods is a demand impossible to meet, in the future just as it has been in the past.

This procedure completely fails to overcome our Great Antinomy. It does not succeed in portraying the variety of forms in history (*v.* Sections A and B above), nor with its cross-sections does it provide a basis for theory (*v.* Section C above). It helps neither history nor theory, and fails in its objective of understanding economic reality. Nor can it be saved by minor corrections, by talking about "styles" rather than "stages" of economic development. All such alterations are irrelevant, for the method itself is fundamentally wrong.

This brings us to the end of our critical survey. Our conclusion must be that none of these attempts to arrive at an understanding of economic reality have been successful. Either they have avoided the Great Antinomy, or else an energetic attempt at a solution has been made, but made unsuccessfully. The accusation that economics is remote from the real world often comes from interested parties who find scientific study of their field of activity inconvenient, and it may therefore be disregarded. But the accusation is not without justification when scientifically supported. Economics is without a perfect method for arriving at scientific experience, for penetrating with the necessary sureness the superficial view of everyday life, and seeing the facts as they really are. This situation is felt by many economists and non-economists. I hope I have made clear the reasons for it.

Every effort must be made to overcome this state of affairs. Because the established doctrines fail before the Great Antinomy, we must make a completely new approach to the subject-matter itself. Simply to continue on existing lines, either "historical" or "theoretical", is impossible. From now on we shall disregard for the time being all existing economic doctrines and hold quite radically to this standpoint. We are not assuming, to start with, any economic doctrine of any kind. We are simply looking at everyday economic life and asking questions about it, seeking to understand it quite spontaneously. This implies no contempt for the great achievements of the past. On the contrary, just because we are turning away from established doctrines to the actual subject-matter we shall arrive in the course of our studies at a true relationship with the scientific achievements of the past.

The preceding criticism has cleared the ground thoroughly for an approach to our subject. In the course of this criticism we have managed to get to grips with our problems, that is, with the *first* main problem of how everyday economic life hangs together, and with the *second* main problem of the structure of the economic system under which everyday economic life proceeds. If these two problems are solved for a particular community or period of time, then economic reality is understood. It has been shown that neither of these two main problems can be answered by everyday experience. An understanding of economic reality as it is to-day, or was at any earlier period, can only come in the form of scientific answers to these two cardinal and closely related problems.[26]

Part III

SCIENTIFIC UNDERSTANDING OF ECONOMIC REALITY

Introduction

The constructors of cross-sections of economic development have avoided concrete detail in order to arrive at what is "essential" or "normal" in economic reality, yet that has not enabled them to attain their objective. We shall try to reach a solution of our two main problems from the opposite direction, by going straight to the heart of the detailed facts. This may seem paradoxical at first, to try to formulate generalised problems for theoretical analysis by studying detailed facts. But we shall see where this leads us.

We want to break completely with those economists who wish to leave factual economic knowledge about the contemporary world to practical men or students of business economics, and knowledge about the past to historians. Detailed conditions are precisely what we want to make a thorough study of, not by diving headlong into a sea of facts, nor, of course, simply by crude everyday observation. A farmer's wife goes to market year after year, yet she knows little of the network of relationships in which she is involved. The scientific approach to economics is from the start distinguished from the pre-scientific by the profundity of the questions asked and the analytical penetration with which the facts are approached. For the reason we have just explained we shall take the two main problems in the opposite order from that in which we first stated them, investigating first the different forms of economic system, and then the interrelationships in everyday economic life.

Chapter I

ECONOMIC FACTS

I. ***Facts about the Present***
II. ***Facts about the Past***

I. FACTS ABOUT THE PRESENT

LET US BEGIN with what is nearest to us in our everyday life and consider what there is to be seen. Here is a greengrocer and other shops, a shoemaker and some other small workshops, some factories, farms, the railway, the household in which I live, a number of other households, and many similar establishments. I shall go into some of these and investigate.[27]

The employee A, who works at an artificial silk factory, lives with his family of three on a housing estate. Two facts stand out after a study of this household. The first is that the household does not live a special existence of its own, but is closely linked up with businesses and other households. The husband goes to the artificial silk works and earns his wages. The wife buys food, clothing, and most of the other goods used by the family from traders, farmers, or craftsmen. Moreover the family is linked with a monetary institution in that it has an account at the savings bank. The second important point is that the family has an economy of its own to manage. The garden is planted according to a definite plan with potatoes and vegetables by the members of the family, who themselves consume the produce. To this extent goods are produced which are not exchanged with other households or businesses. The household thus has two aspects. It is part of a great exchange economy, and it is itself a small self-sufficient economy. Of course, both aspects are linked together. For example, what the family grows in its garden is determined partly by the prices that have to be paid in the market for vegetables and other goods. For the moment, however, we are simply concerned with emphasising the fact of the dual aspect of the household.

At this point the process of abstraction begins, which it is of decisive importance to understand. The individual features of an individual phenomenon—in this case the household A—are extracted and ideal types built up out of them. This is in sharp contrast to the "generalising" abstraction which seeks to fasten on to what is common to *many* phenomena, and with which the constructors of "stages" and "styles" of development work. The method of "isolating" abstraction, or of abstraction of the distinguishing or significant characteristics* starts from the individual fact. (We shall frequently be returning to this extremely important distinction between the two different methods of abstraction.) Von Thünen built up his ideal type of the isolated state from a *single* particular farm. In the concrete case of this single household of A's there are two constituent elements. Extracting each significant element in turn we have two different *types of economic system*,† that of the "exchange economy"‡ and that of the "centrally directed economy".[28]§

Here is a second and more difficult case. The cotton spinning and weaving mill T in the town R in Central Germany was simply a unit in an exchange economy, and was under no sort of central direction. But the kinds of relations which the business had with markets were of many types. For the sale of its thread it had entered into cartel agreements with other German spinners, and thus in these markets it belonged to a monopolistic organisation of a special kind. On the other hand, in the many markets for woven goods in which it was a seller, competition prevailed. Wages were fixed by negotiation between the employers' association and the textile workers' trade union, that is, between two partially monopolistic organisations. Electricity was obtained from the city power station, which had a complete monopoly.

Five years later, in 1934, the picture had completely changed. By the Spinning Industry Act and by other state

* "Pointiernd hervorhebende" oder "isolierende" Abstraktion.
† Wirtschaftssystem. ‡ Verkehrswirtschaft.
§ Zentralgeleitete Wirtschaft.

measures this firm, like all other German textile firms, had been brought under direct central control. In particular, the free purchase of raw materials was no longer allowed, and its cotton and other materials were allocated and distributed by a central authority, instead of being left to anonymous market forces. The installation of new machinery was limited by a veto on investment, another characteristic of a centrally directed economy. In so far as it remained a unit of an exchange economy the firm's situation had also altered. Employers' associations and trade unions had now disappeared, and the state had a much greater say than before in fixing wages. Cartel agreements were forbidden and the prices of most goods were fixed by the state either directly or by regulations for their precise calculation. We have now reduced the real conditions under which this textile firm operated to certain pure forms by extracting the significant characteristics. We thus discover, besides the main types of the "exchange economy" and the "centrally directed economy", particular forms of demand and supply in the exchange economy describable as "competition", "monopoly", and "state control of prices". It is with these pure forms that we are concerned.

Thirdly and finally: the peasant A's farm in Hesse is, like most peasant farms, both household and business unit. In 1938 it contained many of the elements of a centrally directed economy. The farm provided the peasant and his family with meat, vegetables, and fruit, and to that extent was a form of small-scale economy under central direction. At the same time large-scale centrally directed bodies were acting on the farm and shaping its structure. The peasant had to adhere to the restrictions on planting sugar-beet and hops. In these two branches of production the farm is simply a cell in two great public centrally directed bodies operating throughout Germany. At the same time the farm is in many respects part of an exchange economy, with which it is linked in a variety of ways which alter from time to time. In 1938 rye, pigs, milk, and other products were sold at prices and places fixed by the state, while five years before the prices had been formed by the market. In 1938 the peasant could count on certain minimum prices for wine, but the price actually paid depended on auction. The wage rates for agricultural workers were fixed by the state, as were the monopoly prices for artificial fertilisers. All these measures were important for the everyday life of the farm. Had there been no restrictions the peasant would have planted more sugar-beet and hops, while as a result of the price regulations he fattened more pigs and used more nitrogen fertilisers than would otherwise have been the case.

There is an important conclusion to be drawn from this analysis of the formative elements* in the activities of an individual farm, household, and firm. Nearly every household or business to-day has its special characteristics. This multiformity becomes all the clearer the more individual economic units are studied and the more thoroughly they are investigated. But it results only from the different ways in which the formative elements are themselves combined. The number of pure formative elements to be found is limited. This conclusion will prove to be of importance for the whole nature of economics. *Just as a huge variety of words of different composition and different length can be formed out of two dozen letters, similarly an almost unlimited variety of actual economic systems can be made up out of a limited number of basic pure forms.* It is the task of economics to investigate these as thoroughly as possible by extracting their significant characteristics. To study them thoroughly is to discover all those ideal types of economic forms out of which actual economic systems present and past have been, and are, composed.

II. FACTS ABOUT THE PAST

The above description also outlines the procedure which the economist must use in studying the economies of the past or those of different countries or cultures. Here, too, there must be no retreating from the concrete to the general, especially in the early stages. The individual economic fact or particular concrete economic form has to be studied. The sort of history which is of most help to the economist, and particularly the theoretical economist, is not that which consists of large-scale

* Ordnungselemente.

surveys of whole decades and centuries, but that which gives an understanding portrayal of detailed phenomena.

To ask economists to alter their attitude to history as radically as is here shown to be necessary will certainly meet with opposition. They will cling to their old schemes, their "stages" and "styles" of development, and, although it is such an obvious step to adopt a historical method which aims at probing particular individual conditions, it is one that will only be taken gradually. It is also necessary when studying, say, the German economy in 1900 or in 1700, to give up the construction of comprehensive generalising types such as "Mature Capitalism"* or "Early Capitalism".† Instead, individual economic forms must be analysed for their formative elements, with the synthesis following at a later stage.

Having cleared away the confusion in which the old doctrines of types have obscured the actual remarkable wealth of economic forms, let us now look at medieval economic history. We find manors of different kinds, holdings belonging to free peasants, firms of long-distance traders in the cities, the businesses of craftsmen, home-workers, and shopkeepers all closely bound up with their households. Let us study a few of these economic forms more closely.

(1) First take the monastery of Bobbio in Northern Italy, a domain in the valley of the Trebbia, of whose economy in the ninth century L. M. Hartmann has given us such a vivid picture. Bobbio was a rich monastery, owning property in different parts of Lombardy sometimes as far as 170 miles away. Communications were by boat along the Po and the Ticino. Bobbio was by no means the richest monastery of its time, and it can be taken as typical in form of the religious and secular manors of Northern Italy of that day. The centre of this great economic structure was the monastery itself and the thirty-six buildings adjoining it. Here were not only the offices of its administrative authorities, but also the farmhouses of its autonomous neighbouring estates and its business departments. The greater part of the land of the manor was worked independently: this was the manorial land. The property was so scattered that not all the manorial land could be cultivated

* **Hochkapitalismus.** † **Frühkapitalismus.**

directly by the monastery, so that a number of special subsidiary farms were worked (strictly subordinate to the central administration), under the direction of a special supervisor. A certain division of labour was carried out so that particular subsidiary farms specialised in particular goods; for example, that at Lake Garda, whose speciality was the production of oil. A smaller part of the whole property was let out on lease to free or partially free peasants or to serfs. Altogether there were about 650 tenants. The distinction between the independently worked manorial land and that let out on lease was clearly maintained in the economic calculations of the central administration. But the two divisions were closely bound up with one another, for example as regards labour. For the manorial land there were slaves available, but not in sufficient numbers. The feudal services of the tenants were therefore of the greatest importance and were obtained under very differing conditions. The free tenants were obliged, in addition to giving up a percentage of their products, also to pay a small sum in money, and, furthermore, to work for a certain number of days on the manorial land. Sometimes it was only for one or two weeks in the year, sometimes for one or two days per week. The serf, on the other hand, usually had no fixed limits to the services he was obliged to give, while the delivery of produce was of less importance. Here and there feudal service was the one burden of the serf, who differed from a slave only in having his own household.

Manufacturing was one of the main activities of the manor and was concentrated in the buildings adjoining the monastery. Here, in special establishments, bakers and butchers, shoemakers and weavers, saddlers, smiths, parchment makers, carpenters, and coopers were at work. Manufactured goods were also produced on the leased farms partly for their own consumption and partly for delivery to the monastery. It is clear from the documents that the direction of so great an apparatus of production, and the distribution of consumers' goods for the many people co-operating, as well as for cultural and entertainment purposes, was an administrative task of considerable difficulty.

Bobbio was as little cut off economically from the outside

world as were most of the other manors of that time. The payment of dues in money by the tenants amounted annually to about 220 gold *soldi,* and seems to point to links with a monetary economy. Various goods were purchased from outside, for example cloths and spices. Bobbio, also, had received the privilege from the Emperor Ludwig II of holding a market on its property. Thus the manor, as frequently happened, had the authority to hold markets, and it was expressly laid down in the privilege that merchants should pay no duty as they travelled to and fro.

From the point of view of the economist Bobbio represented a peculiar blend of different formative elements. At the centre of this cosmos was a centrally directed economy to which hundreds of small economic "worlds" or units—the economies of the tenants—were attached. These in turn represented small economic bodies mainly under central direction. At the same time they were fused in a great centrally directed economic body. In this great monastic economy freedom of consumer's choice for the dependent slaves, or for the half-free, was scarcely possible. Nor, in so far as they worked on the manor, could they have free choice of work. This fact will emerge as an essential characteristic of the centrally directed economy. The people were in every respect subject to the orders of the central authority. In so far as free men entered into contracts with the administrators of the manor, another typical characteristic of a centrally directed economy was present, which will have to be discussed further. In principle the free worker was not *compelled* to work in Bobbio, but there was no tradition of freedom, which was severely limited by the length of the labour contracts, which usually lasted twenty-nine years.

The prevailing features of Bobbio were those of a centrally directed economy. They predominated, but not exclusively. They were supplemented by elements of an exchange economy, which were blended with them. For Bobbio produced for the market in order to be able to buy from the market, so that the administration always had a certain balance in cash to meet its commercial needs. Its whole economic structure was a complex of structural elements which, in order to distinguish them in their pure forms, we have to extract one at a time.[29]

If we were to make similar analyses of agriculture in the fourteenth century, we would find that it was composed of similar structural elements put together in a different way. In the meantime the large-scale unit in agriculture had been dissolved, the principle unit being now the peasant farm, most of whose produce was used to meet the needs of the peasant's family, or for the manor. The control of production was shared between the head of the family, the provincial co-operative which distributed holdings to its members and made regulations regarding the common land, and finally the lord of the manor. Thus three economic units were linked together in the central control. Some goods were produced for exchange with neighbours or at a nearby town which was a centre for market relations, and for whose contractors some peasants were working as home workers. In this economic system, too, elements of both types of economy were fused, though in a different form.

(2) The medieval crafts were also not as uniformly organised as the theories of the "city" economy hold. On the contrary, we meet here an immense and almost unlimited multiformity. This is of special interest because the question has arisen whether uniformity in the structural elements can be found here or not.

For the individual craftsman in the Middle Ages it was of decisive importance whether his trade was "closed" or "open". The trade may frequently have been a closed one, but the degree and nature of its closure differed. In some towns, for example, the number of butchers', bakers', and shoemakers' shops was fixed by the authorities. Other methods of closing a trade were common, such as compulsory membership of a guild. Then, if the guild had the right to refuse admission, or demand high entrance fees, it, rather than the state authorities, could close the trade. Sometimes craftsmen could even restrict the trade to particular families, as the Paris weavers did in the thirteenth century. On the other hand, guilds were often unable to enforce strictly compulsory membership of a guild, and had to be content with some loose restriction of the circle of members. Frequently the city administration laid it down that no one might practise a trade who did not belong to a guild, but that the guild was not justified in refusing admission or demanding entrance fees. So it was in Padua in the thirteenth century, or in various trades in Cologne in the fourteenth century. Indeed, new entrants often met with illegal obstruction. But the looser obligation to join a guild was economically of quite different significance from a strict law.

At the same time, in many parts during the Middle Ages there were "open" trades, where admission was free and did not have to be acquired through a guild. Certainly, the intervention of the town council in setting up independent master craftsmen if the guilds misused their powers, only gave a limited freedom of entry to the trade. But many city administrations went further. We have already mentioned Nuremberg. Brescia in 1280 laid it down expressly that anyone could practise any craft without needing to join a guild.

It would be a mistake to assume that if a trade was closed monopoly always prevailed, or if it was open, competition. Certainly the limitation on numbers entering a trade was a valuable privilege for those engaged in it, which eased the way to agreements for monopoly control of the market. If the number of bakers, butchers, or shoemakers admitted was large —it was often a hundred or more in some towns—it was not easy to build up monopolies in spite of the closure. The policy of the town government often worked against monopoly agreements.

The reverse might also occur. In cities which followed a policy of freedom of entry the craftsmen in a trade could unite and organise for the monopolistic control of their market. Bologna in the thirteenth century is an interesting example. Like many other towns it followed a policy of freedom of entry, but it tolerated unions in some trades, though not in all. Unions were formed, for example, by the tailors, carpenters, and blacksmiths, and they tried by pressure on competitors to bring them all into the agreement, using methods familiar in the monopoly warfare of modern times. Sometimes several unions would exist in the same trade, as with the shoemakers of Bologna in the thirteenth century, where four different ones were reported, the situation resembling a kind of small-scale oligopoly. Often competition existed in open trades, and in many different forms. Often the creation of any sort of union was forbidden by the town council, as during the thirteenth century in Landshut, Goslar, and Zurich. The craftsmen in a town might sell their wares at large markets in competition with one another and with craftsmen from other cities, like the goldsmiths of Nuremberg, Cologne, and Augsburg, who sold their goods themselves at the Frankfurt fair. But these were special cases. Much more important was the greatest of the medieval craft industries, textiles. For example, the linen and fustian weavers of the south German cities were often in competition with one another, selling their products individually to middlemen who marketed them. The middlemen or "putters out"* were well provided with capital, and individually or in groups often had a monopoly position. The craftsmen were much more favourably placed, where they could unite to deal with the monopsonistic groups of middlemen and conclude collective sales agreements. That happened, for example, in Lübeck in 1424 between the amber workers' guild and a group of long-distance traders who marketed amber goods in west and south Germany and in Italy. This was a case of bilateral monopoly.

Finally, we must remember that the city authorities often fixed prices by law, particularly in markets where monopolies were active. We now have a notion of the number and variety of economic forms in medieval craft industry. We have also found significant characteristics to extract, from which different ideal types of economic system can be worked out.[30]

(3) All the economies in history can be analysed by these methods, not only those of the European peoples of the last thousand years, but also those of ancient Egypt, Babylonia, or China, at different periods in their history. We shall later discuss some of these. (The purest form of centrally administered economy is to be found in the Inca State of the fifteenth century.)[31]

* Händler-verleger.

Our task is always to bring out fully the individual characteristics of each case, say those of the Chinese family economy, taking care never to tone them down by looking for the "normal". We will everywhere see that it is careful scrutiny of each case which, though we may have expected the opposite, leads to the discovery of a certain limited number of basic forms. These basic forms are composed and combined in differing ways in actual economic structures. Which structural elements dominate and which are supplementary will differ, as will the entire historical environment. Nevertheless, in the immense number and variety of economic systems under which men carry on, and have carried on, their economic existences, certain recurring elemental forms are to be found.

We have now achieved an introductory understanding of these forms in their ideal types. This may perhaps serve as a basis for eliminating the Great Antinomy. We have made a beginning, but lack two things: *first,* an exact scientific description of the individual forms in their ideal types, which have up to now only been described in the imprecise language of everyday life; and *secondly,* a systematic survey of all these types in which all the various forms found in actual economic units are worked out one by one and systematically classified.

Chapter II

THE DIFFERENT TYPES OF ECONOMIC SYSTEM

INTRODUCTION

THE BASIC CONSTITUENT forms cannot be precisely and systematically worked out by relying on speculative generalisations or by laying down axioms. This would only widen the gap between the historical facts and our theoretical investigation. Arbitrary model-building is a serious, though a common error. We can only make this new step in the analysis if we keep in close touch with the real economic world. We must continue to stick to the path we have been following. For the task that now faces us we must start from our previous results in the historical field and penetrate further into the structure of particular individual economic units.

Pursuing our investigations in greater detail on these lines, we shall come very soon to a conclusion which will later be shown to be of great consequence. The actions of any director of an economic structure or unit are always based on an economic plan. If we ask why the peasant is ploughing a field to-day, the answer is because it is part of his economic plan. Why the agricultural worker is ploughing on a large farm? Because of the economic plan of the estate manager. Why does the housewife buy a hundredweight of potatoes to-day? Because it is part of her economic plan. Why does B work as a metal worker in a machinery factory? Either on the basis of his own economic plan, or, if on the orders of the state authorities, in order to carry out the economic plans of those central authorities. Similarly, if the administrators of the St. Gallen monastery in A.D. 980 planted particular kinds of fruit, they did so on the basis of their economic plan. Just the same holds for the controller of an Egyptian temple economy in 500 B.C. At all times and places man's economic life consists of forming and carrying out economic plans. All economic action rests on plans. The precision and the temporal range of the plans are very different with different people, as we shall discuss later. But none of men's economic actions are without a plan.

The individual plan and its formulation must be the first objective of the following investigation. This is necessary if we are to determine systematically what are the pure structural elements out of which all actual economic units or structures are built up.

In this way we shall obtain a precise conception of the two pure elemental forms which are to be met with in whatever periods we study: they are, the ideal type of economic system we call the *centrally directed economy*, in which there is no exchange, and the type of system we call the *exchange economy*. The characteristic of the centrally directed type of system is that the control of the entire everyday economic life of the community follows the plans of a central authority. If the economy of a society consists of two or more independent economic units each of which is formulating and carrying out economic plans, then there is an exchange economy.

No other types of economic system, or even traces of others —besides these two—are to be found in economic reality past or present. It is hardly conceivable that others can be found.

I. THE CENTRALLY DIRECTED ECONOMY: ITS TWO FORMS

Some modern economists have asked whether a completely centralised control of the economy of a great community is practicable, and, there are grounds for doubting this indeed. In particular, it has been contested whether, if prices are not formed in the course of the economic process itself, economic calculation of a precise and significant kind is possible (and that without calculation the economic authority in preparing its plans is simply groping in the dark). Were it not possible, the directors of a great centralised economic body would be faced with an insoluble task. Such arguments play an important part in contemporary discussions of economic policy and touch upon a problem of the greatest importance. Certainly the task of guiding a huge economy of a purely centrally directed type, comprising tens of thousands or millions of men, would eventually meet with the greatest difficulties because of the impossibility of precise economic calculation. Here, however, we must leave the problem of economic calculation by large centrally directed bodies undiscussed. In the real economic world this problem is not met with in its full acuteness for two reasons: the economic structures under central direction are usually small, comprising a single family, or perhaps a few dozen or hundred people, where those in control can personally survey all economic events and themselves estimate directly the values of goods and services, and quantify their valuations precisely. The *simple centrally directed economy* or the *independent economy or economic unit*, as we shall call this form of small economy, which is of great importance historically, solves the problem of economic calculation in a comparatively simple way.

We must consider now the centrally directed economy which, because of its size, needs a special administrative apparatus, that is, the "centrally administered" economy. In this case, because of the size of the community and the number of goods to be valued, it is impossible to express the values of goods in quantitative terms. While in the exchange economy scarcities of particular goods are expressed by prices and exchange values, the centrally administered economy has no adequate method for ascertaining precisely the scarcities of different products and means of production. Those in control may therefore direct the available supplies of labour and other factors in a direction which does not correspond with the scarcities actually existing. Historically, elements of the centrally administered type of system are usually combined with those of an exchange economy. It may be that only certain agricultural products are produced and distributed on orders from a central administration. Then, the prices of the exchange sector afford a certain basis for economic calculation. The firmer this basis is, the less dominant is the central administration of the economy, which gives way more to elements of an exchange economy. Otherwise, as history shows, economic calculation, and therewith any precision in the control of the economy, encounters the greatest difficulties.[32]

Study of the different economic systems in history shows that the centrally directed type of system is and has been realised in two forms, that of the "simple centrally directed economy", or independent economy or economic unit, and that of the centrally administered economy. It is clear that elements of this type of economic system are not only present in certain countries and at certain times, for example in the Jesuit community in Paraguay, or with the Incas, or in Russia in the fourth decade of this century, but are present everywhere and at all times. Sometimes they are dominant, and at others only supplementary, but they are always combined with *some* elements of an exchange economy. Here we shall extract them in their pure form and use them as ideal types. Both forms of centrally directed economy are found in the following three variants:

(1) *The totally centralised economy** is characterised by the prohibition of all exchange. The employment of productive resources, and the distribution of their products and of consumption goods, follows central direction. Considerable traces of this variant of the centrally directed economy are to be found in family economies, in the larger centrally

* Die total zentralgeleitete Wirtschaft.

administered economies of non-European cultures, as well as in the housing controls of recent decades.

In its pure and ideal form it may be described as follows. A closed community with about a hundred acres of land is under the economic control of a single "director", who lays down the economic plans. He decides each year what crops shall be sown, how many acres with maize, wheat, barley, or potatoes, and in which job each of the seventeen active members of the household shall work each day. He decides whether and how the house or the tools shall be repaired or added to, which technical methods shall be applied, how and to what extent each field shall be manured, the method of ploughing and what equipment is to be provided. He also gives orders as to which area the different crops shall occupy, and how they are subsequently to be used, that is, what part of the barley or rye shall be used for seed, what for fodder, and what for bread. He also decides on the time at which the barley and rye when harvested shall be sown, or used for fodder or for bread, and how much each member of the family shall receive as clothing, food, and "luxury" goods, and where they shall live.

The central control is exercised so thoroughly that the individual is forbidden to exchange consumers' goods allotted to him for others. If, say, A gets 1 lb. of bread and ¼ lb. of meat each day, then he may not exchange bread for meat with B, who gets the same quantities of each but has different tastes. The rations allotted to the individual must be used up by him, or, if he does not want them, returned to the directing authority. There is no third possibility. Obviously, only under certain circumstances is it possible to prevent the exchange of consumers' goods; that is, when meals are taken in common as in modern households, or in larger economic bodies where consumption is communal, as with the Spartans. Prevention may also be possible with certain goods, such as dwellings, which cannot be exchanged without the permission of the central authority.

When this variant of the centrally directed system exists in its pure form, the most remote corners of economic life are within the range of central orders which cover all economic actions. They control the entire everyday economic life of the community. The totally centralised economy is an extreme case where a single planner is responsible for all economic actions, and it is of special interest for this reason. In it alone the economic system of the centrally directed economy finds its perfect expression.

In the totally centralised economy (and in both the other variants) the central authority orders everyone to his occupation and his place of work and the worker is unable to express effectively his own will about these. Slavery in the form of state slavery, private slavery, or the many varieties of serfdom, is the one essential form which labour relations take in the centrally directed economy. Limitations on freedom of movement and choice of occupation and the tying of the worker to a particular place of work, such as occur in many countries to-day, can be regarded as secondary and milder forms of central control over labour. A third form consists in the economic dependence of the younger generation on the older, as still exists in China to-day, where the profession and occupation of all the members of a family in a family economy depends on the orders of the head of the family. In the centrally directed economy there is no contract of labour, only a relationship of labour to the central authority.[33]

(2) In the *centrally directed economy with free exchange of consumers' goods*, it is the central authority which decides on the employment of productive resources, the time-structure of production, the distribution of products to the members of the community, the technical methods to be applied, and the location of production. In contrast with our first variant, consumers may adjust by exchange the allotted distribution of goods. In this case it is permissible for A and B to exchange, if A wants more bread and less meat and B more meat and less bread. In the real world, it is very common for the allocation of consumers' goods by a central authority to be combined with the freedom of the recipients to exchange. Historically, this kind of exchange between consumers has been practised in very many of the economic structures in which central direction of the economy was the dominant element. Many readers will remember from their military service how the soldiers in a company or battery received rations of bread, fat,

cigarettes, and so on, and exchanged them with one another in order to adapt the rations better to individual needs. During the 1914–18 and 1939–45 wars, rye bread, meat, sugar, cloth, and other consumers' goods were distributed by the central authorities by means of ration cards, though the recipients were able to exchange consumers' goods among themselves.

In its pure form, the centrally directed economy with free exchange of consumers' goods seems to differ only slightly from the first variant we mentioned. There is one fundamentally new condition. The single supremacy of the planner is modified by the possibility of individual needs and plans expressing themselves, though they may only do so to a very modest extent. But pure "monism" is removed and a certain "pluralism" of plans is asserted, in that in the course of exchange certain "exchange values" will be formed. A particular quantity of bread will exchange against a particular quantity of meat, sugar, cloth, or cigarettes. If these exchanges are not simply occasional but lasting, then markets and prices are formed and some generally accepted means of exchange, i.e. money, is adopted. The markets will be completely overshadowed by the central authority and its decisions, and the economic plans of individuals will be completely subordinate to those of the central plan. Nevertheless, this possibility of exchange is of the greatest importance for the recipients of consumers' goods, because they can exchange goods which they need less for those they need more urgently.

One of the difficulties experienced in every community with a centrally directed economy is that of the central authority's inability to obtain reliable data about the needs of the members of the community. There is lack of contact between the economic authority and those receiving consumers' goods, so that their real needs may not be properly known. If the recipients may exchange consumers' goods, it is possible in the second type of centrally directed economy for the effects of major errors in the allocations of consumers' goods to be alleviated to a certain extent, and this is of considerable practical importance for the consumer.

(3) In the *centrally directed economy with freedom of*

consumers' choice, the individual plans of the community assert themselves more effectively.

Let us imagine a closed state of about 100,000 people of whom 45,000 are fit for work, where a central authority directs the economic process, in fact, a centrally administered economy. The central administration orders where the individual is to work, how long he has to work, what mines, water-power, and land are to be used, how they are to be used, and which shall remain unutilised. It also decides how much bread, meat, shoes, machine-tools, and other goods are to be produced. It orders how supplies of steel and iron, half-finished goods, and sheet metal are to be distributed and used, whether new roads or a new shoe factory is to be built, whether and how new investments are to be undertaken, and what technical methods are to be applied. To this extent this variant of the centrally directed economy resembles the totally centralised economy, since these decisions follow from the single plan of the central authority.

But there is one great difference. The individual members of the community have the right to choose freely between consumers' goods. They receive bread, meat, accommodation, and other consumers' goods, not directly from the central authority or by ration cards, but are paid wages and salaries in the form of general entitlements to consumers' goods. (The function of money here is clearly somewhat different from what it is in the second variant of the centrally directed economy.) The citizens of this state can buy freely.

Freedom of consumers' choice consists in the individual buying what he wishes within the limits set by his income. Here is the clear dividing line separating that sort of compulsory consumption by which the individual receives whatever the central authority decides. The central authority, however, has other means of influencing the form consumption is to take than by issuing orders or allocating particular rations. It can alter the raw materials which consumers' goods contain, diverting consumption by substituting artificial fibres and artificial silk for wool, cotton, and silk. Consumption is controlled without direct compulsion of the final consumer by a substitution of materials. Because of the similarity of the new with the old textile goods the consumer may not at once recognise the alteration. Similarly, by regulations concerning the extraction rate for bread, or the composition of chocolate, or by many other similar measures, the central authority can exercise a considerable control of consumption without giving direct orders to the individual consumer. Also by propaganda ("Eat More Fish", etc.) the central authority can often affect consumption.

The consumption habits of a people, formed by its past, its culture, its race, and its climate, can be lastingly altered by the methods we have described. This does not mean there is compulsion of consumers. The individual can decide of his own accord which of the consumers' goods that are offered he will buy. These conditions may be described as limited freedom of consumers' choice, to be contrasted with unlimited freedom of consumers' choice. Compulsion of consumers begins only when overt pressure is used; that is, if they are *allotted* or *have* to buy certain goods because of the orders of a central authority or the force of public opinion—that is, when consumers are completely incapable of effectively asserting their own will.

In a state whose economy is centrally directed but where consumers' choice is free, individuals can in their demand for goods assert their own economic plans against those of the central authority. The size and nature of the requirements for shoes or furniture depend on the extent of consumers' demand for these goods.

Faced by these assertions by individuals of their own economic plans the central authority may act in either of two ways. *First*, it can try to exclude any influence of individuals' plans on its own plan, and it will have powerful means at its disposal for achieving this. In particular, it can act as the sole seller of all consumers' goods and counter the influence of the plans of individuals on the economy by its price policy. Take, for example, the price of shoes: if the demand for shoes increases while the price remains the same, the central authority can meet this increased demand for shoes by raising prices, so that the effective demand for shoes declines, production remains the same, and the central plan is left uninfluenced by the requirements of individuals. In general, the central authority can so devise its price policy that to a large extent those goods are bought which the central authority wishes to produce and get rid of. Certainly it will meet with limitations on its policies which do not exist in the totally centralised economy. If elasticity of demand for a good is small, price changes will have little effect, and in certain circumstances the amount demanded may not be successfully adjusted to the central plans. If, with population and the number of families growing, there is an increasing demand for two-room flats, then a raising of rents by the central administration will be of small effect in decreasing demand. In the end it will have to reconcile its plans with the wishes of the community and increase the production of this sort of accommodation.

Secondly, the central authority can try to use the extent of relative demands as an index of the needs of the population. An increase in the number of shoes demanded each year at a particular price can be answered by an increase in shoe production so that the needs of the population are more fully satisfied. The central authority would then, in drawing up its plan, be concerned to take into account the economic plans of individual members of the community. If it was really fundamentally concerned to do this, then its own economic plan would be dependent on the plans of the consumers. This is where the limits of central direction of the economy are reached or crossed. This second case of our third variant of the centrally directed economy is really to be classified as an "exchange" economy. A monopoly administration in control of all markets is trying to supply consumers according to the principle of optimum output (*v.* pp. 129 ff).

Let us recapitulate. A country in which a "simple" centrally directed economy (or independent economy) exists by itself would look as follows. Thousands of independent economies (or independent economic units) with no economic exchange between them would be functioning side by side. Each single family would provide entirely for itself and would be a centrally directed community subordinate to one of its members. There might be larger and smaller communities, but none of them would be large enough to require a special administrative apparatus. In each case the "director" himself controls and personally surveys the whole economic process. With totally centralised family economies there are no exchange, no prices, and no exchange values for goods. To be precise, in such a country there would be not one economic process, but as many complete and independent economic processes as there were closed family economies, not one economic world, but as many worlds, all similarly constituted, as there were independent economies.

The independent economy and the centrally administered economy are sisters, though very unlike one another.

It is easy to see why the independent economy has always proved inadequate, and why it is regularly forced by modern economic development into a subsidiary role: it is because it is impossible sufficiently to extend the division of labour within that framework. There is no room. In order to add to its supply of goods, family, clan, and village communities from prehistoric times have entered into exchange and extended the division of labour outside the independent economic unit, breaking this up at one point or another and developing other forms of organisation. Modern industrialism, bringing with it an unprecedented intensification and spatial expansion of the division of labour, is bound to a large degree to supersede this miniature form of economic organisation. No modern spinning machinery, blast furnaces, or railway can be employed in it. In the course of history other forms of organisation are bound to arise in which men can enter into economic relations with a more extensive division of labour. As well as the "exchange" economy, there is, and always has been, the centrally administered economy.

Historically, the centrally administered economy has far less often been found in ascendancy than has the exchange economy. But a number of interesting cases have occurred. The modern war economy has brought this form of organisation to a specially high pitch of development. Let us picture it again in its pure form. The country which was previously organised on the basis of independent economic units has now completely changed its appearance. The whole country is now linked together by division of labour. All able-bodied men work daily as parts of a single economic process which comprises the whole area of the country and is directed by one central authority. The size of the population, of the country, and of the productive apparatus make it impossible for a single individual continually to survey in person all economic events and give detailed orders and control their execution. Therefore an administrative apparatus with numerous officials has arisen, which in such a centrally administered economy is the sole framer of economic plans, gives orders to the workshops as to what to produce, allocates raw materials and half-finished goods to the individual workshop, makes decisions about the renovation and alteration of factory buildings, directs labour supplies to their places of work, distributes consumers' goods to individuals, and controls the carrying out of all orders.

We need to be acquainted with both these forms of centrally directed economy and with their variants, if we are fully to understand the different actual economic systems, or to be able to classify them precisely for purposes of subsequent theoretical analysis of the conditions of economic life. In both forms of centrally directed economy there is a concentration of power at one point, less apparent but very potent in an independent economy, and extremely massive in a centrally administered economy. There is no economic system in which power is more strongly concentrated, and this is most of all the case in the totally centralised economy. Here economic power is unlimited. Every member of the community is completely dependent on the economic control of the central administration and its bureaucracy and has for himself no sphere of freedom or independence. Where this form has been even approximately realised, as, for example, for several centuries in the history of Egypt, the individual is a being whose sole task consists of unceasing obedience to the orders of central authorities and officials. The other variants of this type of economic system show a certain loosening and relaxation in the concentrated power of the central authority, the extent of which was more precisely described when we were defining these variants. In defining and analysing theoretically the different types of economic system we meet with one of the greatest of historical problems, that of economic power.

II. THE EXCHANGE ECONOMY

INTRODUCTION

Let us repeat that we do not understand the concept "exchange economy" as covering *simply* the case of the capitalist economy of the nineteenth century. In the nineteenth century elements of a centrally directed type of economy were important even in the so-called capitalist countries. Concepts like "Capitalism", "Communism", and "Socialism" cannot help the economist in his task. The ideal type of "exchange economy" is simply a pure elemental form (just as is that of the centrally directed economy), which is to be found at all periods of human history, and which is arrived at from precise observation of particular economies and by abstracting their significant characteristics.

An exchange economy of the pure type is made up of firms and households which are in exchange with one another. We shall talk of "firms" and their "managers", rather than of "enterprise" and "entrepreneurs", because these latter terms both have a particular historical nuance about them suggesting too exclusively the capitalist period. Such a shade of meaning must be completely excluded from the ideal type of "exchange economy". "Firms" are to be regarded as economic and not as technical units. They are conceived as producing goods and services for sale by purchasing and combining the services of labour and other means of production. The "household" of the typical exchange economy differs in appearance from the usual German or French household of to-day. We have just said that historically the family household was usually a small centrally directed economic structure, in which took place an important part of what to-day belongs to the general process of industrial production. In the "household" of the pure exchange economy no good is produced, cooked, washed or sewn. All goods and services needed by the household are bought ready for final consumption from *firms*, and simply *used* in the household. (It is important to distinguish between the "household" in the sense of actual family economic units, and in the sense of *the consuming unit* in which nothing is produced, in the ideal type of exchange economy.) All traces of central direction are completely excluded from this pure exchange economy. The firms produce and the households consume, and from the households comes a supply of labour or savings which yield income.

The economic plans of the individual firm or household in the exchange economy do not resemble the plans of a centrally directed economic system. In the centrally directed economy in which the economic process of the community is guided from beginning to end by the plan and orders of a single authority, this plan is *complete*, in that the director, as we have shown, takes no account, or only limited account, of other individual economic units and their plans. The economic process of the community is entirely within the range of his power. The director of a firm or household in an exchange economy proceeds quite differently. His individual economic unit is only a small part of the whole process of the social economy. His daily, monthly, and annual plan is therefore "incomplete". It is a *partial* plan. Each individual of the multitude of managers of firms and heads of households has to live together with the others in an exchange economy and in all his plans has to take account of the actions of other individuals and of *their* plans. All individual economic units are in a relationship of mutual interdependence one with another. This fact finds expression in every plan of every individual economic unit at all times and places where exchange relationships have existed or do exist, in every household and factory of America to-day, or with medieval traders, or with farmers at the time of the Roman Empire. In formulating all his plans, the director of an individual economic unit has to consider that he must fit himself into the structure of the exchange economy: "Thus in the exchange economy a new problem arises: the necessity of balancing the parts against one another and of co-ordinating the individual plans" (K. F. Maier). *How does this co-ordination of individual plans and economic actions and thereby of the whole economic process come about under an exchange economy, past or present, in the real world?* This is the question with which the study of the economic system of an exchange economy, and the discovery of its forms, has to start.

Experience provides a twofold answer to this question.

First: in an exchange economy there must always be *a scale of calculation*, or unit of account,* according to which individual plans are adjusted. Occasional acts of exchange between otherwise closed households were certainly of frequent occurrence in earlier European and non-European history, without the existence of any recognised unit of account. But such cases are of minor interest. As soon as acts of exchange become more frequent, and the directors of the individual economic units take part in exchange. a unit of account becomes indispensable. It is the same in the exchange economy in its pure form. Let us imagine a state of 500,000 people in which corn, bread, wool, cloth, and all other goods are produced by numerous firms and bartered against one another, the wages of the workers being paid in consumption goods. If no unit of account existed, then no manager of a firm or head of a household would be able to formulate practicable economic plans. A weaver, for example, might give a worker as his monthly wage a particular quantity of bread, meat, beer, etc., and sell the cloth for a particular quantity of shoes, bread, and wool. Whether these actions have brought him profit or loss, and whether he should continue them or not, cannot be determined so long as he lacks a unit of account, for he is unable to compare individual goods and services. He cannot tell how and what he shall produce for the market. The economic authority in all individual economic units, and thereby the whole economy, is without a steering wheel.

Historically, men at all times and at all places have dealt with this problem by using some standard good as the unit of account, and by this means have co-ordinated the plans of different individuals. The fact that in older cultures non-economic or religious considerations have often affected the choice of this standard good is irrelevant from the point of view of its economic function. In our western civilisation cattle were formerly used as the unit of account. Homer, for example, valued a tripod at 12, a male slave at 100, and a female slave at from 4 to 20 cattle, and a bowl as equal to one ox. Obviously, he had in mind not actual particular

* Rechnungsskala.

cattle, but cattle of an average quality. With most peoples the unit of account was gradually separated off from the standard good, becoming an abstract unit which provided a firm basis for all acts of exchange. These facts force us to include in the *pure* type of exchange economy a standard good as a general unit of account or scale of reckoning, or to introduce *some* unit of account, which may be cattle, fish, or units of precious metal. Only then does the control of the individual economic unit become possible. In the case of the weaver, he is now able to calculate the value of the goods he gives to workers as compared with the value of the goods he gets in exchange for his products. He can ascertain that an ox is equal to 100 grammes of gold, and that in selling his cloth, he is making a profit or a loss. Thereby the economic plans of the individual unit get a firm starting point or basis of co-ordination. The uniform scale of reckoning is an essential attribute of an exchange economy.

Secondly: each individual economic unit which enters into exchange with others either "supplies" or "demands". (We are leaving robbery out of account.) Whether the flint workers at Ruegen in the later Stone Age exchanged their tools in northern and southern Europe for other goods, or whether a modern iron works sells iron and is paid for it, or whether a housewife buys apples and gives money in exchange, all relationships in the exchange economy proceed by way of supply and demand, and usually meet together in a "market". Supply and demand are not discoveries of the nineteenth century, but have existed as long as economic exchange between human beings. Here again we must avoid making the mistake of attempting prematurely to lay down scientific definitions of "supply" and "demand" and "market". Only after a scientific investigation of the conditions can such definitions be arrived at. At the moment, there is no firm foundation for them, and we must still use the words as they are used in everyday life. History shows that the way in which individual economic units "supply" and "demand", that is, how they enter into relations with one another, differs and has differed very greatly. There is the same multiformity which we found, for example, in medieval manufacture, in the economic system of the ancient world, and in modern economic life (*v.* Part II, Chap. II, or Part III, Chap. I), and we must do full justice to it, otherwise the facts of economic history will not be understood. Differences of two kinds are apparent:

(1) The power of the individual economic unit is very different in different markets. Often it has to adjust itself to conditions on the market, as did the head of a household in 1910 in a large town when buying bread or meat. Often the individual economic unit can decisively influence market events, as did the wholesalers or "putters out" in Augsburg in the later Middle Ages, on whom the clothmakers were dependent. Again, the *form of market* will affect the position of the individual economic unit, and this will have an important influence on the whole process of the exchange economy. This leads us on to a large group of problems.

(2) Either exchange takes the form of barter, or the individual economic units make use of a generally recognised means of exchange called money. The shoemaker exchanges shoes for other goods, or receives for his shoes some general means of exchange. Why men often use a general means of exchange has often been discussed. It is easy to show that an exchange economy that makes use of money is more effective than one without money. Every individual economic unit taking part in an exchange economy in which money is used has to hold a certain stock of money, which is of importance in his economic plans. Money has taken very different forms in the course of history. In this field too the pure forms have to be discovered from the wealth of historical material, by abstracting the salient distinguishing characteristics. The basic forms of monetary economy and monetary systems provide the *second* great group of problems. The co-ordination of economic plans, and the whole economic process, takes place differently according to the *form of market* and the form of *monetary system* and of *monetary economy*. This is a brief formulation of the groups of questions with which we now have to deal.

A. THE FORMS OF MARKET

1. *The Two Basic Forms of Supply and Demand*

Throughout history, from the earliest times down till to-day, two different kinds of supply and demand have occurred:

"open" and "closed". Supply and demand are "open" if every individual or group, has access to the market as supplier or demander, and if each individual can supply or demand whatever quantity he thinks fit. If the practice of any kind of job, in manufacture, trade, industry, or agriculture, is allowed free from, or under easily fulfilled, conditions, if entry is not limited to a fixed number, and if there are no vetoes on investment or construction, then supply is "open". It is well known that the industrial legislation of the nineteenth century (for example, the trade regulations of the North German Bund of 1869) established freedom of trade in as many markets as possible, and was intended to and did actually establish "open" supply and "open" demand in very many markets. Similar conditions can be found elsewhere in industry on a number of occasions. They are by no means a discovery of "Capitalism". There were "open" branches of trade and industry in many of the cities of the eastern Mediterranean during the Hellenistic period, in the Roman Empire of Augustus, and in many medieval cities.

Supply and demand are "closed" when access to the market as supplier or demander is not open to everyone, for example, when only a particular closed circle of entrepreneurs can supply or purchase from a particular market, or when there are vetoes on construction and investment, or when only a particular group of workers is permitted to work at certain jobs, or when only a particular group of households may buy particular goods. The closing of supply and demand can be found throughout history, and when economists after the mercantilists either overlooked it or dealt with it only briefly, they were committing a simplification which was bound to lead to an inadequate account of actual economic life when the closed forms began to become more common, as is the case to-day.

The closing of supply or demand can, as our historical sketch showed, take place in very different ways. The exercise of a craft or a trade can be limited to certain families, as, for example, was common in the Byzantine Empire. At that time it was the state which ordered the closure of almost all branches of trade, and also ordered workers and settlers to follow the occupation of their fathers. The state in Egypt had proceeded earlier in a similar way, and the same happened in other countries in the east. The economic policy of many medieval cities is characterised by this struggle over the closing or opening of industry and trade. As important examples from the later Middle Ages we may take Lübeck's policy of closure, and the opposite Nuremberg policy of opening industry, or keeping it open. Until far into the nineteenth century there were regulations restricting access to a craft to those who were related in some way to a master, or who had married a master's widow. In the late nineteenth century, though there were many open forms of market, closed ones also existed. The most important of these was the restriction of the right to issue notes to a few banks or to only one. To-day in most countries a varied and rapidly changing technique has been developed for closing supply or demand, for example, by examinations, vetoes on admission or on setting up in business, or on investment, or on cultivation. Particular branches of production often rapidly switch from being open to closed, or *vice versa.* The method of closure is generally either that the circle of persons admitted is limited, or that the number, size, and productivity of firms is fixed, or both methods are employed simultaneously.

A firm and a household can simultaneously be taking part in both open and closed forms of supply and demand. For example, on the farm W. in J. the production of fruit and wine is open and the farmer can produce as much as he wishes. But the production of tobacco is closed, for in accordance with official regulations only a limited acreage may be sown with tobacco. In J. there is another family R. which, together with a limited number of other older families in the village, has the right to attend the annual parish sale of wood as a buyer. This household is then a member of a "closed" group of demanders, while for food and manufactured goods it is in the "open".

The economic plans and economic actions of each individual economic unit are decisively influenced by whether supply and demand for a good or service is open or closed.

2. "*Open*" *Forms of Supply and Demand*

In order to define the different forms of supply and demand precisely, it will be necessary to carry our analysis of the individual economic unit a stage further. At this point, too, we must try to penetrate closer to real conditions rather than retreat from them.

The manager of an individual economic unit formulates his annual, monthly, or daily economic plans on the basis of facts which he regards as "data". The plan of every individual economic unit is based on these "planning data". The manager of an estate or manufacturing firm takes the size or nature of his plant and of his stores of goods as given, as well also as what may be loosely described as the entirety of his exchange relationships as buyer, seller, and receiver of credit. It is these planning data which are important for our investigation of economic forms. The machine factory A. in F. buys iron from a syndicate and sells its products in a number of different markets. In the one case it is the *price* that is a planning datum, and in the other the *prospective reactions of demand.* In the case of a further group of products the firm takes into account both the expected reactions of demand as well as the reactions of some few competitors.

The data which the manager of this machine factory, or of any other economic unit, takes into account are of different sorts. *As the economic plan depends on the planning data, and as the economic actions of the individual economic unit when supplying and demanding depend on the economic plan, the forms which supply and demand takes are only to be understood if one starts from the differences in these planning data.* Here we have touched upon the decisive point on which our explanation of the forms of market in the real economic world has to rest. The particular cases actually occurring to-day, in the machine factory A., for example, must be distinguished and studied by abstracting the significant characteristics one at a time. In this way, we may discover the pure forms which supply and demand takes, and thus the forms of markets.

(1) The supplier may take *the expected reaction of his customer* as a datum in his economic plan (*vice versa* the buyer). The large-scale farm which is the exclusive supplier of a

region with potatoes, has a potato crop of a particular size in view, and fixes its price for potatoes on the basis of an estimate of demand. So does the machinery trust which alone sells or hires out certain patented shoe-making machines, or the south German wholesaler or "putter out"* in the fifteenth century in respect of his home workers. For in formulating his economic plan he reckoned on a certain behaviour on their part, for example, that they would leave or go over to agricultural work if he lowered their wages further. Though it is a common occurrence historically, it is only possible to formulate one's plans and act in this way if the buyer or seller has his own market. The customers have only *one* supplier, or the suppliers a *single* customer. If the large farm had to reckon with competitors then it would not only have to adjust itself to the reactions of customers, but consider the expected reactions of competitors.

Here we have the case of the monopoly of a supplier or demander. On the basis of his planning data the monopolist fixes either the price, which for him is not a datum, or the amount offered or demanded, letting the price adjust itself.

(2) It may be the price that the manager of the economic unit takes as the datum in his plans. For example, a manufacturer of machine-tools counts on receiving particular prices for his goods, or a household lets one of its rooms and buys daily various consumers' goods. In supplying the room it counts on a particular price, the one which according to its information at the time is usual, and in purchasing food, household goods, and clothes, it takes particular prices as given in its economic plans. Or it may be cotton spinners who take the current market price as given in buying cotton and act accordingly, or a retailer who sells cigarettes of which the retail price, like the purchase price, is regulated by the cigarette factory.

Where does the individual economic unit in a market get the prices which it fits as data into its plan? Under what circumstances does someone in a market take prices as given? When does he disregard the effects of his own actions on prices? There are four cases to be found.

* Verleger-Handler.

(*a*) Several small firms may exist as satellites of a large firm or monopoly. They take the prices these large firms demand as planning data and take no account of the reactions which their conduct causes—in particular of the extent of their own supply or demand. Such cases are frequent in European economic life in this century, and also in the past, as, for example, in the Middle Ages. One could cite the modern cartels in the cement industry whose prices were followed for years by small outsiders, who took them as data in their plans and regulated the size of their supply independently. There is the further example of firms which remain outside employers' associations but adopt the latter's rates, or that of several small transport firms in a town which ask the same prices as those of a much larger railway transport business, and take these as data. To take one further example from the past: several small saffron dealers at the Frankfurt Fair in the late fifteenth century adopted the prices asked by the great Ravensburg Trading Association. The "large" firm does not have to consider the small competitors, for these together only make up a very small part of supply or demand; though it has to do so in its plans and policies if, as often happens, these increase in number. Its monopoly position is then incomplete and may be described as a partial monopoly on the demand or supply side.

(*b*) A firm reckons with a particular price because its supplier has already laid down the selling price at the next stage. Retailers, for example, are under an obligation to the firms supplying soaps and pharmaceutical and other goods to sell at fixed prices. This situation in respect of branded goods is well known in many countries. Such price fixing for resale is by no means a modern discovery. It occurs regularly where the suppliers are strong and pass on goods to weaker "finishers" or dealers. This was the case in Egypt under the Ptolemies with its huge system of state monopoly extending from mining and pig-breeding to perfumery. Private oil mills and corn mills existed which not only bought oil and corn at the monopoly prices, but also had to sell their products at prices fixed by the officials of the monopoly which supplied the raw materials.

With retail price maintenance the supplying firm jumps a stage and brings the final market for consumers' goods within its power. The prices formed in the market for consumers' goods are a direct result of its price policy. This market, therefore, is a case of monopoly or oligopoly and does not represent any special form of market relations.

(*c*) Prices may be officially fixed (a very frequent case). From many possible examples the price edict of Diocletian of A.D. 301 may be taken. This fixed the prices for all services and punished all offences on the part of sellers and buyers, workers and employers, with the death penalty. We shall discuss later this case of the fixing of legal prices by public authority.

(*d*) The supplier or demander takes the "anonymous" market price; that is, not the price of a particular large firm with which he is competing, nor that of officials or of those who supply him, but simply that of the market. The German peasant in 1910 sold his rye or pigs in this way, and it was on this basis that the households made their purchases of vegetables, fruit, and consumers' goods. The supplier does this only if his supply is such a small part of the total market that he takes no account of the reactions his policy entails. A peasant with a crop of 400 cwts. of potatoes regarded his price of 3 marks for 2 cwts., which he could get just after harvest, as a given fact which did not depend at all on whether he sold the whole, or part, or none, of his supply. Perhaps he counted on the price being a little higher next January or February, but this rise in price was not connected with *his* actions. Although *in fact* by his supply he did slightly influence the level of potato prices, the price was for him a given quantity, as it might be, similarly, for someone letting a room, or buying bread in competition with ten thousand others. Here we have conditions of supply and demand which have been realised in many markets present and past, and which we call "competition". It is unsatisfactory to describe competition as a form of supply and demand in which changes in the quantities supplied or demanded by any one individual do not cause any alteration in the price in question. Such a form of supply or demand does not really exist and is scarcely conceivable. What is decisive under competition is not the actual reactions resulting from an individual's conduct (in this it differs little from other forms of supply and demand), but just the fact that, owing to the considerable size of the market and the negligible size of his supply or demand, the individual *does not reckon* with any such reaction in his economic plan, but takes the price as a planning datum and acts accordingly. "Indeed the individual who is anxious to exchange, himself exercises by his demand and his supply a certain influence on the price situation. But in itself this effect is in most cases negligible, and therefore from his own point of view of no importance. His economic plan is formulated as though the exchange values of the goods with which he is concerned are unalterably fixed" (Wicksell).

For the same reasons it is inappropriate to describe competition on the supply side as a condition in which the demand for the products of the individual seller is perfectly elastic, with the demand curve running parallel to the abscissa. This is another formulation that disregards the real economic conditions. The characteristic on the supply side is that the supplier *reckons with* a perfectly elastic demand, that is, sees the price as independent of the size of his supply, and proceeds to choose the quantity which he offers accordingly. It is only in the economic plan that perfect elasticity of demand is given, and because the decisions and actions of the manager of the individual economic unit follow the plan, this fact is of the greatest importance for the economic process. Whether the price is *actually* influenced by an increase or decrease in the supply from this firm is not decisive for the actions of the supplier, nor, therefore, for this form of supply. The opinion that one cannot precisely lay down the number of participants necessary for competition, whether it is 50, 100, or more, on one side of the market or the other, and that competition therefore remains imprecisely defined, misses the important fact that in the real world it is the economic plans that decide.

(3) Interrupting our study of different types of supply and demand, and looking back, we find one important question to put: is it possible clearly and precisely to separate monopoly and competition from one another? The question is important because an answer calls for a precise description, much more precise than in our previous account, of what monopoly and

competition really are. This is also necessary because there is little clarity on this really important question. (Up to now, the conclusion is that in the case of competition price is a datum for the individual economic unit and helps to form the plans and actions of the individual on either side of the market. In the case of monopoly, on the other hand, the expected reactions on the other side of the market become part of the firm's data, and the price is not a planning datum but *results from* the economic plan of the monopolist—in fact, constitutes part of his practical problems.)

Many recent students are inclined to deny that there is any sharp distinction betwen monopoly and competition. The goods of each single supplier—so it is argued—always have their idiosyncrasies for the individual demander and are never homogeneous, either because the goods of each individual supplier, or the suppliers themselves, each have their peculiarities, or because the demanders simply assume such peculiarities to exist. Lack of homogeneity between goods means an absence of real competition. The goods offered by each individual firm must be looked upon as separate kinds of goods. Each individual producer has a "monopoly" for his products. Each trader, farmer, or business man sells *his* goods as a monopolist. The markets in which "competition" is supposed to reign really divide up into a network of interrelated markets (Chamberlin) in which every seller has something of a monopolistic position. If a large number of monopolists sell in a perfect market, then there are conditions which can be described as "competition", but which may also be regarded as a limiting case of monopoly. When approached from the standpoint of monopoly, the multiformity of the economic world becomes comprehensible. The analysis of monopoly "swallows up the analysis of competition" (J. Robinson).

These views may be regarded as a reaction against the predominance of competitive analysis in the earlier works on the subject, and are understandable as such. But they are highly debatable, for they slur over differences which for the individual economic unit, and for the course of the whole economic process, are of the greatest importance. One might compare a sewing-cotton factory which meets almost the whole demand in a country for sewing-cotton, with a lock factory which has to reckon with a hundred similarly situated competitors. The two firms are in completely different market situations. This is a difference familiar in everyday experience which has to be scientifically defined. This is best achieved if border-line cases are brought for decision. These border-line cases arise mainly under the following conditions:

(*a*) *With the availability of substitutes:* for example, a brewery is the sole seller of beer in a certain part of the country, and has secured this position by territorial agreements with other breweries in the neighbourhood. But the population is accustomed to drink mainly wine, which is sold competitively by a large number of merchants and vineyard owners. Wine and beer being substitutes, does the brewery possess a monopoly?

It does *not*, if in fixing its prices it makes them wholly dependent on wine prices, fixing the price of beer in accordance with that of wine, and taking the latter as a planning datum, and also if in fixing its output it takes no account of the effects thereof on the price of wine and beer. It holds its production to be too small to have any effect in comparison with the total production of the more popular drink (i.e. wine). The answer is that the brewery *does* have a monopoly if a sufficient range of prices exists for it to be possible to pursue a price policy for beer; if, that is, an immediate substitution of wine for beer is improbable, and the brewery therefore is not simply fixing its price in accordance with the price of wine. The larger this range in which it can pursue a monopoly policy, the stronger its monopoly position.

(*b*) Often a firm only dominates a certain area, while in other areas it sells in competition with other suppliers. For example, a brown coal producer has a monopoly position in his own neighbourhood. His brown coal here is protected by freight rates against that of competitors, which comes, perhaps, from a considerable distance and so incurs higher freight charges and therefore has higher costs and prices. Up to the upper limit at which competition would become effective there is room for a monopoly policy for this brown coal producer. To that extent the works will take account in its economic plan of the expected reactions of the demanders, and fix price and quantity supplied correspondingly. This upper limit falls as the distance of the market from the works increases, while the distance of competitors narrows. Finally, the boundary will be reached where the contested territory begins, where the works, like its other competitors, takes the selling price as a datum in making its plans. It is clear that the boundary line, where competition and monopoly meet, changes its position with every price change in the competitive area, and also with every change in costs in the monopolistic firm.

(*c*) Many firms possess a certain loyal custom, for example, the retail branches of a textile business in a medium-sized town. Does not the fact that the firm possesses certain loyal customers give it a certain monopoly position? Or does competition still hold between such firms? Where is the boundary?

The fact that a certain loyal clientele exists does not create a monopoly. For the efforts of firms are directed at getting hold of the entire market or even of expanding it. It is just when considering their existing customers that firms are forced to adjust themselves to the market. Sellers who supply only occasionally, and not regularly, can much more easily take up a monopoly attitude, for with them no account need be taken of permanent relationships with their customers. The pressure of competition is usually increased, not lessened, by the need to take account of long-run sales and thereby of a regular clientele, as incidentally Adam Smith pointed out. In such cases, there is usually no considerable scope for pursuing an independent price policy, and the usual market prices are taken as given in their economic plans. Only when the custom it owes to tradition or special location is very closely linked to a firm does it possess a market of its own, and prices of its own, which it will adopt in its economic plans and actions. A village, for example, often has only one shop in which clothing can be bought. By binding custom firmly to this business a monopoly position is built up and a monopoly policy is made possible, but this would have to be given up immediately if by improved communications the villagers were able to buy their clothes more easily in a large town, and the supply of clothing became competitive.

(*d*) It may happen that of two firms in objectively the same situation one will act competitively and the other monopolistically. The manager of a hotel in fixing prices for rooms follows the prices in the town, that is he behaves competitively. His successor holds that this hotel, because of its position and reputation, need not take as given the prices ruling in the market for hotel rooms in this town, but can fix special prices for his hotel, since he possesses a special clientele whose actions can be counted on. He asks monopoly prices and acts differently from his predecessor. If, contrary to his expectation, a strong movement of custom away from his hotel sets in he would be compelled by the facts to return to the path of his predecessor when formulating his economic plans, and to give up the assumption that he possessed a special market of his own.

Wherever monopoly and competition are adjacent it is possible to draw the frontier precisely by a consequential application of our criterion of the nature of the data in the economic plans. The supplier or demander cannot, as this example shows, act monopolistically or competitively simply from subjective guesses, or temperament, or at random. If a supplier selling in competition with many others suddenly and unfoundedly adopts the policy of a monopolist he will be compelled by the facts to change his economic plan, and will learn from them by the loss of custom that his plan does not correspond with the actual market conditions. When we state that economic actions result from plans, and that therefore these plans have to be studied in order to understand economic actions and the economic process, this does not mean that these plans can be divorced from the given economic facts. The planning data certainly very often diverge from the actual facts, but people will usually be compelled to narrow down the discrepancies when they formulate new plans, as we shall discuss later.

(*e*) It would be a mistake to regard cases on the border-line between monopoly and competition as cases of "oligopoly", though this mistake is often made. Often competition and monopoly are directly adjacent. That is clear from the cases already discussed. Let us take a further example. In 1932, there were about a hundred firms in Germany making woodworking machinery, most of which made their own special models. (According to the criterion of identity of products these would have all to be called "monopolists", which would give a completely false picture of the situation.) In spite of these differences, the range within which the individual firm could pursue its own price policy for the sale of the majority of its machines was so small that in practice they sold competitively by following the prices in the market. Only for particular machines which were closely protected by patents did the individual firm count on a considerable range within which it could follow its own price policy. The two positions were adjacent and the same kind of machine moved from time to time from one group to the other, from monopoly to competition and from competition to monopoly. The condition of oligopoly was never present.

From the formal mathematical point of view monopoly is a limiting case of competition, or competition a limiting case of monopoly. *In the actual economic world monopoly is something quite different from competition.*

This vital distinction cannot be defined by asking about the homogeneity or non-homogeneity of the goods which the individual seller supplies. Since Sraffa's well-known article of 1926, the study of the subject has concentrated much too much on this issue. Of course, the products of the individual supplier are mostly not exactly alike, and if one takes the view that competition presupposes complete homogeneity of products, then one is saying implicitly that competition scarcely exists. This conclusion follows simply from the choice of a false criterion and is insignificant.

The scientific definition of competition and monopoly must start from the central point of actual economic life, that is, from the economic plans and their data. Only then will it do justice to the facts of the economic world and make it clear that both conditions, competition and monopoly, are very real and not simply unrealistic extreme cases. It will become immediately clear where the actual difference lies and why it is so important: because the individual economic unit under competition bases its actions on plans, which at all important points take a different element as given than do the plans of the individual economic unit under monopoly. Therefore, the actions in the two cases are different.

It is in the interests of economic pressure-groups to confuse the distinction between competition and monopoly. The effects of monopolies are shown to be harmless and the special problems of economic constitutional law which the existence of such powerful private bodies creates, are concealed. It is all the more necessary that economists should avoid confusing the distinction. By doing so they not only retreat from the facts of the real economic world, but at the same time they are involuntarily serving the interests of particular private pressure-groups.

(4) In its economic plan the individual economic unit may take as given neither the price to be paid, nor the price to be received, nor yet the reactions from the other side of the market. It may reckon with the two factors together: that is, with the expected reactions of the other side of the market *and* of its competitors. This condition has been and often is realised. This will regularly be the case if the supplier or demander has only a few competitors, that is, under oligopoly, where the number of competitors is small in relation to the size of the market. The oligopolist takes account, along with the expected reactions of the other side of the market, not only of the price policy but the whole behaviour, and especially the investment policy, of competitors. If, for example, a competitor extends the lay-out of his works, this fact can have a decisive influence on his economic plans and actions. In particular, the investment policy of competitors was in the Middle Ages and remains to-day a basic element in the oligopolist's own plans.

If in a medieval town three glass makers were supplying the market and had come to no agreements with one another, then oligopoly existed. Or if to-day in Germany two firms produce and sell certain machines, then also there is oligopoly. It is the same condition if in Germany only a few firms produce brushes, or when before the formation of the aluminium-sheet cartel only a few well-known firms sold aluminium-sheet products, or if a few big concerns independently supply the world with petrol. If a limited number of paper factories buy special paper-making machinery, then it is a case of oligopsony.

Whether it is a case of oligopoly, competition, monopoly, or partial monopoly can be ascertained by the methods of observation we have described.

The border-line for *competition,* as has already been shown, is not to be drawn by fixing a number of suppliers or demanders. This is impossible. But whether a supplier or demander is in competition or oligopoly can be ascertained in any concrete case from what each one in the market takes as given in his economic plan. If from previous experience he counts on particular reactions from his competitors and from the other side of the market, then his economic plan is that of an oligopolist.

The frontier between oligopoly and monopoly is to be drawn as follows: three factories making agricultural machinery sell harvesting machines, each of different pattern but serving the same purpose, the production of which each factory has protected by patents. It would be a false description of this case, in view of the differences of the products, to say that each firm had a monopoly of *its own* harvesting machines. The element of competition plays an important part in this case. The three machinery factories consider in their economic plan not only the reactions of the purchasers but also the policy of their two competitors. This, then, is a case of oligopoly although the goods are not homogeneous. The characteristic of homogeneity is useless in this case. Here is another example: if case (3) (*a*) of the beer and wine supply was varied in that in one part of the country the wine was also sold by only one supplier, then the case might be either one of monopoly or oligopoly. It is oligopoly if the seller of wine, like the seller of beer, takes into account in his plans and strategy the reactions of the other. If the customers for wine and beer are so separated that either of the suppliers takes no account in his plans and actions of the other, then he is acting monopolistically. Here, too, it may be the case that the supplier, because of a mistaken judgment of the actual position, acts monopolistically, and is forced by a falling off of custom to act otherwise in the future, that is, as an oligopolist.

The case of oligopoly is nearest to that of *partial monopoly.* With partial monopoly one large seller or buyer dominates, while along with him are working smaller firms, who simply follow the prices set by the large one, without adopting any market strategy of their own. The difference between the small firm and the oligopolist is easily perceived. The oligopolist takes account of the reactions to his policies of the other side of the market and of his competitors. On the other hand, the small supplier working in the shadow of a partial monopolist takes no account of these. There is the following distinction between the partial monopolist and the oligopolist: the partial monopolist knows that the small firms simply follow his prices. For example, the branch of a big chain of grocers may set the prices for certain foodstuffs in a certain town, and the small grocers simply adopt these prices. If, on the other hand, the chain store has to take into account a co-operative store with its own market strategy, then, like the co-operative store, it is an oligopolist.

This particular example leads on to another form of supply and demand. A medium-sized town has two big retail grocers and a few dozen small grocers. In fixing the prices for particular vegetables, the small shops follow the lead of *the two* large ones. Here is a case of "partial oligopoly". The two large shops pursue a partially oligopolistic market strategy, in that they not only take into account one another's reactions and those of their customers, but also of the prospective reactions of all the small shops.

(5) Five potash works form a cartel and fix a minimum price for potash in a certain area. Each now counts on three economic factors instead of on two, as under oligopoly. These are the fixed cartel price, the behaviour of the four other works, whose investment policies will be closely watched, and the reactions of the customers, who, in spite of the price agreement, they will try to bind to them by good service, favourable conditions of payment, and perhaps even bonuses. If the price cartel develops into a syndicate with fixed quotas, the potash being sold through the selling organisation of the syndicate, then the connection between the particular works and its customers is broken. The behaviour of the customers now plays a part only in the plans and actions of the directors of the syndicate, and no longer in those of the individual works.

The individual works now counts, first, on the syndicate price, secondly, on its quota, and, thirdly, on the behaviour of the other four works. Above all, it must keep abreast of the building policy of the others and answer with its own building programme, if it is to prevent a cut in its quota the next time this is fixed.

This is a case of the "collective monopoly" type. Historical investigation shows it to be very common in certain guilds and trader's associations in the later periods of Roman history, in the Middle Ages, and in employers' associations, cartels, and trade unions in modern times. A number of individual economic units make an agreement and come to the market as a monopolist. The analysis of this form has been very much neglected by economic theory and must start from the economic plans of the individual units taking part and from the plan of the directors of the collective monopoly. Out of the difficulty of harmonising the numerous plans of the individual units, each possessing their different interest, arise those inner conflicts with which most collective monopolies have to deal.

(6) It is now possible to return to the fixing of prices by public regulation. Under (2) (*c*) we mentioned that in this case supplier and demander were not in a position to influence the price by their economic action, and that the price was therefore a datum in the plan of the individual economic unit.

One might be inclined to classify the official fixing of prices as being near to competition. That would only be correct under certain circumstances, that is, when the official regulation took place in a market in which perfect competition on both sides had existed previously and followed the previously existing price. If the price of 3 RM. per 2 cwts. for potatoes was previously a datum for the peasant, since he was selling in a large market and took no account of the reactions following from his conduct, then it makes no fundamental difference if the state now fixes the price at 3 RM. per 2 cwts. But the fixing of prices by government does not usually follow on competition, but on monopoly, partial monopoly, or oligopoly, and in that event it has a different effect in that it extends and alters the data of the individual economic unit. The producer of steel previously selling under oligopoly, now adjusts his plans to the official price as well as to the actions of his few competitors and of his customers.

(7) Let us summarise the argument. The analysis of actual economic units in the past and in the present, and of the way they shape their plans, leads to the conclusion that particular forms occur in the real world and must be distinguished in accordance with what is taken as data in the different economic plans. These forms are monopoly, partial monopoly, competition, oligopoly, partial oligopoly, and collective monopoly. By defining the given forms of supply and demand in accordance with *the economic plan of the individual participant in the market,* we shall now have an easily applicable criterion for classification in all actual cases. Governmental price-fixing occupies a special position, for it can take place with different forms of supply and demand in existence and will accordingly have very different significance. It is important in dealing with this case, as we shall show, to remember that elements from the centrally directed economic system are often at work when prices are fixed by the state.

It is the *procedure* that is decisive for arriving at these forms. They must be worked out "from below", that is, out of actual conditions, not at some professorial writing table, but on the farm, in the factory, and the household, and in respect of the past from the detailed information about particular individual economic units.

The old customary procedure must be amended. It approaches the subject by making formal assumptions about it "from above", as when the criterion of the homogeneity of goods is adopted, or it is postulated that "the economic individuals on the same side of the market do not essentially differ in wealth or size" (Stackelberg), that is, that individuals are homogeneous in respect of size and that there is no difference between large and small participants in the market. By using this approach one arrives at three forms of supply and demand: competition, oligopoly, and monopoly. The other forms become mixtures of these three basic forms and they must be treated accordingly by economic theory. Partial monopoly is treated as a mixture of monopoly and competition, or partial oligopoly as a mixture of oligopoly and competition. Many other mixtures are also conceivable.

To start from units homogeneous in size is to fail to do justice to real economic conditions. First of all, this postulate is never actually true, so that "competition" or "oligopoly" in these theories are simply intellectual constructions, having scarcely any contact with reality, and the theoretical propositions arrived at on such a basis have almost no application. Secondly, this is a highly questionable way of treating the mixed forms, which are particularly important because they constitute almost the whole of the real economic world. Let us consider, for example, partial monopoly and partial oligopoly. Neither can be looked upon as a mixture of monopoly and competition. Rather are they independent pure types of their own. A big chemical factory takes up the position of a partial monopolist for a particular drug with many small suppliers working in its shadow. The big factory is not in the position of a monopolist, nor are the small firms engaged in competition. Either the large firm, unlike the monopolist, takes account in his plans and actions of the many small firms, or he does not. The deliveries of the small firms make the supply conditions different from the case of monopoly, and the facts will cause the partial monopolist to consider whether or not to take account of the small firms in his next plan. The small firms follow the monopolist and his prices, and not the prices on an anonymous market as in the case of competition. (Compare case (2) (*a*) with that of (2) (*d*).) *Partial monopoly is economically a basic form of demand and supply complete in itself, and not further subdivisible.* This can best be seen if the behaviour of actual firms in this situation is compared with firms which dominate a market as monopolists, or are participants in competition. It is similar with partial oligopoly. If a few big stove factories supply a market side by side with a number of small ones, which adopt the larger firms' price lists, then these many small firms will usually be an important factor in the market strategy of the large ones. The small firms also behave differently in the case of competition, simply because they are not following an anonymous market but particular oligopolists.

Partial oligopoly plays a considerable role in contemporary industry.

It is the multiformity of conditions that compels the construction of these forms. Analysis by means of abstracting the significant characteristics from actual conditions must decide the nature and forms of supply and demand, *not* deduction from *a priori* postulates. Only by close study of the facts can we deal with this multiformity, and by penetrating to the essential point, the economic plan and its data. In this way we can work out types. There are many typical forms in reality, but not so many as can be constructed theoretically.

After an exhaustive study of the facts, I am unable to find any more forms than those given here.

3. "*Closed*" *Forms of Supply and Demand*

(1) The "closed" forms of supply and demand differ from the "open" in a single but very important respect: that is, the "closure" of supply and demand may be due to governmental prohibition or to the customs and opinions of the people. The closure can arise out of the general economic policy of the state or of a class or city, or it may be due to existing suppliers and demanders having a special interest to obstruct newcomers, or both these may work together.

Of course, there are border-line cases, which are not easily defined as "open" or "closed". It might be asked, for example, whether the attempts of cartels to obstruct access to a market by measures of economic warfare, constitute the closure of supply. Did the German cement cartel in the first decade of this century, when it used very drastic weapons to stop new firms, "close" the supply of cement? The answer is no. Access to the cement market was made very difficult, but could always be, and was in fact often, forced by a powerful firm with capital. Only the veto by the state on the construction of cement works closed the supply and made the entry of further suppliers impossible. If the German craftsmen in 1938 had to go through a particular process of training, pass a difficult examination, and fulfil certain personal requirements to be admitted to a firm, was this a case of "open" supply? Usually the answer will be no. In answering such questions the administrative practices will always have to be closely studied. The same applies to the tests of public need prescribed before the opening of hotels, banks, or insurance companies. It also depends on administrative practice whether the various regulations as to entrance fees to guilds and as to training, origin, and immigration in medieval cities, constitute a closure of wholesale or retail trade or crafts. Then there is the question whether *patents* close supply. They do not, if they cover only a small section of the productive process, as is often the case. But when it is a case of a patent without which production is impossible, then supply is closed for the duration of the patent. The numerous patents for electric lamps of the Osram Company closed the supply until the patents expired.

Boundaries between states, as a well-known formula puts it, are not there in order to draw a frontier line between villages but between empires. The importance of such border-line cases of "open" and "closed" forms of supply and demand should not be overestimated.

(2) What we have here is *two* domains. That of "closed" forms is much larger historically than that of the "open", as our historical sketch showed. Under the heading of "closed" supply or demand come cases of monopoly, competition, partial monopoly, oligopoly, partial oligopoly, and governmental price-fixing. These forms of market have a different significance when they are "closed" from what they have when they are "open", and it is for this reason that this division of the two groups is necessary. For example, wheat production in a country may be closed by distributing certain limited wheat-growing areas among thousands of individual farmers, who need not come to any agreement among themselves. The price for wheat which is then formed anonymously on the market, is a planning datum for the individual farmer, but he takes no account of the reactions to his sales. Competition, therefore, reigns, but it differs from "open" competition. If the price rises, the individual farmer cannot alter his plan and expand the area of his land under wheat. He can only intensify his cultivation of the area allotted to him. This is a fact which subsequently affects the further course of prices, the supplies

received by the population, and the incomes of farmers. Such cases, and similar ones, are of frequent occurrence. Another example would be the letting of accommodation in a city where the authorities do not allow new building, or when investment for retail businesses in a particular country is forbidden. In these cases there will be competition because the plans of the individual economic units take prices as given, but it will be *closed* competition, because, as well as the price, the building or investment vetoes, or the limitations on areas to be planted, are also taken as given.

The towns of the Middle Ages afford numerous examples of "closed" forms of demand and supply. The following is an instance. A craft was closed by restricting its practice to particular families and by limiting the number of journeymen and apprentices. The city authorities expressly forbade collective monopolies, which obviously could easily have been formed owing to the closure of supply, but they refrained from fixing prices. If the number of craftsmen admitted was small, say only three or four, then the following situation arose: the individual bronze-worker or harness-maker took into account the behaviour of his customers and competitors and so was an oligopolist. But it was a closed oligopoly, for he took it as given that the number of suppliers was limited and that he could rely on no new competitors appearing.

Closed *monopoly* also differs from the open form in that its position is far stronger. The law relating to the postal monopoly in many modern states forbids any postal services by the local authorities or by private individuals, and so closes the market in favour of a monopoly. The postal administration counts on this in formulating its economic plans. Its position is different from, and much stronger than, that of a big electricity works which is the sole seller of electricity in a certain area, but whose market is open and whose monopoly power can be broken if individual plants using electricity build their own power stations. Experience has shown that the mere fact that this possibility exists compels monopolies to adopt a different policy. They are always confronted with the possibility of a number of customers making themselves independent by producing their own electricity. Under open monopoly a potential competitor has to be considered, but not in the closed form. To take a further example: the lord of a manor in eastern Germany in the eighteenth century had a closed monopoly on the demand side (or monopsony) for the labour of hereditary and tied serfs and peasants, in the form of compulsory feudal services and manual and menial labour, since the peasants were not permitted to move or to seek employment elsewhere. The lord of the manor was a monopsonist with a closed demand, and commanded a much more extensive economic power than had the industrialist of the nineteenth century, operating in some isolated region whose population may have been dependent on him, yet they had the possibility of escaping by emigrating elsewhere. One could also follow out the monopoly policy of a flour mill, which in mercantilist times had the privilege of the exclusive right of milling in a certain territory and alone was able to supply milling services. After the removal of this privilege in the nineteenth century this mill was still for a time a monopolist, but in an "open" market. It had immediately to alter its price policy, the quantity it put on the market, and its other actions, because it had to reckon with competition, or the possibility of competition. Finally, the closing of the market also affects the character of collective monopolies. The cement syndicate, for example, whose individual members—before the closure—had reacted strongly to each other's actions, in particular in the struggle over quotas and in respect of investment policy, once supply had been closed by a state prohibition on investment, were no longer obliged, when framing their economic plans, to attach the same importance to the acts of their fellow members.

(3) Theoretical analysis of closed supply and closed demand has to consider the different methods of closure which history has to show. First, a distinction must be drawn between whether one single economic unit or a whole circle is permitted to buy or sell. Further, it is important whether the closure is in respect only of the number of suppliers, being those admitted free to employ as much land, labour, and capital as they think fit. A further point arises as to whether supply is restricted by limiting the area which each producer may

cultivate, or the number of workers each may employ, or by a ban on investment, or by a combined limitation on land, labour, and investment together.

The method of closure obviously alters the data in the economic plan of the individual economic unit and, therefore, the whole economic process.

4. *Some Conclusions about the Forms of Market*

A market is a meeting of supply and demand, and so it is from different forms of supply and demand that the different forms of market are to be worked out. Markets are always combinations of different forms of supply and demand.

Having five forms of supply, namely, competition, partial oligopoly, oligopoly, partial monopoly, and monopoly, and five forms of demand, there are twenty-five forms of market. If we take into account whether either side of the market is closed or open, this number will be multiplied by four. Of course, it would be more convenient for the economist if he only had to take account of one form of exchange economy—either competitive or monopolistic. But in economic life, both past and present, the different forms of an exchange economy are blended together in great variety. Because the economic process takes a different course in accordance with the form of the market, owing to the differing power of the supplier or demander, this multiformity must not be neglected. It would also be more convenient in chemistry to have to study, not ninety-six elements, but, as of old, only four. No one reproaches the chemist for paying attention to all existing elements, and the same should hold for the economist. Anyone complaining of the "pluralism" of the forms of the market, and of this whole classification of forms, including the centrally directed economy and its two forms, is misunderstanding the problem. The real economic world shows an unlimited multiformity of economic systems each of which has its individual characteristics, and is of a highly complex construction. How can this multiformity be grasped and understood? The answer to this difficult problem lies in discovering the elemental forms out of which actual economic systems present and past are composed. By doing this, economics can discover regularity or uniformity, where only differences and multiformity seem to exist. By working out a morphological system the problem is immensely simplified. The economist does not create this multiformity; quite the reverse. He tries to reduce an unlimited number of actual systems to a limited number of simple forms. It becomes possible in this way to apply theoretical analysis in spite of the multiformity of history. What emerges from this analysis is that if the economic process is studied as it takes place in some dozen well-chosen forms of market, then the other cases offer no further difficulties.

The forms of market are most succinctly portrayed in a table, and one based on our analysis is given on p. 158.

It is to be noted here that:

(1) These forms of market are actual forms which have been or are to be found in actual economic life (often blended with one another, and existing alongside the forms of a centrally directed economy). They are not given *a priori*. They are discovered with their distinguishing characteristics by studying the planning data of those taking part in the market (*v*. p. 136, Part III, Chap. II, A,2).

(2) Under each particular form of market a man can act according to different principles, for example, that of maximum net receipts or that of optimum output. We shall discuss this subject further particularly in Chapter V.

(3) Each of these forms of market can appear in four types: both open, both closed, or closed on either side only.

(4) Fixing of prices by the state occupies a special position, since it can follow any form of market and has different effects accordingly (*v*. p. 149). For example, the significance of coal prices being fixed by the state varies according to whether perfectly competitive, oligopolistic, or monopolistic supply, or some other form of market, exists, or whether both sides of the market are open, or whether the supply side is closed by an investment veto. Governmental price-fixing is to be treated as a variant of the different market forms and not as a special market form of its own.[34]

FORMS OF MARKET

Form of Demand: / Form of Supply:	*Competition*	*Partial Oligopoly*	*Oligopoly*	*Partial Monopoly*	*Monopoly (individual or collective)*
Competition	Perfect (complete) competition.	Partial oligopoly of supply.	Supply oligopoly.	Partial Monopoly of supply.	Supply Monopoly.
Partial Oligopoly (Oligopsony)	Partial oligopoly of demand.	Bilateral partial oligopoly.	Supply oligopoly limited by partial oligopoly of demand.	Partial monopoly of supply limited by partial oligopoly of demand.	Supply monopoly limited by partial oligopoly of demand.
Oligopoly (Oligopsony)	Demand oligopoly.	Demand oligopoly limited by partial oligopoly of supply.	Bilateral oligopoly.	Partial monopoly of supply limited by oligopoly of demand.	Supply monopoly limited by oligopoly of demand.
Partial Monopoly (Monopsony)	Partial monopoly of demand.	Partial monopoly of demand limited by partial oligopoly of supply.	Partial monopoly of demand limited by oligopoly of supply.	Bilateral partial monopoly.	Supply monopoly limited by partial monopoly of demand.
Monopoly (Monopsony) (individual or collective)	Demand monopoly.	Demand monopoly limited by partial oligopoly of supply.	Demand monopoly limited by oligopoly of supply.	Demand monopoly limited by partial monopoly of supply.	Bilateral monopoly.

B. THE MAIN FORMS OF MONETARY ECONOMY AND THE TYPES OF MONETARY SYSTEM

Introduction

Our analysis of a large number of actual individual economic units has revealed similarities and differences among the numerous different forms of exchange economy. Common to them all was the fact that in the exchange economy, as soon as it attains any size, there must always be a scale of reckoning or unit of account. What differed was the way in which the individual economic units were linked together. The many forms this took varied in two ways. First, in the *form of the market* in which supply and demand came together, and secondly, in the *means of exchange* which the individual economic units used to facilitate their transactions.

History shows that such generally recognised means of exchange have often been lacking, for example, in the pure type of barter economy. But experience suggests that many economists find difficulty in imagining a pure type of barter economy. A highly developed exchange economy without a general means of exchange has recently been held to be "not only practically impossible but totally inconceivable" (W. Lautenbach), but highly developed barter economies have in fact existed, for example, in the Mediterranean area in the ancient world, and in America before Columbus. How could the difficulties in conceiving this type of economy have arisen? There is obviously a misunderstanding which it is important to remove. Presumably what was envisaged was an exchange economy in which no single scale of reckoning existed. Were that so, then certainly exchange could not develop very far. Yet this is irrelevant, for even in the barter economy there may still be a scale of reckoning, which may be cattle or a unit of some standard good, without there being a generally recognised means of exchange—that is, money.

In the pure type of barter economy we have to conceive of a community in which, without the use of a generally recognised means of exchange, all firms and households exchange goods or services against other goods or services, and where each individual economic unit makes use of a scale of reckoning.

It is the simplest system of social economy without central direction. In it all forms of market—from perfect competition to bilateral monopoly—can occur.

In such an exchange economy, there are "exchange values", and all individual economic units are guided by these exchange values. The exchange value of a good is a definite quantity because and only because a scale of reckoning is being used. If wool were being exchanged against flax, tin, bread, labour, and other goods, without the use of a scale of reckoning, it would exchange at as many different rates as there were goods. If copper becomes the scale of reckoning and a unit of copper the unit of account, then all the exchange relations will be described in terms of copper and therefore become comparable. The concept of an exchange economy in this way gets a clear definition.

Some economists call exchange values reckoned in some ideal unit of account "prices". Cassel, for example, says that the sum "at which a good is valued in terms of such an abstract unit of account is a price and the whole scale of reckoning a scale of prices". If, for example, 1 cwt. of wool exchanges for 8 cwts. of copper and 1 cwt. of flax for 2 cwts. of copper, then 1 cwt. of wool would be bartered for 4 cwts. of flax, and Cassel would talk of the "prices" of wool and flax in terms of copper. This terminology is entirely permissible, but its adoption may help to conceal that characteristic of the barter economy which is particularly relevant, that is, that goods and services are exchanged directly without the use of money. The far-reaching effects which money exercises on the course of economic events do not occur in a barter economy, and this must constantly be borne in mind. Therefore, it is better for economists to speak of "exchange values" in a barter economy, and of "prices" only in a monetary system.[35]

1. *The Two Main Forms of Monetary Economy*

(1) The pure type of monetary economy is, as we have said, an exchange economy in which the firms and households use money for every sale and purchase. Money is the generally recognised means of exchange. All individual economic units when "supplying" demand, and when "demanding" supply, money, and for that purpose hold a cash balance.

History shows that the monetary unit is often used as the unit of account—*often*, but by no means always.

During the Middle Ages there was in circulation a great and frequently changing variety of money. The large traders were unable to use as a unit of account kinds of money which were constantly fluctuating in value. They needed a firm and uniform scale of reckoning for conducting their economic calculations, when granting and accepting credits, and fixing prices for purchases and sales: for example, such were the gold *solidus*, and later after the second half of the thirteenth century, the Venetian ducat or the Florentine florin and other units. The unit of account was often hardly used or not used at all. The merchants of Reval at the beginning of the sixteenth century introduced the Riga mark and fixed all contracts of sale and purchase in Riga marks, yet these were very seldom used in wholesale trade. There were many silver and gold coins, dollars, Lübeck marks, Rhenish, Lübeck, and Hungarian guilders, and others, apart from various promissory notes which were also used as money. The long-distance trade of Europe at the height of, and in the later part of, the Middle Ages, when it was of prime importance in the whole economic system of the time, could never have existed had not the money been kept distinct from the unit of account. The only sorts of money used as means of exchange had—and still have in such cases—a fluctuating exchange rate in relation to the unit of account.

Many economists speak of money being both a means of exchange and a measure of value. This definition will not take one very far. If one studies the numerous ancient hoards of money discovered in Greece and Western Asia, one finds often such a medley of coins of different origin in one cash-box that economic calculation could not possibly be carried out in terms of all these different sorts of money. In the cash-box of a long-distance trader of Taranto of the fifth century B.C. money was found from seven different Greek mints, as well as other coins. Most probably one kind of money was also the measure of value and the others not, but surely they were money too? In Hellenic times, too, there existed in the economically highly developed area of the eastern Mediterranean such a chaos of different varieties of money that money and unit of account could not have been identical. Only with the advance of Roman supremacy did the Roman gold *aureus* become not only the predominant form of money, as discoveries show, but also the generally adopted unit of account. This state of affairs came to an end in the third century A.D. with the constant debasing of the coinage which led to a separation of the unit of account from the means of exchange. As is well known, there have been various cases even in modern times in which money was not simultaneously the unit of account, for example, the English guinea or the Austrian *guilder*. In Germany in 1923 the mark in the form of paper notes and bank accounts was used as the means of exchange, but the unit of account was 2 cwts. of rye, a gram of gold, or a Swiss franc. Which was then "money"? Anyone who holds that money is both means of exchange and measure of value is forced to the strange answer that in so far as the mark was not still the unit of account no money at all existed, since the mark had lost its function as a measure of value, and the 2 cwts. of rye and so on were not the means of exchange.

It is also mistaken to hold that money is *in the first place* a means of exchange, though it may *also* perform the functions of a measure of value or unit of account. History shows that in various cultural regions and for many centuries the separation of the two functions was usual, and that separation and union are about equally common historically, or even that separation predominates. It is equally incorrect to look upon the separation simply as a phenomenon of the past, as is sometimes done. *Two pure basic forms of monetary economy are to be distinguished, one in which money is used also as the unit of account, and the second in which money and the unit of account are separate.*

(2) Though these two basic forms of monetary economy have occurred in history with almost equal frequency, there are other reasons why it is important that their significant features should be extracted and emphasised, and a distinction drawn between the two forms themselves. In the first place, the planning and actual course of the economic process is quite different in the two cases. For example, if the Germans in 1918

had not been accustomed to express the prices of goods and services in marks—that is, in the monetary unit—but had used a gram of gold or units of a foreign currency as unit of account, then all long- and short-term credits and debts would not have been in terms of marks. The inflation would have had completely different effects; prices and wages would not have risen to nearly the same extent; but the mark would very rapidly have fallen in terms of the unit of account. The balance sheets of firms would have looked completely different. There would have been no rise in the value of assets with the debit side remaining constant. The plans, actions, and investment policy of entrepreneurs would have been different, as would the whole course of events in those years.

Monetary theory usually starts from the assumption that debts and credits are reckoned in money, and also cost and profit and loss calculations, and that money is generally at the same time the unit of account. From what we have said, it is clear that a theory founded only on this one basic form of monetary economy is not entirely adequate. It fails to explain the relationships between certain everyday economic conditions. For instance, the peculiar and persistent disappearance of gold and silver from the late Roman Empire, which some historians hold to be of such great historical importance, but which in its origin has not been fully clarified, cannot be explained without a suitable system of monetary theory. The same applies to the extensive international trade of the Middle Ages and the direction, composition, and magnitude of the streams of goods which linked together Europe, Asia Minor, and North Africa. Everywhere where money was not the unit of account a monetary theory starting from our second main form has to be applied.

2. *The Types of Monetary System*

(1) In these two pure basic forms of monetary economy we have only dealt with one aspect of the variety of actual monetary phenomena, that of whether or not money is also the unit of account.

The question now arises whether and how the immense range of varieties of money to be found in the past and to-day can be reduced to uniform types, and in that way be made accessible to theoretical analysis. Helfferich distinguishes between "tied" and "free" currencies, and this distinction has been accepted by many economists. According to this classification, the gold currencies as they existed in most advanced countries before 1914 were "tied" currencies, because the money was tied to a metal by free mintage and a fixed relation existed between a unit of gold and a unit of money. On the other hand, all currencies lacking such a connection, in which the quantity of money was freely regulated, as in Austria between 1879 and 1892, or in India after 1893, and all paper currencies, were "free" currencies. This twofold classification has done good service and is adequate for the study of some periods, but it does not suffice to explain the difficult problems of recent times, or even of certain older periods or cultures.

We must put the question again: Which pure forms occur historically in actual monetary organisation? An attempt must be made to work out a morphology of actual monetary systems and thereby to find a basis for theoretical analysis.

(2) Here again we must avoid relying on comprehensive but nebulous and unrealistic generalisations, instead of sticking to actual economic conditions. The questions asked must penetrate into the problems of actual economic units. If we consider a particular contemporary household, or firm of craftsmen, or a peasant's farm, and look at the composition of the cash balance held on a particular day, we shall find there coins of different kinds, paper money, and statements of bank accounts usable by cheque. Or we might study the cash-box of a long-distance trader of Bremen in the eighteenth century, or of the monastery of Bobbio in the ninth century, or the many ancient hoards of money in Attica or Corinth. Let us forget all we know about currencies and monetary systems and simply look at the money, including what we have in our pocket. The first question is: how has this actual money come into existence?

This extremely simple question has nothing to do with that of the origin of money, which plays such a great part in the literature of the subject. It has nothing to do with the question as to where and how money came to be used thousands of years ago, whether the origin was religious or not, where, when, and in what forms, coins were first stamped, how men came to discover and introduce money, and the different kinds of money. All these questions are extremely important, but not for us who have to study everyday economic life. For the same reason we are also not interested in the question which Knapp asked, and prematurely answered affirmatively, as to whether or not money is a creation of the state. We shall consider money as it exists or existed in the cash-boxes of the individual economic unit, and thereby as part of the planning data of that individual economic unit. We have to ask how this actual money came into existence, for example, my 10-mark gold piece of 1910, the pfennigs and Reichbank notes, and the balance usable daily with a private bank. Moreover, the question has to be asked for each piece of money individually.

(3) If we put the question in this way and analyse the significant characteristics of a single case, we shall come to the conclusion that certain monetary systems occur again and again, differing from one another in that money comes into existence and disappears in different ways. In actual fact, most monetary or currency systems are mixed or combined systems, seldom pure types, but the latter may be abstracted one by one for analysis.

In fact, the following types of monetary system can be found:

(*a*) *Money often originates with some commodity being used as money.* This is of what the first pure type of monetary system, or model of one, consists.

In former times, for example in the ancient East between 2000 and 1000 B.C., corn, dates, copper, lead, mussels, and many other commodities were used both as goods and as means of exchange. Corn was used for some transactions as money and then again as a good, as were cigarettes in Germany in 1947. Clearly the commodity had to be reduced to a form more suitable for its use as a means of exchange. Metals were shaped as rings or discs or mussels were fixed together in a special way. Most important was the discovery of coinage by the Lydians.

From such a monetary system money may disappear to be used as goods again, for example, gold or silver as jewellery, copper and lead for tools, cigarettes to be smoked.

It is important to note that this sort of money was produced in widely differing forms of market. Often the creation of money was a supply monopoly. A Greek city state had a monopoly of making and issuing coins, the Roman state after Cæsar set the gold *aureus* in circulation, and the Byzantine emperor the gold *solidus*. The monopolist, in such cases, does not always proceed in the same way. Either, when transforming a commodity into money, he is out for the maximum possible net profit for himself, or he may aim at the optimum supply for the market (*v.* Part III, Chap. V, Section II). An "open" oligopolistic supply is often found. At the height of the Middle Ages, for example, lords of the manor and towns competed as oligopolists with their coins in local trade, as did Lübeck and Cologne with their coins in north Germany.

Finally, there was often perfect competition in transforming a commodity into money, for this is what the right of free coinage must be called. This existed not only in more recent times but earlier too, as in the Frankish empire of the sixth century in which privileged master coiners sometimes carried on travelling businesses, coining for a fee all the gold and silver which came their way. If each individual economic unit can always change as much gold or silver into money as it wishes, there is competition in the production of money. How much money circulates is not decided by one authority or one monopolist who watches the market and acts accordingly. The quantity of money in circulation depends on how far those responsible for individual economic decisions think it profitable to change metal into coins or commodities into money. There is no market strategy. The provision of the market with money depends on the economic plans of a large number of individual units with their individual plans, who create money when it seems to them profitable, exactly as with the production of goods under competitive conditions. Free right of mintage amounts economically to competition in the production of money under our first type of monetary system. The abolition of the free right of mintage means, in this terminology, a change in market forms and the substitution of a supply monopoly for the previously existing perfect competition.

Other forms of market may perhaps have existed for the production of money in this kind of monetary system, but I am unable to find one. Any form of market is possible. Here and in general, it is necessary to think in terms of market forms when studying monetary phenomena, in order to distinguish the *economic* conditions, and not to get caught up in legal categories.

(*b*) *Money may come into existence as a return for the provision of a good or service*: it is absorbed again by the sale of goods on the part of the authority producing the money. This is the second kind of monetary system.

Money created in this way existed in very early times, for example, in the Babylonia of two or three thousand years B.C. The officials of the Temple or of the King's Palace delivered wheat to a private trader on credit, received a promissory note, and used it for making payments. The note was made out to the bearer, circulated as money, and when it fell due could then be presented by the then creditor to the debtor for payment. Again, many centuries later in the fifteenth century, the English wool trader would deliver wool to a Flemish manufacturer and received a promissory note for it. This note circulated as money among wholesalers and counted as money in traders' cash-boxes. (Its circulation was restricted to the economically important. If money is to be defined as a *generally* recognised means of exchange, then only such means of exchange as circulate among *all* sections of the community ought to be included. Many kinds of money are limited in their circulation to a certain number of economic individuals. The present bank money of the Central Bank or of the private banks is not used by, and is scarcely known by, the workers in Germany, though it is the chief form of money for wholesale trade.)

Bank notes or bank money have often come into existence as a form of return payment for the supply of a good. The bank money of the famous Hamburg Girobank was created in this way after 1770. It bought unstamped silver and gave in return to the seller a promissory note which was then used for transferring to other accounts. To-day, when central banks buy gold and pay by cheque into a bank account, the same thing is happening, money is being created out of the purchase of a good, and is removed again if the central bank sells gold.

The state or other public authorities have very often used this method of creating money, but mostly not in the way of the King of Babylon, who was usually a creditor and who only handed on promissory notes made out by others. More frequently it is the state which is the debtor and the real creator of money. Medieval city governments often paid for their supplies with promissory notes that were used as money, as has been described in detail in the case of Como. Also, when the state is not paying for goods and services with newly created money, but is receiving money, it may become the creator of money. To overcome their financial difficulties, Edward III of England and Charles V (and many states and cities before and since), borrowed money from large firms and gave promissory notes in return which circulated as money. The state or monarch very quickly put the money it had received back into circulation so that additional money was created. Both the previously existing money and the new promissory notes were in circulation.

The technical form of the money that comes into existence in this way as a return for the provision of a good or service may differ greatly. Often it takes the legal form of a bill which circulates or of some other acknowledgment of debt on the part of private individuals or of the state, the paying off of which is promised by a particular date. Often the obligation to redeem is not transferred, and then the bearer has no legal claim against the recipient of the goods or services. States especially have often created money in this form when paying for supplies of goods, or for the services of officials and soldiers, with paper money and small token coins.

Also, under this second monetary system different forms of market are possible and actually occur. Often there is a supply monopoly, as when the state gives in payment treasury bills which circulate as money, or when it pays out paper money. It often happens, too, that a number of private individuals put this kind of money into circulation either in competition or oligopolistically, as did the wholesale traders of the later Middle Ages.

(*c*) *Our third monetary system is one under which the granter of credit creates money*, again in varying forms of market.

In most countries to-day bank notes are created by the central bank of issue, that is, by a closed monopoly. In so far as the money is not issued as a return for gold or silver, it is by the bank of issue buying state bonds, discounting bills, or lending against collateral. Similarly notes are daily disappearing from circulation by credit operations in the opposite direction, by the payment of bills and repayment of loans to the central bank or by its selling bonds. Notes and bank money daily come into existence as a result of credits being granted and disappear again as a result of their repayment. The relation between these two processes determines how much of the notes and bank money of the central bank are at any moment at the disposal of the firms and households of the country in question. As is well known, in the nineteenth century in most countries the conditions of production of bank notes were competitive or oligopolistic. Banks were free to circulate their notes and many did so. The famous debate between the supporters of freedom of note issue and those in favour of a central bank of issue (which was the central point at stake between the Banking and the Currency schools), was simply a debate over the form of market most suitable for the supply of notes. It ended in favour of the Currency school, and therefore in favour of a closed state-controlled monopoly of bank notes.

Bank money or bank deposits, particularly in the form of current accounts, has this in common—among other features—with bank notes: it is created either when gold is bought, as under our second monetary system, or when credits are granted, and it is eliminated again by the daily repayment of credits to banks. But the form of market in which it comes into circulation is usually different from that in which the bank note is produced. This is an important characteristic of modern monetary and banking organisation. Let us disregard for the moment the bank money of the central bank of issues (in Germany the day-to-day obligations of the Central Bank), since this has a special role. The bank money of the other banks was until recent times, like the bank note earlier, created under competitive or oligopolistic conditions. In countries in which the opening of new banks was forbidden the supply of bank money is "closed". Under these closed conditions there can be various forms of market, including that of collective monopoly, which is approximately what exists in Germany to-day. The fact that notes, but not bank money, are created by a closed monopoly, the individual monopoly of the central bank, and the further fact that bank money, particularly in the depression of 1929–32, was subject to severe disturbances, have led to proposals that the creation of bank money should also be entrusted to a state-controlled monopoly, and that the private banks should be deprived of the right of creating bank money, as they earlier had been of the right to issue bank notes.

(4) It is now possible to understand the structure of actual monetary and currency systems and to define them precisely. It can be shown how in the course of history our first kind of monetary system has often been predominant, and, less frequently, the second. A commodity becomes money and then becomes an ordinary commodity again. Or commodities are purchased in exchange for promissory notes which circulate as money and disappear again when the commodities are sold. Further, money is created and disappears in the course of credit transactions. The many actual monetary standards of the past and present either consist of a *single* monetary system —say the first—or are some variety or combination of several. The monetary system gives the framework of a country's monetary organisation.

Since the Industrial Revolution the methods of monetary supply have had a decisive share in promoting industrial progress. The creation of money by the granting of bank credits has become of greater and greater importance in this respect. At first gold or silver coins were in circulation, and notes or central bank money was created by the purchase of the precious metals. At that time, therefore, it was our first and second monetary systems that were predominant. With the second half of the nineteenth century the third monetary system became much more important. In the twentieth century notes and bank money have been the most used forms of money, created by credit transactions and costing very little to produce. The supply of money is thus extremely elastic and investment much facilitated. Industrial development is speeded up, but the supply of money is unstable. It depends on the extent of the credits granted by and repaid to the banks, and thus fluctuates between expansion and contraction.

It can be shown how the third monetary system, in its modern form, has gone through various stages. In the nineteenth century the supply of money by credits is closely linked with the gold and silver in circulation and the purchase and sale of these by the central bank. The third monetary system is thus only realised as a supplementary system. The monetary organisation of this period was a peculiar combination of three monetary systems. Since the first world war the first kind of monetary system has disappeared, along with gold coins from the cash-boxes of firms and households. The supply of money by bank credit has grown more important, and our second monetary system—that is, the purchase and sale of gold by the central banks—is only of partial importance. The central bank has now become the controlling factor in credit policy and possesses a certain independence. Since the '30's the central state authorities or finance ministries have taken over and used the central bank as their credit-producing or money-producing machinery.

Certainly there have been set-backs. In Germany, for example, between 1945 and 1948, certain goods such as cigarettes and brandy were used as money, and in this case our first kind of monetary system developed side by side with the third. Furthermore, it may be that the extreme instability of money towards the middle of this century will be the stimulus to reforms in monetary organisation. The supply of money will no longer be predominantly in accordance with our third system but will be linked with the supply of important commodities. This is the direction taken by certain policy proposals.

(5) Our purpose in seeking to discover the different forms of

monetary system is not only to understand *actual* monetary systems, but also to provide a basis for studying how money influences the daily economic process. Everyday experience shows how this influence varies according to the type of monetary system. It was different before 1914 from what it was in 1927, and different in Germany at the beginning of 1948 from what it was at the end of that year. We are able to understand this variety by reducing it to simple forms, as we shall later show. The monetary theory for each particular monetary system asks the question how money influences the economic process. The three types of monetary system represent different sets of conditions. To mention one special problem: in each of the three types of system the balance of payments is equalised out in a different way. We must now try to gain an understanding of the effects of money on the daily economic process in the three types of monetary system.

The classification and study of monetary standards starts from a simple, reliable, precisely definable fact, that at every moment actual firms and households have holdings of cash. When one asks how this money held in cash balances comes into existence and disappears again, one begins to discover certain basic forms for the different monetary standards. The cash holding is the point from which the analysis of monetary phenomena in the real world begins. The same holds for the second question as to how money under a particular type of monetary system affects the economic process. Already, Menger and Walras in their studies of monetary theory started out from the cash holdings of the individual economic unit. The individual unit puts a value on the money in its cash balance, determines the size of that balance, and continually controls its use. Individual firms and households, in making their plans, decide as to their cash balance and how the money is to be used. We have to ask how these plans are formed and what determines the size and use of the daily cash holdings of individual units. Again, it is *the economic plans* on which actual economic events depend and from which, therefore, the theoretical study of monetary phenomena has to start.[36]

III. THE TASK

By analysing and abstracting the significant characteristics of the real economic world, we obtain a comprehensive morphological scheme of the different types of economic system and their numerous different features. These types do not purport to be pictures of actual economic life, that is, they are not real types such as the stages and styles of economic development claim to be, but purely ideal types each representing one single aspect of a group of cases. That does not mean that they are "Utopian", as Max Weber mistakenly called them, for a "Utopia" is something to be contrasted and compared with actual economic conditions. These ideal types are got from the actual economic world and help us to understand it. For this they are completely indispensable in two ways.

First, they are necessary for an understanding of the structure of actual economic systems, that is, for one of the central problems economics has to solve. How this is done will be described when we return to the real economic world and describe the application of this morphological scheme.

Secondly, having worked out these ideal types of economic system with their various distinguishing characteristics, we have a basis both for formulating "general" theoretical questions and for theoretical analysis. They therefore help us with the other main problem of economics, that of understanding how the economic process hangs together. This is the problem we now have to follow up, with the aim of showing how theories can be constructed on the basis of the types we have discovered. (It is of fundamental importance that the dual function of these types be understood. They help us to understand both the nature of different economic systems and that of the economic process, that is, the whole field of economic reality.)

We know why "real" types such as the "stages" and "styles" of economic development are quite useless as a basis for economic theory. It is different with "ideal" types when these are rightly worked out. These contain not only the formal elements out of which all actual economic systems are built up everywhere and at all times, but they represent simple precisely definable sets of conditions, and the interrelations within each set can be analysed and grasped. These ideal types constitute, therefore, a firm link between the empirical view of individual historical events and the general theoretical analysis necessary for understanding interrelationships.

How does the course of economic events proceed in the two types of economic system? This is how our theoretical question is formulated, or, to put it in another way, how in the two systems are scarcities met by supplies of goods?

A. *How does this happen in the centrally directed economy,* or more precisely, in the simple form of centrally directed economy (the "independent" economy),* and in the centrally administered economy? In a centrally directed economy the whole economy of the community is a single economy† directed by a single authority. The individual economy (or economic unit) and the social economy are one and the same. We are now enquiring into the course of the economic process in its five aspects in this "individual economy" or single economic unit (that is, in the simple form of centrally directed economy and in the centrally administered economy). How is the annual social product distributed? How is a particular time-structure of production selected? How are investment and saving done? Why are particular technical methods applied, and how is the geographical arrangement of the economic process controlled? It need hardly be remarked how topical all the problems of the centrally administered economy are at the present time.

B. To formulate the problem for *the exchange economy* is less simple. The reason is obvious from what we have said. In this economic system, several or many independent agents are active, each with his own economic plans, and therefore these plans and actions have to be co-ordinated. This co-ordination will proceed differently according to the form of the market and the monetary system.

(1) The five questions about the control of production, distribution, the time-structure of production, the technical methods to be applied, and the geographical ordering of the economic process have to be asked for all market forms both

* Eigenwirtschaft. † Einzelwirtschaft.

open and closed. The problem has to be formulated in a much more comprehensive way than is usual. For example, it can be ascertained simply from everyday experience that the choice of a location for factories is related to the form of the market, and is different in the case of a supply monopoly from what it is in the case of perfect competition. It is precisely this relationship that economic theory has to clarify. It must not be overlooked that the choice of the technical methods to be applied is also related to the form of the market.

The problem is made more difficult by the following fact. An exchange economy is usually made up of a number of markets, which are all linked up with one another. They are all, therefore, interdependent. Every household and firm belongs to dozens or even hundreds of markets, either on the demand or on the supply side, and its actions in one market will be influenced by what happens in all the others. Of course, the same form of market may not hold in each of the interdependent markets—say, the much studied form of perfect competition, or that of bilateral monopoly. An exchange economy will not be composed of uniform markets. It is unsatisfactory, therefore, simply to enquire about the course of economic events in a uniform exchange economy of, for example, perfect competition. We must put the one question, with its five aspects, also for multiform exchange economies: that is, exchange economies in which markets are of varying forms. This inevitably makes the problem and its solution more complicated, though not so much so as it might appear at the first glance. Theoretical analysis alone can show *how* much more.[37]

(2) The co-ordination of the plans and actions of individual units, and therefore the course of economic events, depends on the structure of the monetary system and the main forms of monetary economy, as well as on the market forms. Therefore, we must investigate what influence the different types of monetary systems and their management have on the economic process of exchange economies, and how differences in the main forms of monetary economy affect them. The different ways in which money influences the whole of the process of an exchange economy must be classified. For example, how far is the time-structure of production determined by the

monetary system and by the creation of or diminution in the supply of money? How far is investment affected as contrasted with the production of rapidly available consumers' goods, and what are the effective savings? Then there is the problem of the influence of money on distribution (for example, on interest and incomes from interest), and also on wages (that is, *real* wages), or the problem of the relation between money wages and the prices of consumption goods. Even the location of production is not independent of monetary influence, not only in international trade as has often been shown, but within a single country. However extensive or small the influence of the monetary supply on the economic process may prove to be, we must in any case enquire about it. How is the economic process in the exchange economy affected by monetary conditions? To answer that is the task of monetary theory, and it is a problem which emerges unavoidably in the study of economic reality.

If monetary theory takes as its problem that of investigating how the value of money, or the price level, is determined, it remains caught up in obsolete formulæ. This narrow formulation of its problem has contributed to the lack of success of monetary theory, which at one time seemed the most developed branch of economics. A theory which studies only how the value of money or the price level is formed, must fail when it comes to be applied. It is unable, for example, to explain the profound effects on the economic process of the cheap money policy in Britain after 1931, or those of the state investment and credit expansion in Germany after 1933.[38]

With a right formulation of the problem of monetary theory, the two elements very soon emerge which determine the way in which the plans of the individual economic units are coordinated. These are the form of the market and the type of monetary system, and they have to be studied not merely separately one after the other but in their interdependence. For example, the outflow of gold under a gold standard will have different consequences when it takes place in any economic system made up predominantly of competitive markets, from what it has in one in which prices are fixed by monopolies or by the government.[39]

C. Now we understand the interrelationships within the two types of economic system, we are confronted by another group of questions. How does exchange proceed between two or more communities with centrally directed economies, or between those with centrally directed economies and those with exchange economies, or between two or more communities with exchange economies? Which goods will they exchange, how will the course of economic events be affected, and how will the credits and debits of each country be periodically brought into equilibrium—daily, monthly, or annually—that is, how does a balance of payments come about?

This completes the formulation of the real problems which economic theory has to solve as they present themselves to the student of economic history.

Chapter III

ANALYSIS OF THE DIFFERENT TYPES OF ECONOMIC SYSTEM: THE DATA

IT IS NOW clear what the main framework of economic theory looks like. It is a very comprehensive framework and very extensive structures have to be built up around it, if there is to be an answer to the problem of the interrelations in the economic process in its five different aspects under each of the two types of economic system in all their various forms. The argument of this book is simply concerned with the fundamentals and not with building up the whole structure, so it should suffice if we consider a single type of economic system in one of its special forms, in order to show how theoretical study can proceed, and add a few points concerning the analysis of the other types of economic system.

I. THE ANALYSIS OF THE TOTALLY CENTRALISED ECONOMY

An economic system totally directed from the centre is, of course, not to be confused with a "communist" economy. We are concerned with an ideal type or pure form which has not been discovered simply from considering communist states but from the study of the whole of economic history. Traces of this type of economic system have been found throughout history, and we have abstracted the significant characteristics for constructing our model.

In this type of economic system, as we described it (p. 120), there is no free consumers' choice, no free choice of occupation, and no exchange between members of the community or family of the consumers' goods allotted to them. All economic actions depend on the plans and orders of a single central authority. It is convenient for the theoretical study on which we are now starting, to imagine this community as not very large, as comprising, that is, not more than about fifty people. The controller can then directly estimate the values of goods and services and the serious difficulties of economic calculation, we have mentioned do not arise. We are not concerned with a centrally administered economy but with an independent economy or economic unit.[40]

A. THE BASIS OF THE ECONOMIC PLAN: THE DATA AND THE EMPIRICAL RULES

1. *The Data*

Since all economic actions follow as a consequence of its orders our study must begin with the economic plan of the central authority. Anyone joining such a community would have to apply to the central authority if he wanted to find out why the economic process took the course he daily observed it taking. What are the facts that decide the leadership to direct the economy in one way rather than another? On what conditions do the economic plans depend?

In a totally centralised economy such as this, one can only understand the interrelated purposes of everyday economic activities by considering the economic plans of the central authority.

In carrying out its plans, the leader of this community is aiming at certain particular goals, that is, he is always aiming at the satisfaction of needs. The ranking of these needs he undertakes himself. He may put his own needs first, or those of the community. If the latter, he may do so in different ways. Either collective needs, such as defence, can be put first, or more consideration can be given to the individual needs of the members of the community. However this may be, there is no economic activity which does not aim at satisfying needs. The impression given by the work of some economists that there have been historical cases of people whose economy was not intended to satisfy needs, always proves false on closer study. We shall return to this subject again when discussing the economic man. Theoretical analysis has to start from this historical fact that the purpose of economic action is everywhere and always the satisfaction of needs. These needs are the first "data" in an economic plan.

The director of the economy has to classify these needs from two points of view, first in accordance with their kind or nature, and then temporally. In classifying them according to their nature, he has to start from the fact that certain needs for, say, bread, rice, or stockings, will be felt in the course of the coming economic year. He has to classify the different kinds of needs in accordance with the means for their satisfaction, and for him there are as many varieties of the former as there are of the latter. The classification of the varieties of needs in accordance with the means for their satisfaction, as developed in many theoretical works, is well founded in that it corresponds to the classification which anyone makes when drawing up an economic plan.

The *temporal* classification of needs has had less attention paid to it, but is not less important. How much of the stock of cattle shall the director of the economy slaughter in the current economic year? As much as will keep the meat supply at the same level in the next year, or at a higher or lower level? How are present and future needs to be weighed up against one another? Are present needs generally to take second place to those of the nearer or more distant future? If so, then the economic plan for the current year will provide for more workers and machines being employed in making steel, roads, machinery, and other productive equipment, that is, for a relatively high level of investment. If, on the other hand, this year's needs seem more important, the plan will provide for more farm workers and means of production being used for consumers' goods. Whatever the decision may be, the director of any economy always has to classify needs *temporally* in giving his present orders.

Already we have come across an essential distinction between the economic process of an exchange economy and that of a centrally directed economy. In the exchange economy needs are established by the individual members of the community who are provided with purchasing power, and are of decisive influence on the productive process. The authority in a centrally directed economy can to a large extent pass over the needs of individuals and can give priority to a single complex of needs—say armaments—and apply a large part of the means of production to this purpose. He does not *necessarily* act like this, but he *can* do so, and historically the centrally administered economy has often on different occasions been managed in this way, in order to make possible a concentration on a particular single task.

Let us consider next what are the means by which needs are satisfied, and what the "data" in respect of needs in the plans of the leader. In planning the production of steel the directing authority will reckon on supplies of suitable labour, stocks of coal and iron ore, and the existing plant available for steel production. There are, therefore, three data, labour, natural resources, and produced means of production. Similarly with the production of bread. The workers available are agricultural labourers, millers, and bakers, and there is the land and all the produced means of production used in agriculture, milling, and baking. Such an answer as this is the obvious one and it is not incorrect. But it is incomplete and can easily lead one astray.

(*a*) To understand the part played by *the stocks of already produced goods*, as a datum for planning, it is necessary again to emphasise the time factor.

First, only from *one* point of view is the supply of goods already produced a datum for planning.

In the short term, that is, when planning for the immediate future, the manager will count on stocks of consumers' goods. All orders for meeting *to-day's* needs must be based on already existing stocks of bread, meat, shoes, etc. No more can be distributed to-day than are ready to-day. Nevertheless, even in short-term plans, provision for the future has an important part. The smaller the stocks of rye and flour, the more cautiously the supplies of bread have to be distributed. All immediately available supplies of consumable and permanent goods from earlier production play a part in short-term plans, consumers' goods being specially important. It is different where the plan extends over a longer period, when the kinds of tools, machines, raw materials, and half-finished goods to be supplied, as they are not yet ready for immediate consumption, can be altered with the co-operation of labour and nature. In their longer-term plans the controlling authorities regard as data the available supplies of produced means of production which will provide the consumption goods of the future. On the other hand, the already finished goods are of less importance. For example, the available supplies of cotton and thread are the main data for the supply of cotton goods until the next cotton crop. In any economic system consumers' goods still in the process of production are not available for consumption, as we have already discussed at length. But as those co-operating in production need consumers' goods daily, *every* economic plan has to start by taking as given the consumers' goods available, as well as those "ripening" for final consumption. *The possession of "capital" is the power of disposing over these consumers' goods*, and in a centrally directed economy it is in the hands of the controlling authority, in an exchange economy in those of the managers of private firms.

Secondly, supplies of produced goods are not *merely* data either in short-term or long-term plans. Because the needs of future years have to be considered to-day, there is a problem of the future stock of produced means of production. It is a most important practical problem dominating longer-term plans. Provision for the more distant future compels the leaders of the centrally directed economy, just as it does the management of a firm in an exchange economy, to make at each present moment decisions as to how many and what sort of houses, machines, and stocks of raw materials, shall be available in a year's time and longer ahead. Decisions as to depreciation are similarly relevant. A person taking over the management of a cotton-spinning mill sees the existing stock of buildings, machines, and supplies not only as a datum, but as a practical problem, in that he has to decide whether to increase or diminish it. Similarly, the leadership of a centrally directed economy also considers the stock of tools, buildings, and raw materials from this second point of view. The fact that the stocks from previous production, at their existing level and in their existing form, are always a datum in economic plans must not mislead us. This is only one of their necessary aspects. From other equally essential points of view the economic authority is forced to face the practical problem of the future form of the produced means of production, for without a solution to this the supply of goods in the future is endangered. The greater the extent to which durable goods are employed the greater is the apparatus of buildings, machines, and other equipment, and the more important it is to take account of both aspects simultaneously.

The stock of goods already produced must be regarded as both a datum from which an economic plan has to start, and as a problem for the plan to meet, in that it has to decide whether and in what form this stock shall exist in the future. Both aspects are essential, though some economists ignore one and some the other. If it is only labour and the free gifts of nature that a theory regards as "given", and not also the existing stock of produced means of production, then it is certainly in this respect unrealistic. This is the mistake that Böhm-Bawerk made when he described "production without capital" simply by means of a combination of labour and nature. In fact, production of this kind must be very rare.

At the present time it is particularly this second aspect of the stock of production goods that it is necessary to emphasise. Some theoretical economists are inclined to take the stock of durable means of production, such as machines, houses, roads, etc. *simply* as given and to disregard problems of its maintenance. This makes for a distorted view of contemporary events and of the history of the last century with its huge investments, and thus again for a lack of realism. It is only necessary to look at the management of a single firm to realise the importance of the maintenance and renewal of productive equipment in actual life, and how conscious the management of all firms are of the existence of this problem.[41]

(*b*) *Land and Natural Resources*. The plans and orders of the central authority determine which mines and galleries shall be exploited, which fields used, which workers employed in mining, agriculture, and all the other branches of production. Which of the services of labour and natural resources shall find employment depends on the economic plan, but the services are not themselves a datum in the plan. Rather the central authority has to decide in its plan *which* of the services of nature and of managerial and other labour are to be used.

The data of the plan are, therefore, labour and natural resources, *not* their services. This distinction is not merely a question of splitting hairs: it is of the greatest importance for understanding the construction of an economic plan and the course taken by the economic process in the centrally directed, as well as in the exchange, economy in all its forms and throughout economic life. The common habit of regarding the services of the factors of production simply as a datum unjustifiably narrows the field of study for economic theory and leads to the exclusion from economics of problems which are of the utmost importance in the real economic world.

Let us imagine as representative of a totally centralised economy an isolated family of fifty people. The director in all his economic plans, whether long- or short-term, takes the available labour force as a datum. He has to reckon with a certain number of able-bodied workers each with the particular capacities of a man, woman, or child. One may be suited for agricultural work, for looking after cattle, and for carpentry, another for butchers' or bakers' work, and so on. Each individual has his special abilities. In his economic plan the director has to decide whether each one has to work, and if so how many hours or days, and which of his abilities are to be made use of, whether, for example, our first worker is to be employed as cowherd or carpenter. The more trained the labour force, the more employments into which they can be directed. How they are to be employed depends only on the orders of the director. The decision is inextricably bound up with the general aims of his plans and the other data. If the director, with the intention of increasing future supplies of goods, builds more extensively, or produces new agricultural equipment, then he has to withdraw supplies of labour previously employed elsewhere—say in agriculture—and put them to work on building houses and making machinery. The labour supplies remain the same but different services are being used. In actual economic life the right direction of available supplies of labour to their best employments is a problem of the greatest practical importance. The manager of a firm can never regard the *services* of labour simply as a datum. The economist must proceed in the same way.

The same is true of the natural resources. *They themselves* are given, but not their *services*, which have to be *chosen*. Here, too, the economic plan decides which services are to be employed. Day by day various services are available from natural resources, those of the agriculturally useful land owned by our community, those of the water supplies, stone quarries, and so on. Which land shall be cultivated and which not, and which for corn and which for turnips? How are the water and wind power and the resources of the earth to be used?

The description of the economic process as it takes its course can only show that particular services of labour and natural resources *have been* employed. But this is not sufficient. We have to understand how the economic plan is constructed, and the purpose of economic activity. Therefore, at this point we must ask the questions that the economic planner himself asks, that is, which services are to be chosen out of the many which *can be* provided by the existing supplies of labour and natural resources. The labour and natural resources are given, but there is still the problem of choosing the services they shall give.

Up to now we have taken as data of the central authority's economic plan the needs which the director wishes to be satisfied, and on the other side, natural resources, labour, and (from one point of view) the stock of previously produced goods. The central authority combines together the services of labour, natural resources, and the existing goods on the basis of existing *technical knowledge*, which is the fifth datum in the construction of an economic plan. What methods in agriculture, manufacture and transport are practicable depends on the extent of technical knowledge. "Technical knowledge" is not the same thing as "the technical methods applied", which present a problem both from the point of view of the practical business man and the economist. Certainly in some fields only one known technical method existed for centuries on end, as, for example, in many branches of medieval agriculture using the three-field system. In such a case there is only one technically known method to be applied. Often, and not merely in recent times, technical knowledge has made possible many methods of growing corn, milling, baking, or of producing steel or shoes. The controller of a centrally directed economy, just like the manager of a firm in an exchange economy, has to choose which of the many known methods are to be applied. It is a choice which can only rationally be made as a part of the plan as a whole. A clear distinction is, therefore, necessary between technical knowledge and the application of particular technical methods, the first being an economic datum and the second an economic problem. With technical knowledge must be included *commercial* knowledge, that is, the existing knowledge of methods of economic calculation, balance sheets, profit and loss accounts, book-keeping, cost accounting, business statistics, and in an exchange economy, of market research, budgeting, purchasing and sales organisation, financial organisation, and so on.

Finally, the totally centralised economy has its legal and social organisation, the existence and rules of which are an economic datum. The same holds for this as for all the other data. Economic theory gives no answer to questions about how needs arise, why the land and its climate are as they are, or about the working ability of a people or family, or their technical knowledge. Nor can it explain why this totally centralised economy has come to exist. This sixth datum, the legal and social organisation, must not be interpreted too narrowly. It not only includes traditions, laws and customs, but the spirit in which men live and keep to "the rules of the game".

2. *The Empirical Rules*

The data with which the central authority reckons are, so to speak, the bricks out of which its economic plans are constructed. As soon as this work of construction begins, it becomes clear that account must also be taken of certain empirical rules which have been shown always to require attention in framing actual plans and orders.

Much has been written about these empirical rules, often called "laws", but their character and economic role have not always been clearly explained. To begin with, we must lay it down that empirical rules are not axioms. Nor are they rational truths which can be deduced from axioms with absolute certainty. They are rather "factual truths", known from everyday experience to the practical man and taken for granted by him without further reflection. Science makes consciously known what the practical man knows vaguely, and describes precisely what to him is nebulous. Precise observation shows the validity of these propositions, and in doing this often offends the naïve man in the street who does not realise that he is actually always behaving in accordance with these empirical rules. Confronted with their scientific formulation he behaves like the *Bourgeois Gentilhomme*, who was astounded at the information that his whole life he had been speaking in prose.

First, we are concerned with Gossen's First Law, which as formulated by Wieser states: "In the case of every divisible need the satisfaction from the first unit applied will be desired with the highest intensity, and every application of further units of the same kind will be desired with less intensity until the point of saturation is reached, beyond which desire will turn into aversion."

This is a perfectly simple condition valid always and at all times. Everyone knows that his daily needs of meat, bread, and other consumers' goods decrease as they are increasingly satisfied. Every household follows this principle daily, and the director of a totally centralised economy must do so as well. We can observe the validity of the rule for ourselves and understand how it operates for others.

There may be some argument about how the rule should be formulated. Its validity has, in particular, to be confirmed both when it is applied to men's plans for the future, as well as when applied to their actual satisfactions *ex post*. This distinction is important. Also, the period of time for which the rule is valid has to be specified. The shorter this is the more obvious the rule's validity, but there are difficulties introduced by the time factor, and these have to be got over. For example, there is the case of tobacco, where consumption increases the need for it. The need, satisfied for one day, recurs with increased intensity on the following day. What is important is that at this new stage the rule is again valid. Further, certain not insurmountable difficulties arise out of the fact that the intensity with which a man desires a unit of a good does not depend only on the extent to which he is supplied with *this* good, but also on his supply of other goods. The intensity with which a pound of brown bread is desired depends not only on the supply of brown bread, but also on that of white bread and potatoes (that is, of substitute goods), and on that of butter and marmalade (that is, of complementary goods).

Here there is room for debate, but the basic fact with which we are concerned is not debatable.[42]

Secondly, the law of diminishing returns (or more correctly the law of diminishing marginal returns) holds good always and everywhere in economic life. No farmer uses a year's labour on half an acre of land, leaving his other five acres uncultivated. He knows that his labour will bring in larger returns if he distributes it over a number of acres, and that concentrating it all on a small piece of land will lead to sharply decreasing returns to every successive day's labour. The same holds for every other branch of production. A shoe factory has at a particular moment a particular stock of buildings and machines. It is of little use employing only two, three, or four workers. At first the return for each successive worker employed increases, but after a certain point, say 350 workers, it falls again, and finally, after about 420, it is impossible to employ any more workers. This empirical rule holds for any combination of natural resources, labour, and production goods, and men act in accordance with it. Unlike the first rule, knowledge of it is not obtained from the "inner" observation of oneself, but from observing "outside" facts.

Economists have tried to state this rule precisely. Perhaps it can be represented most shortly—following Edgeworth—by a simple table setting out the returns on a given piece of land and given equipment.

Here the rule is given in the form first of increasing and then of decreasing returns to labour—not to land. It would also be possible to vary the quantity of other means of production—for example, fertilisers—in order to see the resulting curve of returns.

A.	*B.*	*C.*	*D.*
13	220	16·92	—
14	244	17·43	24
15	270	18	26
16	294	18·38	24
17	317	18·65	23
18	339	18·83	22
19	360	18·95	21
20	380	19	20
21	396	18·86	16

A. Labour in man-days.
B. Total rye crop (kilos).
C. Average return (kilos) of rye per man-day of labour.
D. Additional kilos of rye resulting from an additional man-day of labour (marginal return).

Scientific observation of the facts confirms the everyday experience that this rule is of universal validity and not simply applicable to agricultural production. For getting coal from a coal mine or making clocks in a clock factory, a similar course of returns can be ascertained. If the management of a clock factory, with a given equipment in buildings and machinery, and with a given organisation, invests in raw materials and takes on labour, there will be first increasing and then decreasing returns.

At this point doubts may arise. What if the management of a factory increases its capital investment and the size of the firm as a whole, adopts improved technical methods, buys new machinery, and constructs new buildings? Does the law of diminishing returns then hold? This is what was in the minds of those who contrasted increasing returns in manufacturing production with decreasing returns in agricultural production. There is a twofold error here. In the first place, the law of returns remains valid if the increase in the size of the firm is continuous. As is well known, there are optimum sizes for firms beyond which any further increase in size must lead to diminishing returns. Exactly the same holds for agriculture. If the field on which the returns are represented in our table is improved, and new capital invested in it, then returns increase *there also*. But it holds, too, that further new applications of capital lead to diminishing marginal returns, and secondly that after a certain new stage has been reached, for example, after a new drainage system has been successfully installed, our empirical rule will again hold at this new stage for the employment of labour, seed, fertilisers, and so on.

The controller of a centrally directed economy counts also on the effectiveness of this rule at all times and in all branches of production.

Decisions, as we know, have continually to be taken as to the time-structure of production. In the making of these decisions the following *third* empirical rule is important.

The controller of a centrally directed economy knows that to employ all the workers and available means of production on providing consumers' goods for this year, would be to run the risk of so using up buildings and tools that insufficient means of production would be available next year. Markedly less would then be forthcoming from the labour and natural resources. He will regularly have to decide to employ labour and means of production on maintaining or extending the means of production—buildings, tools, raw materials, and so on—which only become "ripe" for consumption in the future. He has to decide, that is, about capital investment. He does this because he knows that given supplies of labour and means of production as a rule produce more consumers' goods the longer the interval between their first employment and the final maturing of the consumers' goods. Everyone knows this rule and acts according to it even when he is debating its validity. Everyone knows that to employ machinery and tools raises the productivity of labour, and that one moves faster on a bicycle than on foot. To employ labour and means of production for making machinery and tools, is simply to employ them at a point where the temporal interval until the ultimate completion of finished consumption goods is longer. It is employment of factors available *to-day*, for making consumption goods that will only be available in the distant *future*. The construction to-day of a blast furnace from the products of which bicycles will later be made which will be of use for transport over a long period, means putting a long interval of time between the first expenditure of services and the maturity of the final consumption goods they produce, with the object of increasing the yield of these services.

The fact underlying this well-known empirical rule must be described in a scientifically precise way. It is clear that between the application of the labour and means of production necessary for making a consumption good and the ultimate readiness of this good for consumption, there is an "average period of gestation". There are special but surmountable difficulties in measuring this period, but it is a fact that if it is lengthened an increased yield may follow. These facts are not to be confused with those underlying the second empirical rule. In *that* case, in the production, for example, of crude iron in a blast furnace with a certain combination of coal, ore, other materials and labour, the increasing of *one* of these factors will lead first to a rise and then to a fall in the marginal return. But in the case of this third empirical rule by employing more time-consuming methods of production, for example, by building and using a blast furnace, the productivity of labour and the other means of production is appreciably increased compared with their direct application for consumption purposes.

The lengthening of the period of gestation in actual economic life comes about in two ways. If we follow the use to which a potato crop is put, we may find one-third being used for human consumption, one-third going to pigs, one-seventh kept for seed, and the rest for feeding cattle, making starch, spirits, and other products. Looking at these uses, as one must, from the temporal aspect, it is clear that using potatoes as food for human beings is to put them on the shortest route to final consumption. To feed them to pigs is to "put them back", that is, the potatoes are moved away from final consumption and used in another productive process, that of pig production. They are used at a point further in time from final consumption. Similarly the potatoes kept for seed next year, or those which are used in industry or are fed to cattle, are "put back" to different distances from the final stage of consumption. This "putting back" involves lengthening the process of production, the second method of extending the period of gestation. In so far as the potatoes are used for feeding pigs, the services of the farmer, which could also have been used for satisfying present needs, have been put into a longer process of production. Similarly the labour of a man employed in building a blast furnace is, in combination with the "putting back" of iron and other materials, being used in a longer process of production.

We would get corresponding results from following out the possibilities for a piece of leather or other material. The leather can be used for shoes and thus soon come into final consumption. Or it can be used for leather driving belts and in combination with labour be used in longer processes of production. Why do men extend the period of gestation in this twofold way? Why do they "invest" or refrain from consuming in the near future, putting consumption off till later? Because the yield from labour and the material means of production is raised.[43]

The planning data and the empirical rules, as they are known to the controller of the centrally directed economy, form the foundation on which his economic plans are constructed. A whole system of plans will exist, because a total plan for one year or several years is the basis for all the orders, actions, and plans for the following month or day, which are fitted into this total plan as it is carried out and adapted. This total plan is a unity. (Even if a man acts mainly on momentary impulses without formulating any comprehensive plan, on *some* questions he has to take effective long-term decisions, as, for example, the farmer about the fruit he is to grow and how he is to grow it. Such decisions fix the direction of his further economic activities for the year ahead.)

In the total plan, and in the subordinate short-term plans, the central authority brings together labour and the other means of production in the combinations which seem most suitable. In making its economic plans the central authority has to estimate the importance of the different goods in different uses, that is, the services provided by labour, natural resources, produced means of production, and consumers' goods. It has to make valuations on which the whole plan rests. *The centrally directed economy is a system of valuations.* How the central authority shapes the plan, what functions the notion of the margin has in practical economic life, how costs influence decisions, how each plan is constructed, and how the economic process in everyday life is determined in its five aspects, this is what economic theory has to explain, and what to some extent it already has succeeded in explaining.

B. RISK

As soon as the authority's plans are carried out in practice a highly significant fact emerges. It usually appears that there is a divergence between the "planning" and the "factual" data. Either the authorities may have made a mistake when framing their plan, or the data may have altered while it was being carried out. Any of the data may diverge in this way, all of them together or singly. An unexpectedly cold winter alters people's needs or causes the winter seed to freeze. (The data regarding natural resources are different from what was expected.) Or there may be disease and therefore the labour force available is unexpectedly small. Fire may destroy or diminish the stock of previously produced goods on which the plan was based, or a new building technique may prove less serviceable in practice than had been expected. Naturally, the "factual" data can also turn out to be more favourable than those assumed in the plan. The weather may be better or the wastage of stocks smaller than had been forecast.

The estimates in the plans and the orders of the authorities are only in exceptional cases completely justified by the facts. There is generally a greater or lesser degree of uncertainty. Expectations are only partially realised. It is because of the imperfection of expectations that the risk element makes itself felt.

To the fact that the planning data are not generally fully realised by events men react in two ways. ***First,*** they often feel it necessary to alter the original plan and adjust it to the new situation. If the winter crop is killed by frost, then the farmer has to make it good, as far as possible by additional sowings in the new year, which will mean changing his plans and activities for some months. If some of the workers are absent the whole deployment of the labour force for this period has to be rearranged. The short-term and daily plans and orders have constantly to be revised as compared with the original outline plan. Just because such revisions are necessary, it is impossible to plan out economic actions in full detail for a year ahead.

The main plan usually fixes simply the general direction. The short-term plans carry out constant revisions of the main plan as a result of continual trial and error with the facts as they develop.

Secondly, the risk element affects the shaping of the main plan. As far as possible it is treated so as to keep the divergence between planning data and factual data as small as possible. Our sketch of the basic elements in the plan here needs to be supplemented. *Also, the risk element has constantly to be considered*, in addition to our six kinds of data and the three empirical rules. If the element of risk is held to be considerable, either no long-term plans will be made, so that risk is evaded, or there may be an attempt to lessen the risk. Under the influence of magic a man may try to ward off bad weather, crop failure, and disease by incantations, sacrifices, and prayers. We could describe this as an attempt to prevent too wide a divergence between factual data and planning data. The plans take into account the performance of these sacrifices and incantations as well as the employment in this way of the people specially qualified. When magical ways of thought have not the same influence, other means of reducing risk are used. The plan provides for the production of a variety of goods with the specific purpose of reducing risks. An unforeseen spell of cold weather, for example, does not usually hit the different crops equally severely. Therefore the number of varieties of crops to be planted is increased. Special buildings and equipment can lessen the danger of fire, floods, or disease. Finally, it often happens that because of the risk element a man feels obliged to stick to plans he has already begun to carry out. He knows the factual data better in respect of his present plans, and if he adopts new methods he has to run the risk of a greater divergence between planning and factual data. Sticking to previous procedures is not always "irrational", but may be based on a careful weighing up of the risk element.

The divergence between the planning data (*ex ante*) and the factual data (or *ex post* facts) has at all times, and is still to-day, of essential significance in all economic conduct. What has been and is of decisive influence on actual economic plans, and conduct cannot be ignored by economists without their theoretical apparatus being in that respect useless. Most of the earlier economists paid little attention to imperfect foresight, uncertainty, and risk in their analysis. Recently, however, a change has set in, and much that is of importance has been written about "expectations", "anticipations", calculations of returns *ex post* and *ex ante*, and about risk.

It is now necessary to fit this complex of facts into a place in economic theory corresponding to that which it occupies in actual economic life. Just as economists have to explain precisely the data and empirical rules and discern their nature so that they fit together in theory in exactly the same pattern as they are observed to have in a particular economic system, so it must be with the theoretical treatment of the risk element. Risk (or risk bearing) is not, as it has sometimes been called, a factor of production, nor is it a datum, nor an empirical rule. It consists rather in the *fact of divergence between the planning data* (ex ante) *and the factual data* (*or* ex post). As soon as economists realise that the facts require this distinction between planning data and factual data, the risk element will get its right place in economic theory. This systematic definition of the place of risk holds also, *mutatis mutandis*, for the exchange economy, and its correctness can easily be proved in everyday economic life.[44]

II. THE ANALYSIS OF THE EXCHANGE ECONOMY: A PRELIMINARY SURVEY

In the exchange economy it is the plans of a number, small or large, of economic organisations, firms, and households, and not simply those of a single authority, which decide the course of the economic process. Millions of independent firms and households work side by side in a great community linked together by division of labour, with each economic unit carrying out only a small fraction of the total economic process. As we were previously discussing, this is how the great practical task arises of co-ordinating individual plans so that the actions of individual units fit together and the process as a whole fulfils its purpose. While in the centrally directed economy only the problem of scarcity has to be overcome, in the exchange economy that of the co-ordination of individual plans and actions has to be solved too.

In a monetary economy this co-ordination of individual plans and actions comes about through the price system. It is the task of theory to show how, as a consequence of the forming of prices, the whole exchange economy in its five aspects is controlled and the individual plans co-ordinated.[45]

(1) An obvious method of approach is to survey the world of prices as a whole, as did most of the classical writers, for example, Ricardo, Say, and J. S. Mill, and as many more recent economists such as Clark or Cassel, have done. This procedure, when all the interrelationships are before one, and one does not start from single firms or households, is not without its dangers. To attempt to portray the entire cosmos of the price system as a whole, may well mean starting from too narrow a foundation of real economic facts. There is not sufficient emphasis on the fact that in an exchange economy everything happens in the firms and households, and it is difficult to link up such analysis with everyday life. A student of Cassel's account of modern economic theory who happened to be manager of a factory, would find it difficult to see the connection between his theoretical knowledge and his everyday economic life. In his theoretical studies he would find nothing about what goes on in a firm. It ought to be precisely the function of a scientific theory to show how the activities of the individual firms are linked together and how the activities of the firm fit into the whole interdependent economic system. In his analysis the economist is always in danger of losing sight of the cause of events in the real world and of ending up in unrealistic speculation. Economic reality requires that analysis must start from the study of the individual economic unit, as Thünen did with so much success.

The recent tendency to prefer study of the theory of the individual economic unit is a justified reaction against the "general" theoretical systems. The theory of wages will only be put on a sound basis and be of use in explaining real problems, if it starts from the analysis of firms and households and explains the special forms which demand and supply take in the labour market. But even this part of economics is in danger of becoming one-sided and sterile. Exponents of mathematical theory are fond of confining their analysis to a detailed study of models of particular single firms or markets. Cost curves for individual firms are drawn up, but no attention is paid to the question of the function of the costs of the individual firm in the control of the whole economic process in an exchange economy. The main task of theory, which is to make comprehensible the interrelations between all the individual economic units, is not faced.

This trend also explains the complete lack of appreciation of the work of the great system-builders of the past shown to-day by some theoretical economists, who do not seem to realise that the interrelationships in the real economic world can only be discovered as part of a system. The analysis of single firms or households, or of the relationships between particular individual quantities, scarcely constitutes a theoretical economics. It is impossible to understand particular economic events without understanding how they all fit together. For example, for the individual entrepreneur the existence of interest is not a problem. It is simply something he has to pay. He knows when the rate of interest rises and falls but cannot survey the causes of this from within his individual firm. With a fall in interest rates he goes in for more mechanisation and does not have to think out the changes this brings about elsewhere, how in doing this he is altering the productive process elsewhere. Capital is of key importance in his balance sheet, but he is not interested in why all firms aim at balancing their accounts, why it thereby follows that the entire production of the economy is deployed in a particular way, nor in what meaning the balancing of accounts by the individual firm possesses. That the entrepreneur sees things in this way and acts accordingly is right and comprehensible. But it is wrong if the economist makes the horizon of the individual entrepreneur his own. It is his task to discover the interrelationships throughout the whole economy. He has to ask *why there is* a rate of interest, what the function of capital is, and what significance calculations of capital have. If the economist neglects this task and confines himself to precise accounts of what happens within the firm, or of the relations between particular groups of economic units, his picture is bound to be patchy and to fail in its real purpose.

We have come here upon another point in which the one-sidedness of economic theory often cuts it off from the real world. Systems which do not start from a precise analysis of individual economic units and markets are built up on unrealistic foundations. On the other hand, an analysis of single firms, households, or markets, which does not organise the interrelationships of the economy as a whole into an analytical system, fails to explain the real economic world, which is not simply a number of adjacent individual firms, households, or markets. Only by combining together analysis of the individual economic unit with that of the economic system as a whole can we discover the interrelations we are looking for.

(2) How can this problem be solved? The analysis of the individual economic unit shows that the actions of the individual firms and households are based on plans. It is also clear that the planning data on which the director of the individual economic unit counts, only partially correspond with the planning data on which the plan is constructed in a centrally directed economy. The plan of a centrally directed economy is based on *data from the point of view of the economy as a whole.** *The plans of firms and households, which are only a fraction of the whole economic process in an exchange economy, are themselves "incomplete"* (*v.* above, Part III, Chap. II, Section II, Introduction, p. 129) *and only at certain points are they concerned with the data from the point of view of the whole economy.*

Let us take, for example, a farm of 250 acres producing and selling wheat, pigs, milk, hay, flax, and various other agricultural products. (The elements of central direction often found in such a case are left out of account here, as we are concerned with the ideal type of exchange economy.) What here decides the economic plans, the direction which production is to take, the employment of the labour supplies and other means of production available, the level of investment, the technical methods to be applied, and the location of the different crops and buildings? Partly the nature of the soil and

* **Gesamtwirtschaftliche Daten.**

the climate, the variety and efficiency of the labour supplies available, and the decisive factors in legal and social organisation.

These facts can also be described in this way: The data as to natural resources, labour, technical knowledge, stocks of goods, and legal and social organisation, determine the decisions of the manager (who formulates his plans in accordance with the data *as they seem to him* to be). Here the firm is concerned directly with what are data from the point of view of the whole system; but as a purchaser of labour, seeds, fertilisers, and fuel, it is surrounded by prices and as a recipient of credit it has to pay interest. Under conditions of perfect competition these are data from the point of view of the individual firm, and it is clear that at these points the firm's plans are "incomplete" or "partial", and that it is only indirectly concerned with the data for the economy as a whole. The same holds for the cash balances that the management keeps. Prices can also be regarded "as representing the frontier line between the exchange economy as a whole and the individual economic unit". At those points "the firm is not *directly* concerned with the data for the system as a whole, but only in so far as it takes account of the actions of all the other individual units" (K. F. Maier).

This way of looking at what are the data from the point of view of the individual economic unit, and of dividing them into two groups, is familiar to the practical business man. He is also accustomed to distinguish between what he takes as given regarding the characteristics of his firm, himself, and his workers, and data on the nature of the connections of his firm with the market. At the same time he takes account of the empirical rules as far as they relate to production, that is, of the second and third rules. He is aware, though only somewhat vaguely, of the law of diminishing marginal returns, for it does not occur to him to try to plant all his crops on one small section of his land and leave the rest uncultivated. He is aware of the empirical rule involved in employing, e.g., available supplies of labour for making paths or a drainage system instead of on hoeing, thus diminishing this year's harvest in order to increase those of future years. The plans of the manager are built up on what are data from the point of view of the single unit and on these two empirical rules. In doing so the manager follows the principle of substitution as explained by Jevons, Marshall, and others.

We have not yet described all the factors that decide the plans and actions of the head of this firm (or farm). Here, too, what is expected according to the data of the plan often fails to correspond with what actually happens or the factual data, though this divergence makes itself felt in rather a different way than in the centrally directed economy, corresponding to the difference in the data. Uncertainty and risk arise not only because of changes in the weather, fires, and so on, but because of movements in prices. The farmer in producing pigs counts on particular prices for fodder, young pigs, and porkers. These prices may be partly realised but partly not. Hence there are price risks because the management of a firm cannot exactly estimate in advance what the other economic units with which it is directly or indirectly in touch will be doing. The manager of a firm knows that this kind of twofold risk exists and he takes account of the risk element in his plans and actions by sowing a variety of crops, by insurance, anti-flood precautions, maintaining stocks of goods and money, and by avoiding far-reaching plans and large investments. Political confidence is also a relevant factor, important for economic action and everyday economic life and its changes and for cyclical fluctuations. A consequence of confidence in the political order is that the managements of firms can count on certain data, for example, on the approximate rates of taxation being lasting, and on there being no likelihood of anything from this quarter coming to disturb their long-term plans. The less reliable the data seem to be, the less will plans be made for the distant future.

The same applies, *mutatis mutandis*, for every household. Each household is surrounded by prices. The worker's household, for example, has on one side its income, and on the other the prices of consumers' goods. At the same time the plans and actions of the head of a household are determined by its needs and the stocks of good available, these stocks also, like producers' stocks, having two aspects. In part the household does not affect the data for the whole economy, since it simply pays and receives prices. In part what are data from its own individual point of view—its needs, etc.—are at the same time data from the point of the whole economy. The first empirical rule, which is the only one of the three which is relevant in this purely consuming community, always remains effective. The plans of the household are therefore all dependent on these two kinds of data, on the first empirical rule, and on the risk element.

The analysis of the firm and of the household comprises the first stage of theoretical investigation.

Study of the individual unit shows the direction in which research must proceed if it is to approach its goal. There is no room for arbitrary choice here. The fact that firms and households are surrounded by prices and hold cash balances forces the economist's studies in two directions. He has to study their relationships with markets and with monetary systems.

First, we have to study the behaviour, let us say, of the farm we were describing, when it is supplying rye and pigs under perfectly competitive conditions, how it reacts to price changes and fixes its supply, and also how it plans and acts when selling under monopolistic conditions or in other forms of market. The time factor has to be taken into consideration. In the short period supply from any unit to a market, say to the wheat market, comes out of the stocks on hand, that is, out of the stocks available till the next wheat harvest. In a somewhat longer period, for, say, the next year, the scale of production of the farm unit being given, supply will come out of current production. Over still longer periods the scale of production can be considerably altered, enlarged, or diminished. This kind of time-scale is important for most branches of production. The monopolist supplier of a good over the quite short period does this out of stocks, over a somewhat longer period he takes as given the existing apparatus of production and looks for Cournot's maximum point, and over a still longer period he selects and constructs out of all the possible scales of production that which seems the most favourable for him. Theoretical analysis of a supply monopoly has to study not only the case of the particular cost curve for a given productive apparatus, but also that for given stocks, and that for an alterable scale of production. All three time periods are interconnected. The important problems of the reaction interval between changes in data and movements in prices and their effects, and those of the so-called time "lag", must be studied with the aid of a time-scale such as this threefold one.

Total demand and supply in single spatially and temporally defined markets are made up of the actions of single firms and households within the framework of the different market forms. For example, in the wheat market of a country supply over short periods comes out of a given stock; for medium periods supply is from a given apparatus of production; and over long periods the scale of production is variable.

The analysis of the individual firm and household demonstrates the interdependence of all markets. The third stage of the analysis has to trace back total supply and total demand in particular markets to the data for the whole exchange economy. Then if we add the conclusions obtained from monetary theory—which is also based on the analysis of single firms and households—we can get a clear understanding of the interrelationships between events in the exchange economy as a whole.

Further study will show that what are data from the point of view of the exchange economy as a whole, correspond with those for the centrally directed economy as a whole. Here also they are six in number—needs, natural resources, labour, stocks of finished and semi-finished consumers' goods, technical knowledge, and the social and legal organisation of the exchange economy. These, together with the empirical rules, determine the workings of the interdependent exchange economy as a whole. On them depend all issues of the direction of production, distribution, investment, technical methods, and the choice of location. Economic theory has to show how they interact, in the exchange economy as well as in the centrally directed economy. Certainly in the exchange economy they interact in quite a different way from in the centrally administered economy, where the needs to be satisfied are fixed by the central authority, where consumers are powerless, and where it depends on the plans of the central authority what effects the data have.

Everything that we said about the data for the centrally directed economy applies also to those for the exchange economy, for example, with respect to natural resources, the various needs, the distinction between natural resources and the services they yield, labour and its services, and the stock of goods being both a "datum" and a "problem". There are only one or two important additions to be made. *First*, the distinction between what are data from the point of view of the individual firm, and what from the point of view of the economy as a whole, of course, applies only in the exchange economy and not in the totally centralised economy. *Secondly*, in the exchange economy there is no one taking as the data for a plan the entire range of what are data from the point of view of the whole economy, for there is no "total" plan, and there are also no total "overall" risks. *In the exchange economy there are planning data from the point of view of the individual units.* *Thirdly* and finally, the social and legal organisation of the ideal type of monetary exchange economy must be taken to include the monetary system and the monetary policy actually being applied, as well as the existing forms of markets, which it cannot do in a centrally directed economy.

Let us assume that in a centrally directed economy, or in an exchange economy, all of the six data for the economy as a whole remain for a long time unchanged. That is, no changes take place in needs, climate, quantity of labour, size and composition of stocks, technical knowledge, and the legal and social order. What would happen in such an economy? The answer must be that the same processes would be repeated over and over again. Year after year the economic process would present the same picture. Values and prices would remain completely unchanged. The divergences between planning data and factual data would gradually disappear. The controller of a centrally directed economy and the heads of firms and households in an exchange economy, would take as their planning data the realised *ex post* "factual" data of the previous year, and these planning data would regularly be confirmed. There would be no divergence between expectations and reality, and risk would disappear.

Such a condition may be described briefly as the "static" state. Obviously, it has never been realised historically. Large changes in data have been constantly occurring, occasionally only small changes, but never no change at all. The same things do not recur year after year. But it is permissible to work analytically with such a notion. The static state is a *possibility.*

In fact, the notion of the static state is indispensable for understanding the interrelationships of the real economic world. It is important because for an understanding of the economic process it is necessary to discover in what direction the economy as a whole is moving from any given initial conditions. At the same time it provides a basis for analysing changes in everyday economic life. By varying one datum at a time an understanding can be got of economic development, and in this way the notion of the static state is especially helpful. This topic and the method of variations in general will be discussed later.

There are also dangers in this notion of the static state, which can easily be misapplied. Two misconceptions have proved specially harmful.

In the *first* place often a simple description of an assumed static state is all that is given. Then the notion of the static state is used to conjure away the real problems of economics. If one imagines a totally centralised economy in which the six data are unchanged the controller has almost nothing to do. He repeats year by year his plans and orders, and the various parts of his community repeat their activities with the same regular rhythm. The authority is not faced with any new problems for solution. It can devote itself to other non-economic tasks. Constant repetition of the same conditions would provide the solution to economic problems. It is the same in any form of exchange economy. If all the data for the whole economy remains the same, heads of firms and households have nothing to do but to repeat their orders, and in such a monotonous world all actions would similarly be repeated. The theorists who describe such a static state imagine an exchange economy in which the equipment of produced means of production, such as buildings, machines, and raw materials, is always kept at the same level, never being either increased or lessened. *Why* these produced means of production are kept at the same level is apparently of no interest. Having excluded this problem by assuming a static state, one discovers that the problem no longer exists. This rather jejune conclusion is unfortunately often used to deny the existence of the important problems of the time-structure of production. Similarly there is no problem in the static economy of why particular technical methods are applied. They are just "assumed", for *why* they are applied cannot be explained by simply describing a constantly repeated economic process. Of course, the problem of risk, in reality of central importance, also disappears. The economically static state, which takes all this as given, is of very little interest. Static analysis becomes interesting and important, in fact highly important, when the question is asked of how one particular combination of productive methods and resources is chosen from out of the billions possible.

Secondly, there are two quite different kinds of static state. It may be that all the means of production are used to the optimum extent and all workers employed fully and in the best possible way. This would be a static state describable as one of "complete general equilibrium". On the other hand it may be that there are workers permanently unemployed, equipment unused, stocks stagnating, while those employed are not being used in the best way. That would be a static state without complete general equilibrium. It is a common mistake to think of the static state of the Lausanne School simply as one of full general equilibrium, which in fact only comes about under certain *special* conditions, that is, under perfect competition in all markets, and by no means under *all* conditions. The assumption that the static state is always one of general equilibrium is unfounded.

To combine both these errors and simply describe a given condition of complete and general equilibrium, is to be content with a static analytical apparatus unsuitable for the solution of real economic problems.[46]

III. INTERDEPENDENCE IN THE DIFFERENT TYPES OF ECONOMIC SYSTEM

To study the two main types of economic system in all their different variants and how the economic process in its five aspects works itself out in each, is certainly a very extensive but not an impossible task.

The question at once suggests itself of whether all forms of centrally directed economy and all forms of market and monetary system must be treated separately from the start. Must the analysis of each be carried out separately, or can the solution of the problems for a single ideal type be applied for the analysis of other types? Further, can economic relationships as a whole be studied for a few ideal types and the results be applied forthwith to other types?

The answer is a threefold one.

A. Solutions to the problems of one type of economic system are often not merely useful but quite indispensable for solving those of another type of system. The history of economic theory offers a wide range of examples. The treatment of price problems is obviously a relevant case. A study of the exchange economy on the lines of Walras or Marshall with the purpose simply of describing the price mechanism will yield some very precise conclusions, but will not explain the full significance of the interrelationships of an exchange economy. It will not get behind the scaffolding of the structure of prices and rewards—as Schumpeter describes it—which conceals the living social process. It is quite different if one first studies the world of the simple centrally directed economy and after that comes to that of the exchange economy. Because the simple centrally directed economy is controlled by one head, the purpose and relevance of all the valuations and actions are clearly explicable. The means of production are obviously valued and used in accordance with the needs to be satisfied. This method achieves what a simple description of the pricing of the means of production in an exchange economy does not achieve, that is, an understanding of the purpose behind the forming of the prices of the means of production and therefore also of costs. The study of the simple centrally directed economy not only serves to explain the actual processes of that type of economy as they have occurred historically, but also clears the way for an understanding of the exchange economy. To have seen this is one of the greatest services of the Austrian economists.

Again, anyone who has understood the interrelationships and valuations in a simple centrally directed economy is on the way to understanding how valuations are made by the forming of prices in an exchange economy and the meaning of changes in price relationships for the whole economic system.

There is one case in which studying together several different economic systems or forms of market has a special significance. This is in the study of an exchange economy in which the powers of government are used for fixing or partially fixing prices.

This case is a very common one. We have shown that it is not to be regarded as a special form of market, because the fixing of prices may follow upon any of the different kinds of open and closed markets. It is therefore a special case. In this case too the price is a datum for the whole economy and is no longer a problem. It is not for the economist to follow out how it may have been arrived at, for in such a case as this, and in this case alone, he would be passing beyond the boundaries of his given subject-matter. There is simply a direct decision by political authority. Nevertheless, it is often not understood that theoretical analysis of this case is indispensable. The question remains as to how large supply, demand, and production are at the prices fixed, and how in general the course of economic events is influenced by price-fixing.

Let us assume that the wages for textile workers in a certain country are from a particular date onwards fixed officially, being raised from their previous level. How does the rise in wages affect the economic process? Before we can answer this question we must have an answer to the question as to the previous form of market and the way in which wages were fixed. It may have been monopsonistically, that is, the workers in competition with one another faced a mill-owner with a monopsonistic position in the labour market able to force down the wage below the marginal product of labour.

Alternatively, conditions of perfect competition may have existed. Also of importance is the question of how the textile firms marketed their goods, whether competitively, monopolistically, or in some other way. The level of wages and the extent of employment and of labour offered will differ according to the answers to these questions. It is senseless to study the official fixing of wages, or any other form of official price-fixing and its effects, without having in advance a thoroughly clear picture of the previous conditions on which the authorities intervened with their official price-fixing.

The study of official price-fixing also requires a previous theoretical analysis of the centrally directed economic system. Halting the price mechanism leads in certain circumstances to a central authority directly controlling the economic process. Raising the price of timber by official price-fixing is then followed by the distribution of timber to purchasers by a central authority. Selecting which requirements are to be met and which not is no longer done by pricing, nor left to accident, but is done by rationing, and that, as we know, is a procedure belonging to the centrally directed economy.

B. Among the different forms of centrally directed economy and the many varieties of exchange economy, two models have a special importance. The analysis of them is of little direct but of great indirect value, since they serve to prepare the way for the analysis of a very wide range of types. I refer to the smallest variant of the centrally directed economy, *the simple economy of Robinson Crusoe*, and secondly, the primitive variant of the exchange economy, *the barter economy.*

(1) It has been disputed whether Crusoe analysis has the slightest value. Diehl, Spann, Cassel, and many others agree that he is a useless conception. Men conduct their economic life together in society and the economy of human beings is essentially social. In no period of history have men lived their economic lives in isolation from one another, neither in prehistoric nor in historical times. Certainly, there have always been single cases of men living for days, weeks, or years by themselves, like the prophets of old in the desert and airmen of to-day who come down in remote regions. But these are exceptions of no importance historically. The conclusion may

therefore be drawn, as was argued by Diehl, that "For the purposes of our science only individuals living in a community are of significance, and Robinson because he lives his economic life alone, is of no interest for the social economist." What is the use of Crusoe analysis for solving the economic problems of contemporary industry or other questions of social economics?

Crusoe analysis arose particularly in the eighteenth century out of the philosophy of the Enlightenment. He was intended to prove that a natural impulse towards religion, morality, and law was alive in men. If contemporary economists were to work with Robinson Crusoe they would have to take a particular individualist point of view as their starting point.

Although men seldom economise in isolation, this particular ideal type is of special value for an understanding of the social economy. Two characteristics make the concept of Robinson Crusoe a specially valuable theoretical instrument. For a man who has to answer the basic economic questions by himself alone, the facts of economic life emerge with special force. The subject–object relation is here quite clear and recognisable. This is closely connected with another valuable quality of the Robinson model. In this small-scale variant of the centrally directed economy it can be explained without difficulty how every single economic action fits together as part of a whole interrelated system. It is comparatively easy to work out the system of ideas by which interractions in the economic process are alone to be understood. The Crusoe type of economy has therefore a far greater significance than its comparatively rare historical occurrence suggests. Crusoe analysis is not simply an unreal theoretical pastime, but provides analytical tools by the aid of which difficulties in the study of social economies can be overcome. Not that we imagine that the social economy consists of a number of Robinson Crusoes. That is certainly not the case. Crusoe analysis is relevant for the system as a whole and for its interrelationships. From the study of Crusoe's system as a whole we can gain a far clearer insight into the much more obscure interrelationships of the social economy, whether of the centrally directed or of the exchange type.

Crusoe analyses are, then, preliminary studies, and regular and persistent use should be made of them. It can be very soon seen that they are worth while when used as an auxiliary method. This is something quite different from the former "Robinsoniad" philosophising, with the value or lack of value of which we are not concerned here.[47]

(2) In the barter economy we recognise one of the main forms of exchange economy and a predecessor of the much more important monetary economy. We know that men have bartered with one another in prehistoric times in Europe, in the ancient world, during the Middle Ages, and partly also since the Renaissance, as well as in other cultural regions. We can construct the type of a barter economy by abstracting from history this aspect of such economies. At one time the barter economy was of great importance historically, but this has dwindled away with the advance of money. Here again, however, the importance of such analysis is not measured by the historical importance of this type of system. The analysis of the barter economy is specially significant as a preliminary study for that of the monetary economy, which is how the classical economists used it. In order from the outset to exclude the influence of money on the economic process in an exchange economy, they analysed a barter economy. In order to keep vividly before them the streams of "real" goods they imagined themselves in a world without money, that is, without any generally recognised means of exchange. They had much success with this model. They successfully disproved the mistaken doctrine of general over-production, which had been based on the false notion that total supply and total demand were two quite separate quantities, and that the former was apt to run ahead of the latter. Say and James Mill, among others, by treating the problem in a barter economy could show where the error was, an error which in the form of so-called purchasing power theories is still influential to-day. Anyone who offers goods on the market, say shoes or cement, can be shown at once in the barter economy to have *the will* to demand, otherwise he would not appear on the market. At the same time he has the *ability* to buy goods in that he is offering cement or shoes. Disturbances in the barter economy can only arise through particular mistaken estimates of demand and supply.

The classical economists have been accused of holding that the barter economy corresponded with the normal form of economy, and that all economic problems could be solved by its study. Also, that they only allotted money a subsidiary role, and did not recognise that in the monetary economy it is an extremely active factor. However, even Say and James Mill added to their proposition the rider that changes in monetary circulation could bring about general losses, though they did not follow up this argument. Others like Hume or Ricardo realised that money was not simply like a veil covering the actual movements of real goods, and that the economic process in a monetary economy cannot be explained simply by applying the results of barter analysis. Others, like the later theorists of the currency school, laid great emphasis on the influence of changes in the quantity of money on the entire course of events in an exchange economy, and have described them in detail. Against all these writers the accusation is quite unfounded.

Modern students have examined the relationships between the monetary and the barter economies more closely. Swedish economists, in particular Wicksell and Lindahl, have shown that the differences between a monetary and a barter economy are very great, and that a monetary economy cannot be regarded simply as a more advanced stage of barter economy, but rather that in consequence of the use of money the economic process takes quite a different course from what it does without it.

Nevertheless the analysis of the barter economy remains valuable as a preliminary study. Without it there is a danger of the real basic relationships between goods being overlooked. The discussion of "saving" and "investment" would certainly gain much from not being conducted purely in terms of monetary and banking technique, being started instead from a study of the basic fact of the time-structure of production in a barter economy.

C. To arrive at a theoretical solution by first putting one's questions in respect of a series of skilfully chosen models, has proved a heuristic method of the first importance in the treatment of most problems of economics. The application of this procedure, by which the question is formulated and answered first for simple and then for increasingly complicated sets of conditions, calls for much scientific discretion.

Because the sets of conditions in particular economic systems or particular forms of market or of monetary system, are never the same, the theoretical results of the analysis of a single type can never be directly taken over as propositions about interrelationships in other types of system. The courses taken by the economic process in the two extreme forms, the totally centralised economy and the perfectly competitive economy, show certain similarities. It can be shown that the controller of a totally centralised economy can in some circumstances direct the economy in a way similar to that in which it proceeds under perfect competition. This should not mislead one into believing that the course of economic events must necessarily always be the same, nor that the analysis of one model can be substituted for that of another. Great differences remain. In the one case a single will and a single plan decides to the exclusion of all others, in the other case *all* the households and firms decide. The distribution of power is quite different in the two cases, as we shall later be discussing. In the former case there is no free consumer's choice or free choice of occupation, as there is in the latter. Men live in two quite different economic worlds. The whole course of economic events proceeds quite differently. These great and various differences cannot be removed or smoothed out by false theories of equalitarianism.

The analysis of different economic systems and their various characteristics must be used mutually to assist each other, but the results must not be directly taken over, nor should certain conclusions be regarded too hastily as universally valid. Such universally valid results, that do not depend on the variety of forms in the real world, do exist, for example, certain propositions regarding costs. But which results are universally valid only becomes clear when the different individual forms have been analysed.

The history of economics is full of attempts to find a short cut which avoids the tedious study of the numerous different forms of organisation, and which leads to a uniform theory beyond, or without regard to, the existing multiformity in the real world. In many cases it is the economic system of perfect competition in all markets that is studied. Such "monistic" systems are misleading because of the simplicity of their construction. They do not correspond to the actual multiform economic life of the present day or of the past. This divergence is important when concrete problems have to be solved, that is, when the theory has to be applied. The struggles for power, for example, of partially oligopolistic oil combines, or of those many varieties of powerful bodies so important in the economic world of to-day, cannot be explained by means of a "monistic" system.[48]

IV. THE DATA

A. It is of essential importance in all theoretical studies to grasp what the data are, to realise their limits, and to be able to work with them.

As we saw, data must not simply be "assumed", and in ascertaining them everything arbitrary must be excluded. The basic fact about all economic actions is that they are determined by plans, and this brings one to the distinction between planning data and "factual" data. We can now arrive at some further general propositions regarding the nature and functions of the different kinds of data.

(1) Data, from the point of view of the economy as a whole, are those facts which determine the nature of the economic world without themselves being economic facts. On coming up against these data theoretical explanation has to break off. The task of theory is to follow out the necessary relationships as far as the particular set of data, and in the other direction to show how the course of economic events depends on the data. Economic theory cannot show how these data come to exist.

Countless facts of nature and history and all sorts of illusions and imponderabilia affect the day-to-day course of economic events. All these factors exercise their effects through the planning data and the "factual" data, and only in this way. One natural or historical fact can shape a number of data; for example, when a cold winter affects the data for both needs and natural resources. Or it may be that the differences in racial characteristics between, say, Norwegians and Negroes affects the data for the supply of labour, for needs, for technical knowledge, and for social and legal organisation. Similarly the abolition of illiteracy and the introduction of compulsory education in Europe during the last hundred and fifty years constitute a change in the data for labour, needs, technical knowledge, and social and legal organisation. The victory of Calvinism certainly had the most profound effects on the course of economic events, and altered such data as the supply of labour, the social and legal organisation, technical knowledge, and needs (in that greater emphasis was laid on future needs, that is, on saving).

(2) The argument that economic theory must stop short when it comes up against the data also applies to cases where two or more data are interacting on one another.

An historically important example is that of inventive activity. The history of technical knowledge shows very clearly that its extent is closely related with the social and legal organisation of a community. The revolutionary changes in the economic order at the end of the eighteenth and the beginning of the nineteenth centuries, and the removal of the countless restrictions on technical methods, were a vigorous stimulus to the invention of new processes. Also, the passing of the new patent laws which afforded a certain limited protection against imitators, probably increased the number of inventions. The change in one datum resulted here in the changing of another. But the causal connection was between the data only. There was no economically necessary relation between a change in social and legal organisation and an increase in inventive activity. Other assumptions of an intellectual, psychological, or material nature had to be satisfied in the countries concerned, if legal reforms were to be followed by an increase in the number of inventions. The causal connection is not of an exact theoretical kind. For the theoretical economist, the social and legal organisation and technical knowledge are both given, independent quantities or data.

(3) Economic facts or events, themselves the result of certain conditions or data, can in turn react back on the data for the economy as a whole.

This reaction always follows indirectly and is therefore not accessible to theoretical analysis, which at best can only show the direction in which a change in data *could* arise. For example, in a local labour market for the clothing trade the wages of home workers may be kept down at a very low level by monopsonistic conditions. The low level of wages causes the state to intervene and fix wages for home workers. Here we have the data for social and legal organisation being changed by the economic fact of the level of wages. Nevertheless the economic fact does not shape the data in the same way in which the data shape economic events. The reaction is indirect *via* the policy of the state. Whether the state authorities react to the low level of wages by removing the monopsonistic conditions depends on the constitution of the state, the political policy of the leading statesmen, the attitude of the officials, or the influence of the workers on the political authorities. Consequently, the connection between the low level of wages and the change in the organisation of the labour market cannot be explained by economic theory, which at the most can indicate that intervention by the state *might* result.

Let us take a further example. Because of a change in data the price of coal falls markedly and numerous mining enterprises get into difficulties. Some enterprising technicians and chemists try successfully to find cheaper methods for getting coal and better uses for it. "Technical knowledge" has changed, and in this way costs are reduced and profits raised. In this case also, according to a pattern which has been repeated many times and in many branches of production during the last century, an economic fact (that is, a fall in coal prices) resulted in a change in data (that is, in technical knowledge). Here too it is clear that while technical knowledge has a direct influence on economic events, the reverse influence of economic events on technical knowledge is indirect and not inevitable. They are often not fully operative and depend to an important extent on the ability, enlightenment, and energy of the technicians and on many other non-economic circumstances. The theoretical economist cannot, of course, maintain that a fall in price in relation to costs *must* lead to an increase in technical knowledge and a lowering of costs. He must confine himself to pointing out that the economic facts, which he can explain precisely as a result of the data, *might* give a stimulus to a change in one of the data—that relating to technical knowledge.[49]

(4) The data from the point of view of the system as a whole constitute the frontier line up to which theoretical analysis is to be pursued and at which it has to break off. They are not data from the point of view of economic policy.

It is rather the reverse that is true. Economic policy, whether interpreted in a broad or narrow sense, takes effect by altering the data. When the state prohibits cartels or expands credit, or reforms technical and business education, it is altering the data. Pressure groups are similarly striving in their economic policies to bring about changes in data by means of state-regulated prices, or by prohibitions on movement into a trade or on imports.

Also, the efforts of economists in preparing the way for an effective economic constitution are directed at shaping the data for the social and legal organisation in a particular way. Naturally, the results of theoretical analysis are used; but theoretical analysis itself breaks off at the point where it reaches the data for the society as a whole.

B. In dealing with the data and fixing their limits the following mistakes are particularly common.

(1) The frontiers are sometimes fixed too ambitiously, so that problems are subjected to theoretical analysis which cannot be solved by such methods.

An example of this is the Ricardian theory of wages. Ricardo treats the supply of labour according to exactly the same principles as the supply of goods, on the extent of which price is dependent. In the long run that quantity is supplied which results in a price which precisely covers the costs of production. Ricardo treats the supply of labour in exactly the same way. The natural price of labour enables the working class to exist and reproduce itself without either an increase or decrease in numbers. A rise in the market price for labour above the natural price brings an increase in supply, since the higher level of wages stimulates the growth of population. A fall below the natural price results in a decrease in the numbers of the working population owing to distress and poverty. At every point Ricardo simply applies his reasoning about the production of goods to the labour force.

Here is an inadmissible violation of the frontier between what is given and what is not given. The growth and decline of population depend indirectly on so many natural political and psychological facts that a necessary relationship between the level of wages and the size of the population does not exist. Ricardo takes the size of the population as a "problem" to be answered with the aid of economic theory, and not as a datum for theory, which is what it really is. No wonder that this theoretical doctrine has not been confirmed and that the connection he claimed to exist between movements in wages and movements in the number of workers is, on the whole, disproved. The theory fails because it applies its methods of analysis to problems beyond the frontiers of what are data from the point of view of the economy as a whole.

(2) The frontier may also be drawn too narrowly. A fact which presents a problem for the economist is postulated as a datum. This is a mistake that is often met with and which has had dire results, for example, on the treatment of problems of the stocks of produced means of production. It must be recognised that the frontiers here are being drawn unduly narrowly and that what is being postulated is not really given to the economist. If the produced means of production are regarded as an inexhaustible fund of income, or if the process of production is seen as one in which so-called durable "real capital" has the role of an original factor of production, then the produced means of production will be treated as a datum. Some theoretical economists argue that there is no reason why one should not proceed in this way. The manager of a firm does so. He regards the existing buildings and machinery as given. The economist, therefore, should not proceed with his analysis beyond the given capital goods. He will only get caught up in pseudo-problems or in some infinite historical regress of no economic interest.

The problem is, of course, not of the past but of the future. The stock of produced means of production is never from the economic point of view simply a datum. The managers of a railway, for example, in their daily and longer-term plans reckon with the existing stock of wagons, track, and engines, but they must also in their present plans make decisions about depreciation, maintenance, extensions to the track, and new rolling stock. The productive apparatus at any given moment is not only a datum, for at the same time its maintenance, that is, its immediate and more distant future, has to be cared for.

Economists must not evade this fact, as they do if they take so-called "real capital", that is, the durable produced means of production, simply as a datum. It never is that in any economic system. It always presents an economic problem. The equipment of durable means of production, which will be in existence in one, two, or three years' time, depends on economic plans and actions which are being initiated or completed now, or which will be formulated and carried out in the immediate future. The nature and extent of this equipment will be the result of economic actions. It is therefore inadmissible for the economist to take it simply as a datum.[50]

(3) Changes are postulated which are not changes in the data for the whole economy, but are themselves economic facts. This is a misuse of the method of variations which makes for superficial and incomplete answers to the problems involved.

The most frequent but not the only form in which this mistake appears, is that of studying the problems of an exchange economy by starting from variations of particular prices.

For example, in seeking an answer to the problem of how the payments and claims between two countries are brought into equilibrium, that is, of how the balance of payments comes into balance, the following theoretical argument has been used since the days of the classical economists. The exchange rate for a country's currency rises or falls for some unspecified reason and the question is then asked as to how the adjustment will work itself out. Following on this kind of formulation of the problem there will come a description of how a fall in the exchange rate leads to an increase in exports and a decline in imports, and how gradually a lasting equilibrium in the balance of payments would come about. It was thought that by doing this a problem had been solved. This was hardly so, for the question was incompletely formulated and therefore the answer was also incomplete. The change in prices in the foreign exchange market was ultimately the result of an alteration of one or of several of the data. This aspect of the problem is simply avoided by separating off the economic events in *a single* market and then simply showing what equilibrating forces are active in this single market and no more. "It must be quite clear that with the question formulated in this way a complete theory of the mechanism of adjustment in the balance of payments can never be worked out. Only a partial solution can be arrived at if the question is left open of how the original equilibrium in the foreign exchange market was upset. The answer is bound to be superficial, as it does not go into the changes in the economic process which brought about this change in the foreign exchange market" (F. W. Meyer).

The question must be framed in a different way and more comprehensively. The whole economic life of the two countries must be kept in view, and what must be assumed is the variation not of a price but of one of the data for the whole economy —for example, extreme cold resulting in a bad harvest, or the discovery of large ore deposits, or an invention applied first in one country only, or a strike, or changes in the needs for foodstuffs, meat, or vegetables. The question then is how, in spite of this variation in data, the payments by and to a country will be kept in balance, and what equilibrating forces are at work. It is now clear that shifts in the prices and economic processes in the two countries are the main equilibrating factors, and that the mechanism of the exchange rate is simply residual in bringing about equilibrium. Only if the problem is formulated in this complete way, starting from an alteration in the data for the whole economy, can a solution be obtained, which incidentally is in this case of great importance for economic policy.

(4) There is a fundamental misunderstanding in the objection, which might be and has been made, that if theoretical explanation of economic events stops at the data for the economy as a whole, the important and really relevant relationships are missed, that is, those between economic phenomena and history and politics.

Exactly the opposite is the case. Only with the aid of a system of data can the connections between historical, political, and economic events be clarified. All political and historical happenings can be summarised as changes in data: whether it is Rome gradually becoming the master of the Mediterranean lands, or the French Revolution creating a new type of modern state, or the Russian state at the beginning of the nineteenth century being transformed by new political principles, or the much more extensive claims of defence policies in all the great states between 1914 and 1918 and in the subsequent decades. In all such cases a change in data for the whole economy has taken place, in particular in the data "legal and social organisation", "needs", "labour", or "technical knowledge".

In so far as theory by means of abstraction and ideal types shows how the data determine economic events, it is a suitable instrument for explaining the relations between historical and political facts and economic events. Exactly the same is true about particular economic policies. They too represent changes in data, as, for example, when a Greek city-state of the fourth century B.C. sets up a wheat monopoly, or when Queen Elizabeth fixes wages at a particular level, or when the German Reich gives a bank the exclusive right of note issue or reorganises the labour market or the taxation laws. Economic theory cannot demonstrate *why* the Greek city-state introduced a wheat monopoly, or *why* Queen Elizabeth intervened in the fixing of wages. These are questions which can only be understood from the general historical situation of the country and the epoch. Because economic theory demonstrates precisely how economic facts result from the data, its application makes it possible to understand the economic effects of these changes in data. There is no other way.

There must be a distinct frontier line between what is to be taken as given and what not. Unless there is, and unless theoretical analysis keeps within this frontier, history and theory cannot be combined.

The result is a fatal confusion, of which an appalling example may be found in the economic doctrines of Adam Müller.[51]

Chapter IV

THE ECONOMIC SYSTEM AND THE COURSE OF ECONOMIC EVENTS: THE THEORY APPLIED

THE FIRST OBJECTIVE of the economist, let us repeat, is a scientific understanding of real economic life. He has reached this when he has answered two questions for every country and every period: that of the structure of the economic system, and that of the relationships in the course of economic events under that system. Both questions have proved difficult to answer. It is clear that the usual path of taking cross-sections of economic history and constructing theories for each, does not lead us to our objective. We therefore started on another path.

Those who work with cross-sections of history construct their types by means of "generalising" abstraction, that is, by standing back from reality and disregarding detail. Because they do that the results they achieve do not correspond with the facts of the economic world and are unsuitable as a basis for theoretical work. From the start we have taken the opposite direction, trying to penetrate as far as we could into the workings of actual households and firms, and concentrating on detail. We might compare the "stages" and "styles" of economic development, intended as they are to represent the normal economic life of a particular period, with the silhouette of a town as one sees it at a distance. Our method, on the other hand, is to penetrate to the heart of the town and study the individual houses from cellar to roof. Each single economic phenomenon must be thoroughly studied. By abstracting the significant characteristics we have arrived at the ideal types of economic system, the various forms of centrally directed economy, the market forms, and the types of monetary system. Examples of the different forms of organisation were found in history and discovered by studying past and present facts.

It may be asked what we intended to do with this morphological system? The single forms we have combined together, although taken from actual observation, are not replicas of actual economic phenomena. They are not photographs or pictures and are not intended to be. Nor do they seek to describe a particular historical milieu. We have shown that because they represent simple and clear sets of conditions they serve as a basis for arriving at theoretical conclusions, that is, general propositions about necessary relationships. This completed one essential step in our analysis.

We are now concerned with the question of the use of this morphological scheme of ideal types of economic system and their variants; and of the use of theoretical propositions in understanding the real economic world. Can we do better than the numerous procedures we have already criticised, and arrive at a scientific understanding of the economic world, and have we therefore been justified in taking the path we have?

Our answer is in the affirmative. *We maintain first that by applying this morphological scheme we can successfully understand the framework and structure of the economic system in every period and of every people.*

Secondly, we maintain that when the theoretical propositions are applied they are found to be suitable instruments for understanding the course of the economic process under any actual economic system.

In these two ways we can get beyond superficial everyday impressions to a scientific understanding of economic problems, and not only of present-day problems. It remains to be shown how this is to be done.

I. THE UNDERSTANDING OF THE DIFFERENT ECONOMIC SYSTEMS

(1) Anyone visiting Japan to-day to study the economy of the country would, quite rightly, first try to study the structure of the Japanese economic system. If he confined himself simply to looking at households, farms, industrial undertakings, banks, etc., in their almost unlimited interrelations and interdependence with one another, and relied simply on direct observations, he could not discover any *system.* If he tried to make use of the "stages" and "styles" of economic development, he would find that they were inapplicable to his case and contributed nothing to a knowledge of the contemporary Japanese economy. From the start he would fail in his attempt to understand economic reality.

Having discovered the different types of economic system, the market forms, and the main forms of monetary economy and monetary system, we start from a different position. This morphology gives simply the basic forms of organisation which are not arrived at by speculation or deduction. Sombart tried to deduce them from the notion of an "economy", opening the way to every kind of subjective arbitrariness. Here they have been worked out from precise observation of the facts of economic history, and from analysis of how actual economic plans are arrived at. These types are the basic forms to be found in the real economic world.

A successful understanding of the structure of an economy can only be achieved when we have understood and applied the basic forms.

Let us take a recent example to show how this can be done, namely, that of the German economic system of 1940. Whatever part of it we study, we find combinations of central direction and the exchange economy. Every head of a family was aware of this direction, for if he wanted to buy food, clothes, and other goods, he had to have not only money but also ration cards. Similarly a manager of a firm in making his purchases required not only money but a licence. Closer study shows that central direction was the predominating element in the structure of the economy. It was to be found partly in the simple centrally directed economies of the farms or in urban households, but above all in the central administration of the economy. In agriculture, the individual farms certainly still formulated their own economic plans in so far as they were still operating in an exchange economy. But this multitude of individual plans was decisively affected by the "total" plan of the central authority created by the comprehensive administrative apparatus of the Food Authority for the Reich (*Reichsnährstand*). As a consequence of the official price regulations for goods and foreign exchange, the economic system was mainly controlled in its industry and trade not by prices and price fluctuations, but by the central administration, which allocated raw materials and half-finished goods with the help of a system of quotas. The direction of the labour force was also largely in the hands of the central controlling authorities and only partially dependent on the plans and intentions of entrepreneurs and workers.

Many widely differing forms of central direction and of markets and monetary systems were to be found. In so far as consumers only received goods in rationed quantities the first or second form of centrally directed economy existed, and the third form inasmuch as they obtained unrationed goods according to their own choice, though the production of these was mainly under the control of the central authorities. The state control of prices was exercised in many different forms of market, in open and closed markets and under bilateral monopoly and perfect competition, and in each case had a different significance.

This method of approach, that is, the application of our morphological system to actual cases, enables us to understand the details and character of each economic system. *Individual detail does not disappear, but is fitted into a system and thus becomes properly comprehensible.* If we compare the economic system of Germany in 1940 with that of the same country in 1930, we would notice a number of differences. Many important decisions had been transferred from the entrepreneur to the Reich authorities or to organs of the central administration. There had been changes in the functions of cartels. The importance of the banks had diminished. Money had a changed significance. Details such as these, and many others, would be put in their right context by applying the morphological system and understanding the framework of the German economy in 1930 and 1940. Each single point would help to reveal this framework in the two cases. By 1940, with the rise of the centrally administered system and the decline of the market system, the decisive plans were no longer being made, as they had been in 1930, by individual units, but by officials of the central administration. The entrepreneur had become simply the executive organ of these authorities, possessing certainly some independence in the making of his plans, and also—as in the exchange economy—bearing risks.

In 1930 cartels were associations of independent undertakings for purposes of excluding competition, that is, they belonged to an exchange economy. In 1940 they were mainly instruments of the central administration. In the different economic system, though they retained something of their original purpose, their role had altered. Further, if the banks in 1940 were of much less importance in the control of the economic system than they had been in 1930, the explanation is partly that the extent and direction of investment in 1940 depended on the officials of the central administration and no longer on entrepreneurs, and partly that businesses had become extremely liquid and therefore in no need of bank credit. This was connected also with the freezing of prices and with rationing. We know how the function of money changes with increasing central direction of an economy and this change of function was very noticeable in the years before 1940. It is easy to understand the single phenomenon and its changes when one sees it for what it is, part of a whole system.

It would be a mistake to want to construct further pure forms in addition to those we have already found. We might want, in order to characterise the German economy of 1940, to construct another pure form, that of the controlled market economy, as a third form along with those of centrally directed and exchange economies. The peculiarity of the German economic system of 1940 really consisted in its representing a particular combination of pure forms. Elsewhere and at other times these same pure forms have been combined in other ways, and it was not in 1940 a case of a new form. It was the contrast between the elements of central direction in the economy and those of the exchange system, which was the essential characteristic of the German economic system in this case, and it cannot be understood, if this contrast and the variety of forms realised in it, are disregarded.

One must guard against being so impressed by the characteristics of a contemporary economic system as it exists at the moment, however varied the forms represented in it may be, that one interprets it as a new form. A comparison of the German economic systems of 1940 and 1946 shows them both to be "controlled market economies", which is the sort of description which conceals essential differences. In 1946, too, the forms of organisation to be found in centrally administered and monetary economies also existed. What was important was that they were in a state of collapse. The failure of money and the central administration of the economy had led to increasing self-sufficiency of economic units and to the emergence of a system of barter, two things incompatible with an extensive division of labour. The economic system is reduced to a primitive condition. This feature of the development becomes clear when the different pure forms represented in the two economic systems are abstracted and distinguished and the particular way in which they were combined is understood.

Bach, Mozart, Beethoven, and other masters created their works by combining together a limited number of tones which they all used. The special character of a great musician or of one of his works lies in his combinations of tones, not in his creating new tones. It is the same with economic systems. Each has its individuality, though their variety is immense. But the individuality of any particular one does not consist in its embodying a new pure form, but in its particular selection from the limited number of already existing forms, and in the way in which these are blended. In this way alone can economic systems and their changes in the course of history be precisely defined and understood. In order to avoid repetition I would ask the reader to call to mind at this point what was said in Part II, particularly in the second chapter (p. 164), or better, to read it again. We were then obliged in order to define the economic system of a country or a period to abstract the formal elements of which it was made up, whether it was the Egyptian economy in the age of Augustus, the economy of Nuremberg in the late fifteenth century, or that of the French Revolution. We were then simply making use of the more important of the pure forms. This was premature but inevitable, as there is no other way of getting to understand the economic system of a period. But now we have discovered how these formal elements are obtained, and we are in a position by applying our morphologicial apparatus to give a precise definition of different economic systems. It is now possible to understand the structure of all economic systems, whether they are the product of natural growth or fixed by an economic constitution. At the same time we can now give a more precise definition of the term "economic system" (or "economic order"). An economic system (or order) comprises the totality of forms through which the everyday economic process at any particular time or place, past or present, is actually controlled.

Whatever economic conditions one is examining it is always necessary first to ascertain the structure of the economic system. Let us take as a further example, that of the famous Jesuit community which existed in Paraguay from 1609 to 1767. The sources provide a rich supply of facts. There is information about the fertility of the soil, about family life, about the economic activities of the Indians, details about agricultural and manufacturing production, and so on. How is the economist to approach this confused mass of individual facts and distinguish the essential from the unessential? How can he discover the purpose of the whole system? He must first ask about the structure of the economic system, making use of our morphological scheme. He would then find, in brief, that the responsibility for the economic process in this community of altogether about a hundred thousand inhabitants was with the villages, which were about thirty in number with between two and seven thousand people in each. Each separate village was a simple centrally directed economy controlled by a senate whose plans were decisive for the economic government of the village. Economic calculation was carried out by the senate in "real" barter terms. This was practicable because the village economy was so small and the varieties of goods so limited. Each village was a totally centralised economy with a few traces of free exchange of consumers' goods. The centrally directed economic bodies occupied a considerable proportion of the land of the village and of its manufacturing workshops. Beneath them numerous smaller centrally directed units existed, the family economies of the Indians with their family fields. The senate had an important influence on the economic control of these family economies, which were by no means independent.

The dominant forms of organisation were those of the simple centrally directed economy, which were only partially combined with those of the exchange economy. The forms of market in the surrounding world with which the villages traded, varied widely. In the trade of the villages with one another the peso was used as the unit of account, though not as the means of exchange. This was a case, then, of our second main form of monetary economy, and of the first type of monetary system, for certain goods, mainly tea but also tobacco, maize, etc., were used as money.

The much discussed question as to whether this famous community was "communist" or not usually peters out in a quarrel over the concept of "communism", and leads nowhere. What we want to know is its structure and the formal elements of its economic system. The special features of this economic community can now be seen against the background of its historical environment and in its relationship with other economic systems. A comparison with the Inca state makes it clear that they were related to the extent that in both cases the dominant characteristics were those of a centrally directed economy. But in the Inca state, which consisted of eleven million people, the economy was mainly centrally *administered* and was not, as in the Paraguayan community, a simple centrally directed economy. In both economies the dominant form of organisation was combined in a particular way with various supplementary forms of organisation.[52]

(2) From the point of view of scientific method, the procedure by which we can come to understand an economic system can be described as follows. To apply the different

ideal types of economic system with their numerous variants it is necessary after defining and working out a morphology to return to the real economic world. But this time we approach it differently. Formerly we examined the individual phenomena, the farms, estates, households, etc., studied them from every standpoint, and in the course of our analysis extracted one by one the forms realised in each case (the varieties of centrally directed economy, the market forms, and monetary systems). Now we survey the whole economy of a period or of a nation or of an area, for example, the French economy of to-day, or the Siberian economy of a hundred years ago. Previously we worked by abstracting the significant characteristics from the particular phenomenon, now by "generalising" abstraction. That is, we now survey, say, the French economy and ask what are its main forms of organisation. By combining together the various forms of organisation to be found in it, we build up a realistic picture of the French economic system.

In the process of applying one theoretical scheme, we make a twofold synthesis. First a number of purely formal elements are combined together into one economic system, and secondly the economic system is fitted into its geographical, intellectual, political, and social surroundings. We compared our morphological system with an alphabet without using which we are unable to write a word. Only when we know the different pure forms and the structural elements of the different kinds of economic systems, can we fully understand the system in any actual economy. Just as each single word only contains some of the letters of the alphabet, so only a part of our alphabet of pure forms is sufficient for describing any actual economic system. In a description of the contemporary German economic system there are almost no open forms of market. All these forms are not "applicable" in this case. In a study of the contemporary Germany economy they would remain unused in the economic tool-box. They are as little applicable as the letters "a" and "b" are if I write the word "type". But they *will become* applicable, and other types applicable in contemporary Germany will become inapplicable, if we are trying to understand the economic system of another people or another period—for example, that of Germany in 1890. The economic system of Germany at that time was predominantly an exchange economy with "open" forms of market. The concept of a "closed" market was for that period largely inapplicable. Certainly there were elements of a centrally directed system existing at that time, but no central administration of the economy, only the simple centrally directed economies (the independent economy) of the households and farms. We can see a great difference in the "applicability" of the various ideal types simply in making a comparison of these two German economic systems. It is just these changes in applicability which make it easy to recognise clearly the real differences between the two systems. (The question might be asked as to how long economic systems continue to exist. The answer is as long as the structure of the economy remains in essentials unaltered. If in palæolithic times a tribe remained organised in the same way for many thousands of years, then its economic system existed for many thousands of years. The economic system of ancient Egypt also survived for thousands of years. During the French Revolution, there were four economic systems in one decade.)

This synthesis of pure forms which is necessary for defining any economic system must be combined with another kind of synthesis. In analysing economic relationships we temporarily detach them from their historical context, and have subsequently to fit them in with their background again. If we are describing the economic system of Diocletian's time, what we find is not *simply* a combination of different pure forms, but we find this system to be part of the intellectual, political, and social life of the Roman Empire at that time. In concentrating to the full on analysis we temporarily took our eyes off the historical facts, to which we now have to turn our whole attention again equipped with the conclusions of our morphological analysis. We now have to give due attention to the interconnections between all sides of human history, for example, to the relations between the historical situation of our time and the economic system as it exists to-day. We shall give examples later.

(3) An important consequence follows for the co-operation

of economic history and economics. That co-operation is necessary has been felt for a long time. The question is how it can fruitfully develop. The view ruling among economists that the economic historian is concerned with individual facts while the economist has to discover major relationships, is not merely false, but even meaningless. The historian who collected together single economic facts descriptive, say, of thousands of the tenant farms of northern Italy in the sixteenth century, would be acting senselessly. He would be proceeding like a man who had to describe a house, but instead described each single stone out of which it was built and gave no idea of the ground plan, structure, and architectural style of the house. Also, the historian must understand the different economic systems, and see the single economic unit and economic fact as part of a whole. Otherwise he is unable to define an economic system, since he knows of no characteristics by which he can do so. In addition there is the further question of the criteria by which he should distinguish and separate the economies of two different peoples or periods.

If the historian turns to the economist and asks how this problem is to be dealt with, he does not receive any very satisfactory answer. What use could the historian make of Bücher's stages of development, if he was describing the German economy at the time of the great reforms of Stein? A "city economy" would not be correct, and a "national" economy tells us much too little. He would be unable to describe the huge change which took place between the beginning and the close of the nineteenth century with such terms as "National Economy", "Early" or "Mature Capitalism". There would be nothing for the historian to do but to use his own concepts taken from everyday experience and therefore inadequate for the purposes of economic history.

The highly justifiable demand of the historian must be met in another way. Above all, the economist must demonstrate that the question which must be asked is that of the *structure* of the economy, and that it is necessary to think in terms of different economic systems. The historian must ask about the structure of the Germany economy in 1800 and 1900, if he wants to understand and portray the revolutions that took place in the course of that century. Furthermore, the economist must explain that the economic system of a period can only be understood by using the different ideal types of economic system. Then the historian can himself complete his study of any particular real economic system. The ideal types in their pure form are only analytical conceptions, but any actual system is made up of a combination of them. In order to understand the economic world he is concerned with, the historian needs the system of ideal types provided by the economist. Only in this way can he get beyond the mere unscientific recording of single arbitrarily selected facts. What the economist has to provide are not models falsely claimed to portray the real economic world, but pure forms the application of which makes it possible to understand *any* economic system.[53]

II. UNDERSTANDING THE COURSE OF ECONOMIC EVENTS: THE THEORY APPLIED

(1) To understand the different economic systems is to understand an important part of, though not the entire, economic life of any period or place. Whatever the existing system may be, economic life goes on day by day. How it does this is, as we explained, the second main question of economics. Mere everyday experience with its bias and its contradictions is even less able to understand the daily economic process than it can the economic system under which the daily process takes its course. Here also the great epistemological antinomy lies across the path. How can history and theory be combined in the explanation of everyday economic life so that its interrelationships can be scientifically understood?

After what we have said above, the answer is clear. It cannot be done by constructing a special theory for every economic system that has existed. (This would certainly fail because each actual system represents a particular combination of forms, whether it is the economic system of America to-day, the Jesuit system in Paraguay, or any other of the various systems past or present. No descriptions of different economic systems can provide a limited number of sets of conditions on the basis of which a theory can be constructed.) The pure forms or ideal types are rather to be used as "models" on the basis of which theoretical propositions can be worked out. The interrelations in the actual course of economic events can be discovered by applying the theoretical propositions arrived at in this way. *Just as our understanding of different economic systems is obtained by means of the morphological scheme, similarly the understanding of the course of economic events comes by applying theoretical propositions.* The uniqueness and particular historical environment of each economic system are fully recognised, but it remains possible to apply the results of theoretical analysis and to understand the interrelations within the actual course of economic events, whatever this course may be, at any time or in any country.

(2) At this point, we come up against an obstacle. Most people to-day would regard it as a grotesque claim that propositions of economic theory should not only be applied to contemporary problems but to those of the Middle Ages, of the ancient world, and of other periods and cultures. From all sides we are warned that abstractions and theories only have meaning in the context of a particular historical situation, that any economic theory has simply a relative validity, and—whether one likes it or not—is relevant only to a particular period. It is argued furthermore, that we have ourselves lived through too many historical changes to be able to believe in the lasting validity of theoretical conclusions. After the change in attitude to, and in our consciousness of, history that came early in the 19th century, we can no longer maintain the timeless validity of theoretical economics, or fall back into the old long-exposed rationalist errors. We should rather be content with a scientific understanding of the economy of *a single* period, say that of "capitalism". Because we want to understand the course of history and its political and social relationships and to do justice to each different epoch, we must discard the sort of theoretical proposition which claims "timeless" validity. There may be some difference of opinion with respect to details and as to whether all or only some theoretical propositions are to be regarded as relative to a particular historical period; in general, however, there would be agreement that their validity is limited to a particular time and place.

I maintain that this "historical prejudice", as it may rightly be called, obstructs our understanding of the economic world, past or present, and of its individual phenomena, an understanding which is to be obtained precisely by applying theoretical propositions which are not limited in relevance to any particular period.

There are two points to be made here.

First, it must always be remembered that the propositions of economic theory rightly understood say nothing about what actual conditions exist. They do not describe anything and do not give a picture of the German economy of to-day, or of any other period or country. "If perfect competition exists then . . .", or "If a crop failure occurs in one country, the balance of payments alters and then . . .". This is what the propositions of economic theory look like. Theory has nothing to say as to whether, when, and where this happens. It consists of "hypothetical propositions about necessary relations under various possible sets of conditions".[54]

Secondly, a distinction must be made between "truth" and "relevance". This is essential throughout the whole study of economics, yet it is often disregarded. Every theoretical proposition correctly arrived at is true, but it only becomes relevant if at some particular time and place the set of conditions obtains for which it is valid. As I have written elsewhere, "The relevance of theoretical propositions is continually changing. If a gold standard does not exist, then the theory of the equilibrium of the balance of payments between two countries on the gold standard is not relevant. But it remains *true* and will become relevant again as soon as the gold standard exists again. The theoretical propositions about bilateral monopoly or the centrally directed economy simply gain in relevance, not in truth, if these conditions occur and have to be investigated. Theoretical propositions are only limited to particular periods as regards their relevance, not their truth."

Economic theory is a set of analytical instruments. Which of these instruments is to be used in working out some particular concrete problem, and which are to remain for the time being unused, is decided by the special characteristics of the particular case. It is by using these instruments that we can understand the interrelations in everyday economic life at any time or place. Let us, by means of a few examples, discuss *how* this is to be done.

We described just now the structure of the German economy in 1940. Now we have to study everyday economic life in the German economy of that time. It would be impossible to construct a special theory for the course of events in the German economic system at that time, for it was far too complicated. Undue simplification would be unavoidable, and the results that would finally appear would not fit the German economy of that period.

For achieving our task we have, on the one hand, an understanding of the structure of the economy of that time, of the typical basic forms out of which it was made up, and of the way in which they were put together. On the other hand, we have the comprehensive scheme of theoretical propositions about inevitable relationships under the different ideal types of systems, that is, the different forms of centrally directed economy, of markets, and of monetary system. If these are combined, it becomes clear how economic theory has to be applied if we are to understand the real relationships between economic events. *The clear perception of the structure of the system which the scheme of pure types helps us to obtain, makes it possible to apply the theory, which is itself built up on these pure forms or types.*

It has often been said that prices had an entirely different significance in the German economy of 1940 from what they had in that of 1930. This is quite true, and we can now easily see why. It was because central direction of the economy was much more important than in 1930. Valuations were largely made by the central authorities, and took effect through the allocation of foreign exchange, raw materials, finished and semi-finished goods. The control of the German economic process worked differently in 1940 as compared with 1930, that is, not so much through the price mechanism as through the valuations of central authorities. Value theory had become *more* relevant, but price theory less so. But it would be quite wrong to describe the theory as "untrue", as some modern "relativists" might wish to do. Furthermore, in 1940 also, the influence of prices was not entirely negligible in controlling the economy.

Let us take a second example. In explaining the everyday economic life of Germany at the end of the nineteenth century we proceed in exactly the same way, but apply different theoretical propositions. Prices played a different part in Germany in 1898 from what they did in 1928 or 1940, because then there was a different economic system. At the turn of the century there were many fully competitive markets, along with others in which many different varieties of competition existed. Thirty years later, when monopoly had spread through much of the German economy, another department of economic theory became of greater importance in explaining everyday economic life. In order to study how real wages were fixed forty years ago we have to start from conditions in the labour market of partial monopsony, or of bilateral monopoly between trade unions and employers' associations, or of perfect and open competition, or of other open conditions in the labour market. Similarly the markets for goods were "open" and predominantly competitive with very little central direction. Theoretical propositions about the state regulation of prices, closed forms of markets, and a centrally directed economy, which are relevant to-day, are seen to be irrelevant for a study of this earlier period.

Here is a third example. "In the Middle Ages were prices formed in accordance with the doctrines of Adam Smith or of our contemporary economists? Were prices in the Middle Ages freely arrived at in a form of market in the main determined by supply and demand?" (W. Mitscherlich). This question is based on a point of view widely held by economists, but which does not do justice to the historical facts. There was no more one single process of price formation in the Middle Ages, than there was a uniform medieval economic system. To see this we must look at history more closely. There were towns under the rule of an autocrat, where the guilds in return for the payment of dues received privileges assuring them a monopoly position on the local market. In other towns the economic and political leadership was with a commercial aristocracy. Then the craftsmen neither worked for wages, nor worked under the "putting out" system, but were home workers receiving raw material from long-distance traders and wholesalers to whom they delivered the finished goods. In such cases guilds were sometimes forbidden, and in any case were difficult to organise, particularly if the home workers were scattered over the countryside. When the craftsmen's guilds came to power in the cities, that is, with the coming of democratic leadership, economic policy was different again, being more friendly towards the guilds, while price-fixing became less strict. There were, therefore, four kinds of systems under which prices were formed in different ways—under competition, monopoly, price-fixing, and so on. The key position in the system was held alternatively by an autocratic governor, the long-distance traders, or by the hand workers. Where guilds existed they had a widely differing significance. There were guilds of wholesale "putters out", of hand workers, home workers, and retail traders. The significance of the particular guild only appears when the structure of the economy is understood. Only by applying the relevant theory can the functioning of the system and the great battles between the groups of long-distance traders, craftsmen, and home workers, be understood, and therewith the purpose of the whole system and of the medieval economy as it really was.

Let us look at the Flemish cities of the late thirteenth century as described by their celebrated historian Pirenne. Bruges was then enjoying its greatest period, and there were also Ypres, Ghent, and others. We must first understand the unusual economic system of these towns. Until about 1280 the patrician cloth traders were the sole governing class. The weavers, dyers, cutters, and other craftsmen often lived in houses belonging to the wholesale merchants and were not permitted to combine in guilds. On the other hand, the wholesalers' guilds were closed to outsiders. The labour market was a clear case of a closed monopsony and gave the wholesalers a powerful position, which was protected and strengthened by the government of the town being in the hands of the merchant aristocracy. The power of the merchant aristocrats was so great that they created the post of official overseer to control the work of the craftsmen in their own houses. The cloth was sold in the cloth halls to which purchasers streamed from all over the western world. There was not much competition between the wholesale merchants of the same town, but there was between the guilds of the different towns, so that supply was to some extent oligopolistic. So much for the economic system. By applying the theory of monopsony we can explain how the wages of the workers were fixed under this system, and how the huge incomes of the merchant aristocracy were obtained. But parts of the theory of international trade and of monetary theory have to be used to explain why particular quantities of cloth were exported from Flanders each year, and why wool, dyes, and food were imported into Flanders from abroad.

After the first great rebellion of the weavers in about 1280, and after the battle of Kortrijk, the political and economic system of the Flemish towns altered. The craftsmen gained in political and economic influence, they formed guilds, took part in the government of the towns, and in Ghent actually governed alone. The economic structure changed. The closed monopsony in the labour market of the merchant aristocrats was abolished, and in its place there was closed bilateral monopoly between guilds and unions. To explain the changes in production, as well as the levels of wages and profits, we must turn to the theory of bilateral monopoly. That is, we change our theoretical instruments.

We might here ask of the economists of the historical school why economic theory should not be applied in this way to the economic process in Flanders in the thirteenth century? There is no reason why it should not, just as there is no reason why what is suitable and relevant in our morphology and theory should not be used to explain the economies of Nuremberg, Lübeck, or Paris in the fifteenth century, where open and closed markets and competition and monopoly of the most different varieties existed. There is no other way of understanding economic life and its interrelations. Why should it not also be used to explain economic life in quite other kinds of historical environment, say of America before Columbus, of Ancient Egypt, India, or Japan? There is no reason why the forms and effects of the great monopolies of Ptolemaic times should not be explained by applying our theoretical apparatus. There is no ground for this strange hesitation in using theoretical analysis for the explanation of the historical problems of a period when this analysis was unknown. This historicist prejudice is unfounded and harmful. It is based not only on an underestimate of the potentialities of theoretical analysis but on a false notion of history, the result of a hypertrophying of the ideal of historical development. There is, perhaps, no surer way of getting rid of it than a closer understanding of historical conditions.[55]

(3) At this point we reach the limits of the applicability of theory, and at the same time the limits of our knowledge of the real economic world.

The application of theory, and the discovery of the interrelations between economic events, always requires that the structure and particularly the *predominant* forms in the economic system are already known. *Only if one knows what pure basic forms have been, or are, realised in any economic system, is it possible to decide what parts of the theoretical apparatus are to be used.* If we do not know whether an economy is totally centralised, or centrally directed with free consumers' choice, or whether a market in the exchange economy is monopsonistic, or oligopolistic on the supply side, or of some other form, we are unable to apply to it the relevant theoretical propositions.

We have already said that lack of information makes it impossible to understand the structure of the economic systems for long periods of world history. In ancient times it was possible to understand the structure and forms only of some particular economic system, as, for example, those of Egypt, where the manuscripts provide an unusual degree of insight, or for different countries in the later classical period about which well-grounded hypotheses are possible. But in the main the sources for the ancient world are insufficient, as they also are for long periods in the early Middle Ages, and for cultures in other parts of the world. It is important to remember what we have already said, that information about legal institutions does not permit firm conclusions to be drawn about the structure of a system. The information we have about Babylonian law at the time of Hammurabi does not give us any real picture of the Babylonian economic system of about 2000 B.C. How far the central administration of the economy actually reached in the countryside and the city, in what forms it was realised, where elements of an exchange economy were present, who were the mainly responsible parties in exchange relations, what market forms or monetary systems were predominant, would all have to be known if we were to understand the Babylonian economic system and then, by applying our theory, to understand the interrelations between economic events. So long as information about the structure of the economy is incomplete, no full scientific knowledge of the economic system of a period or nation is possible.[56]

(4) From all this we can conclude that it is possible to overcome the great antinomy by a scientific understanding of everyday economic life. This great antinomy arises because the economic world has no one unchanging form or style. Economic life at different times and places takes very different forms, but the interrelations in an economy can only be discovered by theoretical analysis. There seems to be an irreconcilable divergence here. There is not the same uniformity as exists in the natural world and which makes it possible to formulate, for example, the "general" theoretical questions of physics. It was possible to resolve the antinomy because an exact study of individual economies showed that economic systems with their almost unlimited variations and multiformity are made up of a limited number of pure forms, so that this multiformity can be reduced to uniform types. In this sense there appears to be a certain special kind of invariability of the general form of the economy as a whole, that is, a uniformity in the basic forms of organisation. This is what makes theoretical analysis and the application of theoretical propositions possible, and thus the solution of the real problems of the economic process.[57]

A further conclusion is that a knowledge of the pure forms and their characteristics has two epistemological functions. *First*, when it is applied it serves as a means for understanding the structure of the many different forms of economic system of which history tells us. *Secondly*, these pure forms provide the basis for working out theoretical propositions.

The one function of economic theory is that when applied it explains the course of economic events, and how they all fit together and interact on one another.

In the next three sections we shall show more closely how by using our morphology and theoretical propositions we can understand the problems of the economic world.

III. A SIMPLE CASE

Let us now take a simple example in order to bring out some of the essential points in arriving at a scientific understanding of the real economic world. Let us take the problem of the economy of Silesia, and in particular the position of the handloom weavers in the middle of the nineteenth century.

To start with one finds a confused collection of economic, social, and political facts and the contradicting opinions of the weavers, merchants, and other parties concerned. How are the true relationships and the true state of affairs to be discovered? Obviously, we can get no help from concepts like "capitalism", a "regional economy", or other "stages" or "styles" of economic development.

Let us assume we did not possess a classificatory scheme of the different types of economic system and of theories based on them. We should then first have to study particular firms and households and work out the many different formal types of economic system. This might enable us to understand the basic forms of organisation of which all actual economic systems are compounded. Then we should have to study the relationships between economic events within the framework of this system; that is, to work out theories, which we could do on the basis of the simple and limited sets of conditions given by our system of types.

Equipped with these analytical instruments, we should return to the historical facts about the Prussian state in the middle of the nineteenth century, to the religions and social ideas prevailing in Silesia at that time, and to the economic and political position and power of the different individuals and groups as they then existed. Then we would be able to understand the facts scientifically.

In the *first* place, we can now describe precisely the economic system in Silesia at that time. In agriculture, with which craft industries were closely connected, various kinds of central direction existed. At the same time there were many of the elements of an exchange economy in the forms of market and in the monetary system. In the labour market, for example, there was monopsony. Thus certain ideal types were relevant for Silesia at that time, by means of which a unified account of the Silesian economic system could be given and its place in the historical situation of the country as a whole explained.

Secondly, we have to study the everyday economic process, and in particular the position of the weavers. At this point we apply those of our theoretical propositions that are relevant, for example, those relating to the centrally directed economy, to monopsony, and to international trade. In this way we can work out in what way the everyday life of the weavers was determined by non-economic political factors, by the social structure of the country, its natural resources and conditions, and by the technical knowledge the weavers possessed; in short, how it was determined by the data. Further conclusions would follow as to how the everyday economic life of the weavers and their wages and standard of living were determined by the interrelations ramifying throughout the whole economic system, of which the Silesian weaving firms and the weavers' households were only a small part, and how it was affected by events in other parts of the Silesian and Prussian economy, by the competition of woven goods from England and elsewhere, and by the suppliers and customers on whom the Silesian weavers depended. In this way we would explain everyday economic life with its relations both on the non-economic and the economic side.

Our problem is thus solved, and we have an understanding of the economic system and the course of economic events in Silesia. A seeming chaos of individual facts is reduced to a unified interrelated picture.

IV. ECONOMIC DEVELOPMENT

(1) All real economising is always dynamic. In earlier periods cultural stability has held for thousands of years at a

time and historians have rightly warned against projecting into other periods the ever-growing pursuit of novelty and change characteristic of contemporary mankind. In many cultures and for many thousands of years during the Stone Age—by far the longest section of human history—economic life seldom changed at all rapidly and for most of the time only very slowly. Economic institutions remained the same for hundreds and thousands of years at a time. But then also there were wars, climatic fluctuations, and plagues, which were continually bringing about shifts in the course of economic events.

Any economic development can take place in two ways, in a change in the economic system itself, or in a change in the economic process, or in the way this takes its course, within the framework of this system. On the one hand, the framework of the system may alter, or on the other, everyday economic life may not repeat itself in exactly the same way. The nature and quantity of the goods supplied, the way the means of production are employed, the extent of productive equipment, the technical methods, and the location may change. Every change in the economic system brings a change in the economic process. But the reverse does not hold. Not every change in the economic process brings a change in the system.

The progress and decline of economic systems and the expansion and contraction of everyday economic activity alternate throughout history. Economic decline took place in the later Roman Empire, or in the old German Empire at the end of the sixteenth century and the beginning of the seventeenth century. On the other hand, economic expansion occurred in the eastern Mediterranean during the third century B.C., and in Germany during the thirteenth century in connection with the great political and economic expansion in the east. Finally a huge process of development in economic forms and activity took place with the coming of industrialism, which began in Britain at the turn of the eighteenth and nineteenth centuries, and which since then has shaken the whole world. Enough has been said on this topic in other sections of this book. One point only need be made here. This is concerned with the problem of the *trade cycle*, that is, with fluctuations in the economic process.

We are concerned only with the fluctuations characteristic of modern industrialism, not with the trade fluctuations that have certainly existed much earlier, in the ancient world, in the Middle Ages, and after the Renaissance. We shall concentrate on the trade fluctuations of the nineteenth and the beginning of the twentieth centuries. It is clear that industrialisation involves capital investment, the construction of factories, railways, machinery, blast furnaces, roads, and houses. (The nature of investment has been discussed briefly on p. 191, along with the lengthening of the period of gestation, partly by "putting back" means of production, and partly by lengthening the productive process.) Since its beginning, industrialism and the consequent investment have developed spasmodically. The growth of investment has taken place at different speeds. Increased rate of investment over a period we refer to as a "boom" and a slackening off as a "slump". This is not to say that the trade fluctuations of the last hundred and fifty years have exclusively and in every case consisted of changes in the rate of investment. That was not the case—whole countries and regions have been plunged into economic depression by crop failures, changes in needs, or discoveries. Nevertheless, the main distinguishing characteristic of modern trade fluctuations is the change in the tempo of investment, and in this respect they mostly resemble one another.

Why and how these fluctuations in investment took place is determined by the entire historical situation of a country and period. *There is no single necessary and inevitable course for fluctuations which follows its own laws.* The direction and nature of investment depends first on the economic system. In Russia in the thirties of this century the process of investment was quite different from what it was in England, or Germany in 1927, or Germany in 1935. It is of decisive importance for the direction and extent of investment projects, and therefore for the shape of the fluctuations in individual countries, whether central direction or the exchange mechanism is predominant and in what way, or in an exchange economy whether it is monopoly or competition that is more important.

The other data of the economic process are also constantly

being altered by historical developments in every sphere. The war of 1914–18, for example, profoundly affected the economic process in many countries, not merely by bringing about changes in their economic systems, but by altering needs and by uprooting millions of workers from their previous work. All the subsequent political events, national and international, affected the fluctuations of trade in different countries. In Germany this was the case with the Versailles Treaty, the Dawes Agreements, the wage policy of 1923 (which was dictated by considerations of internal politics), the cartel and foreign credit policies, the state borrowing after 1933 for the purpose of stimulating and speeding up investment, and the special policy of a fixed exchange rate. In England there was quite a different economic policy with the devaluation of 1931 and the cheap money policy. Economic conditions in Germany and England after 1931, with their profound differences, can only be understood as parts of a quite different total historical development, and must be related to the different structures of the two countries.

Certainly it is true that with the structure of the modern state as it is, an economic crisis always threatens to become a political crisis. But, *vice versa*, political factors are of decisive effect on trade fluctuations. This was obviously not only the case for the period after the war of 1914–18. The German Empire of the last four decades before 1914 had a particular law of property and of contract, and a particular industrial and company law. It was firmly attached to the gold standard and a particular system of trade treaties. In this way the state created certain "rules of the game", the nature of which had an important part in determining the process of investment. This is so even in respect of many details. For example, if Germany in 1892 had not introduced the limited guarantee company (the G.m.b.H.), without public balance sheets, then there is no doubt that the quantity of investment would have been smaller and the tempo of the upswings in German activity would not have been as lively as it actually was. At that time, too, though the state did not intervene directly in the course of trade fluctuations, it exerted a strong influence by its economic policy.

If one considers that in addition to politics other historical factors, such as changes in population, determine the economic data (as have, for example, the differences in the population changes in Germany and France in the last half-century), it is clear why it should be noticeable that each fluctuation in trade or each change in everyday economic life is something separate, or, as W. C. Mitchell puts it, "a unique historical episode differing in important respects from all others and never repeated". Every economic situation, whether in Germany between 1926 and 1933, or between 1903 and 1907, every boom and depression, wherever and whenever it may be, must be seen in its particular temporal and national setting. Trade fluctuations are not of a single uniform pattern. *There is no normal cycle of trade fluctuations.*

(2) The conclusion follows that dynamic theories or trade cycle theories, which aim at reaching generally valid propositions about allegedly regularly repeated movements in everyday economic life, are bound to fail.

If industrialism was an independent process which, once entered upon, inevitably took a certain definite course, like a chemical process which after a certain mixture has been made necessarily develops in a certain way, then one would be more inclined to think that "dynamic theories" might have something in them. Doubtless, it is a notion of this kind that the many new creators of dynamic theories have in mind. Confronted with the immense process of expansion that has taken place in economic life in the last hundred and fifty years, they want to discover laws of development for this period and for what is called "capitalism", just as the chemist discovers chemical reactions, or the biologist the laws of development of plants. Many are so captivated by this notion that they take it for granted, and so economic life is studied as something separate from other departments of life.

Dynamic theory can also be based, as it is by Marx and his disciples, on what is called the materialist conception of history, according to which all the religious, political, and other phenomena of history are dependent on a technical and economic foundation.

The religious, cultural, and political "superstructure" which is raised on the basis of hand-tools and handwork, will be different from that which is based on machinery and factories. All history is related to certain basic technical–economic facts. If this view of history is correct, not only would a foundation be provided for dynamic economic theory, but for the general understanding of all history. Dynamic economic theory would become the basic science of history. The development of religion, politics, culture, and everything else would be discovered from the course of economic development.

The scientist cannot accept this analytical segregation of economic life, nor can he with Marx regard it as the sole basis of history. Still less can he countenance the attempt to combine the two points of view. His refusal is not subjective, but necessitated by historical experience. Every day he receives confirmation that all economic development can only be understood as a part of history as a whole. Dynamic theories or trade cycle theories are all of them unable to take account of the decisive influences economic events are continually receiving from non-economic factors.

The failure of purely economic theories of "dynamics" and of the trade cycle became particularly obvious after the outbreak of war in 1914.

Year by year we have ourselves experienced how important economic events have been determined by national, international, and political happenings, and by war. It has become obvious that not only the great political events of this epoch, but even the element of political uncertainty at home and abroad, is alone enough to influence the economic plans of entrepreneurs, their expectations and actions, the rate of investment, and all other economic events. The most careful refinements of dynamic theory or of theories of fluctuations are of no assistance in this respect. The basic defect of all these theories is irremovable, as the facts overwhelmingly confirm.

Let us take a further example of world importance. The break-up of the international order of foreign policy, trade, and money of the pre-1914 world economy was an essential cause of the collapse of international economic relations. This collapse again was a cause of the severe depression which began in 1929. The entire economic development of the world in these decades was decisively determined by the collapse of the international political order. How can so extensive and unique a political factor be accounted for by economic theories of fluctuations which seek to give universally valid explanations of the course they take?

It might well be asked how anyone could ever attempt to formulate propositions of universal validity about allegedly inevitable developments of economic events. The main reason was because for decades people have been accustomed to a sectionalised treatment of history. Historical science has been divided up into political, economic, legal, religious, and art history, with dire results. We have forgotten how to look at events in their full historical context. At the same time, there were two other special errors which affected the study of economic changes.

First, the logical character of economic theory was misunderstood. The belief that theory describes concrete events is very near to the notions on which dynamic theories and theories of fluctuations are based. The description of a static state obviously does not correspond with real conditions. The economic process does not really repeat itself year after year. Static theory is clearly inadequate, and the facts seem to require the discovery of dynamic theories which describe actual economic life. It is easy to understand how the constructors of dynamic theories believe they are coming nearer to reality, when in fact they are moving away from it. As soon as it is understood that theoretical propositions have nothing to say about facts but are hypothetical in character, and that, like the static state, they are analytical instruments for understanding the real economic world, not for describing it, then the character of economic theory becomes clearer.

Secondly, the creators of dynamic theories believed that economic events could themselves be observed to change the economic data, and they therefore concluded that static theory was to that extent inadequate. Dynamic theory is supposed to investigate the break-up of the previously existing set of data by economic events, and the subsequent effects of this on economic development. For it is clear that many economic phenomena, even when themselves determined by outside data, subsequently react in their turn on the data and their form. I believe that most of the theoretical economists, who have tried since Marx to construct dynamic theories, had this fact in mind. Such a relation often occurs. An increase in the size of firms can lead to the formation of cartels, that is, can bring about a change in the form of the market. A big outflow of gold can lead to a suspension of the gold standard.

At the end of the previous chapter (p. 215) we were discussing two other cases: too low a wage gave ground for intervention by the state, and for changing the form of the labour market; and a fall in the market price of coal stimulated technical invention. It is obvious that there is no *necessary* connection between the economic facts (a lower wage or a fall in price) and the changes in data (a different form of labour market or new technical knowledge). Many different kinds of non-economic conditions must also be fulfilled if this reaction is to take place. What these two examples show is of general validity. The data for the system as a whole are constantly and simultaneously being shaped by many different kinds of non-economic facts. Therefore, no *necessary* relationship should ever be claimed as holding between economic events and a change in data. A fall in the price of coal, giving rise in one country to technical discoveries in coal mining, fails to have this effect in another country where scientific and technical initiative is less. Whether the enlargement of firms actually leads to the formation of cartels depends on the mentality of the entrepreneurs, on legislation, the administration of justice, and on other factors. Universally valid theoretical propositions of dynamics about the effect of economic events on the outside data are not possible.

It is true that there do exist unstable systems which tend to transform themselves. A market, for example, in which there is bilateral monopoly, or bilateral partial monopoly, or oligopoly on the supply side, frequently changes in form. The absence of equilibrium in these forms of market results in a deliberate effort to reach some more stable form, and often a supply oligopoly transforms itself into a collective monopoly. Cartels develop out of the oligopolistic struggles of a few firms.

The development of the labour markets in many countries since the beginning of this century provides examples. Where bilateral partial monopolies of employers and workers had been formed which fought out their battles by strikes and lock-outs (important manifestations of an absence of equilibrium) the state often found itself obliged to intervene, or to fix wages, or even to direct the employment of labour through the central administration. In this case bilateral partial monopoly was replaced by a centrally administered system. The economic process with its lack of an equilibrium position was affecting the form of the economic system. But here again there is nothing inevitable about the development. It is not inevitable that a cartel should arise out of oligopolistic supply conditions. There are also governments which are not moved by strikes and lock-outs to alter the form of the labour markets. This fact also, the existence of unstable markets and economic systems, does not provide possibilities for a dynamic theory.[58]

(3) So much by way of criticism. What is the positive answer? How can economic developments, and above all fluctuations in trade, be investigated successfully? What applies in other fields is valid here. The investigation must penetrate into the special characteristics of individual phenomena. This prepares the way for historical and theoretical study and leads on towards the discovery of the relationships we are seeking. The special characteristics of particular fluctuations are not to be pushed into the background, as happened with attempts at creating a "normal" cycle. On the contrary, such special characteristics must be specially emphasised.

By way of example let us compare the upswing in the German economy from 1903 to 1907 with that between 1933 and the outbreak of war. The fact that the German economic system after 1933 took on increasingly the characteristics of a centrally administered economy gave to the detailed changes in economic conditions quite another course than they had between 1903 and 1907. The two cases had this in common: the rate of investment was accelerated, but the *way in which the increase took place* and in which the whole economic process, including the distribution of income, changed, was completely different. In the years following 1933 prices and wages were fixed by the state, but not between 1903 and 1907. Furthermore, prices had a different significance, a much smaller one in the later period. In the earlier period the economic system was predominantly of the type of an exchange economy, and the economic process was regulated by the forming of prices, but not so after 1933. The more the economy came under central direction, the more prices became simply units for accounting purposes. The economic process was controlled by the central administration or its organs, with their economic plans, valuations, orders, and instructions. This applied to all prices, even to interest rates. In the upswing of 1903–07 the movements of interest rates on the different capital and money markets helped to decide the extent and course of investment. After 1933 the rate of interest was of little significance. Its role became more and more subsidiary, the more investment depended on the stimulus and sanction of the central administration and the less it expressed the actual shortage of capital. Banks and banking policy also had quite a different significance in the two periods. Earlier, it was the banks, and the private entrepreneurs to whom they lent, who controlled investment. After 1933, under a different economic system, the banks surrendered more and more of this function. Differences in the system of international economic relationships were also influential in both cases. The gold standard, along with long-term commercial treaties and the few restrictions on trade, still preserved at the beginning of the century an international trading community, which had an important effect on the German upswing and its ending. It was quite otherwise in the second period, in which there was no international economic community, and when the economic process in the individual countries was considerably influenced by the independent trade cycle policies of their separate governments.

Certainly the differences between the two economic systems at the two dates were not the only reason for the different courses taken by the two upward movements. There were other special occurrences shaping the data which were of great importance for the course of the movements in Germany. In the years between 1903 and 1907, for example, there were a number of good harvests, a big increase in population, and the

Russo-Japanese war. In the thirties there were other well-known occurrences, above all a growth of armaments. The two upswings we have compared were not the same phenomenon differently dressed up. The upswing of 1903–07 was something quite different from the upswing thirty years later, in spite of the same word being used for each case.

(4) We must ask now what will be achieved by extracting the special characteristics of each fluctuation with the aid of our morphological scheme. Two important results will be achieved. In the first place, we shall be led directly to an understanding of the interrelations between economic events and those of history as a whole. The difference between the German economic system in the first decade of this century and in the thirties is very closely connected with the changed structure of the state. As soon as the structure of the different economic systems is understood it becomes possible to see such interrelations as those between the old international order and its economic effects, and those between the international political conditions of the thirties and *their* economic effects.

Secondly, the discovery of the special characteristics of each case has effects of quite another kind, which again lead us up to the crucial point. If the individual characteristics of each trade fluctuation and the economic structure in which they develop have been fully worked out, they can be analysed theoretically. In this way it also becomes possible to understand how economic changes are related to one another. In this way and in this way alone, are the conditions created for a successful application of the apparatus of economic theory. If we are studying the upswing of 1903–07 we use the theory of the exchange economy. Price theory, the analysis of the time-structure of production, and the theory of interest in an exchange economy are all relevant. In the theory of international trade and in monetary theory, the relevant propositions which have to be applied are those fundamental to the gold standard. In studying the upswing between 1933 and 1939 we have to change our theoretical tools. In this case the decisive influence on the economic process is the valuations of the central authorities. The theory of price loses in actuality and its place is taken by the theory of value for a centrally directed economy. The theory of the time-structure of production in a centrally directed economy becomes relevant. The relevant parts of the theory of international trade and of money also change. In this way it becomes possible to understand how the single phenomena in economic fluctuations, that is, the detailed changes in everyday economic life, mutually determine one another, and how they depend on the data. The facts then appear, not as a mere confusion, but in their interrelations with one another. This opens up a field of problems of especially vital importance for which theory has to be applied, that is, the whole field of trade cycle problems. Only by applying theoretical propositions will it be possible to understand this side of economic life, namely that of the changes in the economic process in the real world.

However, theory can only be successfully applied if an important pre-condition is established. If a theory is to be suitably applied to economic fluctuations and the problems of economic development, it has to be equipped in a special way. It is not sufficient that the theory should aim at describing merely a static state. Rather it must contain a sufficient number of hypothetical propositions about the effects of changes in data, if its application is to explain actual changes. The "method of variations" must be used.

The method of variations is that of breaking up a hypothetical static state by varying one of the "outside" data for the system as a whole. Then one studies what alterations in the whole system of economic relationships have to follow, in which order they take place, and what frictions will take effect until a new static state is arrived at. The final situation is then compared with the original static situation and in this way the entire economic effect of a variation in data is obtained. We start, therefore, from a static condition in an exchange economy with a particular mixture of monopolistic and competitive markets and with a particular monetary system. We assume, *ceteris paribus*, that a technical discovery is made. We then study what changes occur, compare the new static state with the old, and so understand how the discovery and its application change the quantity and nature of production, incomes, the time-structure and the location of production, and so on. We may start and end either with given static conditions of complete general equilibrium, or with static conditions in which parts of the productive apparatus of the labour force and of stocks are unused, in which case equilibrium is not complete and general. It may also be that by the change in data a static condition without equilibrium is transformed into complete equilibrium and *vice versa*. Both must be shown to follow from theoretical analysis of the course of variations. But at the start and at the end of the variations a static state must always exist. There is no tenable economic basis for the view expressed by, among others, Keynes and Pigou that after a static state has been disturbed a new static state *cannot* again be reached. To abandon the notion of the static state would be to give up all understanding of economic development.

It is true that in real economic life the movement to a new static state is regularly interrupted by fresh changes in data. But this is not an objection against this method. For only with its aid can it be known in what direction a variation in data will take effect. Let us take a case where because of unfavourable weather there is a crop failure in a country, whose trade balance and equilibrium balance of payments alter. The tendency to a new static position is interrupted by a rise in tariffs, the consequences of which in their turn are affected by a change in credit policy in the original country, and so on. Nevertheless, to know what new static position would follow on a bad harvest, if all other factors remained undisturbed over a long period, would be of great interest, even though this position would never actually be reached because of changes in other data. One would see in what direction the movement is at the moment of the original change in data (that is, the crop failure).

The statement that a new static position is reached in the long run must not be misunderstood in the way it so often is. That the new static position is never actually reached does not mean that it is not of interest. Rather it answers the question of the direction of the movement which follows immediately on the change in data. If I have worked out theoretically with the help of the method of variations the effects that the payment of reparations must have on everyday economic life in an exchange economy, the application of these results to the case of the German economy after 1929 enables me to understand the connections between the different phenomena, such as, for example, a fall in the exchange rate, an increase in unemployment, a fall in prices, and a shift in the balance of trade. This is so even if the reaching of a new static condition is hindered by numerous other changes in data.

The method of variations fails if it is not carried out in the right way, for example, when it starts from a position of complete general equilibrium, which is very seldom even approximately realised in real economic life, and simply neglects disequilibrium positions. It fails also if the sequence of individual events which leads to the new static position is not precisely studied and is simply set alongside the original position. This is a mistake that Ricardo made and which he himself discussed in a letter to Trower, and which has often been made by exponents of the Lausanne version of modern theory. As each change in everyday economic life is a transition, the juxtaposition of a series of descriptions of static positions does not suffice as an explanation. If, for example, theoretical analysis of the general economic effects of a large once-and-for-all reparations payment by country A to country B simply puts the final static position side by side with the starting position, much of importance is left out. The changes on the foreign exchange markets, the capital markets, and labour markets, and in the streams of goods, the interconnections and duration of these changes, are not studied. How can such static theoretical schemes be applied to concrete cases? It depends on the direction and extent of the changes as well as on the frictions that occur. But it is not the whole method of variations that is failing here. The inadequate use of the method simply discredits its correct and thorough application.

Thirdly, the method of variations fails if the theoretical system is incomplete. For example, if economic theory does not start from the economic plans, and does not keep the *ex ante* planning data separate from the "factual" data, or in an exchange economy what are data for the individual unit and what are data for the system as a whole, then it is disregarding the essential element of mistakes, uncertainty, and risk, or is not giving them the key position they deserve. Alternatively, the theoretical system may be inadequate because it may leave out certain problems. If the time element is omitted, a theoretical system will be quite unsuitable for explaining contemporary economic developments and fluctuations. It will fail to analyse the process of investment. The "timeless" theories of this kind, which were widely adopted during a period notable economically for the gigantic scale of investment being undertaken, have widened the gap between theoretical studies and the real economic world.

(5) The conclusion we come to is that it is pointless to try to construct a "normal" cycle of upswing, crisis, and depression in the hope of arriving at a theory and explanation of the trade cycle. To do so would be to lose sight of the real economic world behind a theoretical scheme. In studying the trade cycle one must not withdraw from the facts, but penetrate into them. The comparison of different fluctuations is very useful, not for the purpose of constructing a normal cycle, but in order to bring out the special characteristics of each, which must be the first step in one's work. As our examples show, this can successfully be achieved if our morphological system is applied. This provides a basis for further investigations, both historical and theoretical. It is then possible to appreciate the general historical context, to apply the relevant parts of the theory, and thus discover the real economic relationships.

Here it may be objected that though the German upswing of 1938–39 looked quite different from that of 1903–07, that does not hold in all cases. Many upswings have been very similar to one another, as have many depressions and many complete cycles. Only those cycles that resemble one another must be brought together. Then a normal cycle can be discovered for each epoch, and a theory of the trade cycle which explains this normal cycle can be worked out, limited in application to this particular period. For example, in the century before 1914 the fluctuations were all similar, and not accidentally similar, but similar because the economic order remained approximately constant. It is therefore possible to construct a normal cycle for this period and a theory limited in relevance to it, and there is some point in doing so.

Two remarks should be made about this kind of argument. *First,* the approximate constancy of the economic system claimed for the period before 1914 did not exist. In some periods it has been completely lacking, especially for the period in which we are living to-day. Consequently, to-day the individual characteristics of each single fluctuation in each country are so marked that it is impossible to take account of all of them at once. The older method is bound to fail to-day, and this failure gives rise to the unfortunate impression that a scientific solution of the problem of the trade cycle is impossible.

Secondly, fluctuations in the century before 1914 did not resemble one another as closely as is often assumed. If the upswing of 1903–07 is compared with that of 1869–73, essential differences will be found and these must not be overlooked. The economic systems at the two dates were different. Certainly an exchange form of organisation predominated at the two dates; but in 1870, particularly in rural areas, central direction of economic life was much more strongly represented than at the beginning of the twentieth century. More important was the transformation which had taken place in the form of the exchange economy itself. By the beginning of this century in the coal and iron industries, and in other important industries, cartels had been formed which did not exist in 1870. The large markets were of other forms. How this difference affected the course of fluctuations is debated, but *that* it did is certain. If one also takes into account the war of 1870–71 and the French reparations payments it is clear that the German upswing and its termination had special features to which there was nothing to correspond in 1903–07. Thus the two upswings can be very clearly distinguished. The theoretical tools to be applied in explaining the upswing of 1869–73 are by no means the same as those relevant for 1903–07. In the one case the theory of monopoly, and particularly of collective monopoly, is relevant, but not in the other. The unique character of each particular cyclical movement is the result of two factors, the uniqueness of each particular economic system and the special features of the non-economic events which alter the data.

The reader can try for himself. He can study the contemporary cyclical position at the present moment and put it under the microscope of our morphological system, that is, the system of different forms of centrally directed economy, the market forms, and the monetary systems.

(6) This does not mean that trade cycle and dynamic theories are without value. But they must be interpreted differently, not as their creators have regularly conceived them as explaining some normal cycle. *They are rather to be regarded as dealing with hypothetical variations, based on assumptions about various changes in the basic conditions.* Looked at and interpreted in this way, they are valuable as theoretical studies which make use of the method of variations.

It is not the function of the monetary theory of trade fluctuations to explain and describe the actual course of fluctuations in the last hundred years, or what is called the trade cycle. If it is treated as a study of the effects of the hypothetical variations in a single datum, the quantity of money, that is, as a theoretical instrument only to be applied under certain conditions, it can render good service. Some phenomena, particularly cyclical movements, can be explained in this way. Certainly much of its relevance disappears if we are concerned with fluctuations within economic systems in which central direction of the economy is predominant, and where money and interest play a quite different and much smaller part. This is also the case for economic systems which though of the exchange type have a different kind of monetary system from that assumed in trade cycle theory.

The "harvest" theories and psychological theories of the trade cycle should be interpreted in the same way. They should be regarded as studies of possible variations in one datum and their effects, and if applied in the appropriate place where such a variation actually occurs they are useful. (If a crop failure occurs, its effect on the economic process will vary according to the nature of the economic system in which it occurs. If future prospects are considered more favourable by entrepreneurs, and they alter their investment plans accordingly, the consequences will differ in an exchange economy according to the forms of market and the monetary systems prevailing. This is the way to apply these theories.)

The important studies of time-lags between changes in data and prices, and the consequent reactions, are also studies of models. Only when they are applied does it become clear what importance time-lags have. It is always clear that changes in data have very different effects under different forms of economic system.

(7) In recent decades the influence of consumers on the economic process has diminished, a characteristic fact of the greatest importance in contemporary economic development. Since Carl Menger economic theory has been demonstrating how the needs of households backed by purchasing power, that is, consumers' demand, control the productive process even in its most distant recesses. Perhaps this theory is now obsolete and incorrect and a new one must be worked out? This is what Keynes attempted when he sought to explain, among other things, how and why the entrepreneur and not the consumer occupied the central key position in the modern economic process. Should the attempt be made to construct a special dynamic theory to explain the shift in the centre of gravity away from consumers?

This shift came about in two stages. At the beginning of this century, the entrepreneur gained considerably in power. Previously dependent on markets and prices, his position changed with the decline of competition and the spreading of other market forms, and with the advance of amalgamations, concerns, trusts, cartels, and other powerful groupings. He now pursued his own market strategy and as monopolist controlled important markets. Monetary changes also strengthened the position of the entrepreneur. To an increasing extent money took the form of notes and bank money, granted as credits to the entrepreneurs. Our third form of monetary system came to be the prevailing one. The extent and tempo of investment markedly increased, and forced saving grew in importance. Industrial entrepreneurs with powerful monopolistic or oligopolistic positions were large-scale recipients of bank credit and gained control of large areas of the economy. They were no longer merely agents acting on the orders of consumers. In those parts of the economy in which this twofold change had not taken place, or was not so marked, as, for example, in agriculture, firms remained to a large extent dependent on markets and consumers.

The shift in the centre of gravity away from consumers continued and entered upon a second stage of development. Central administration of the economy gained ground in many countries and the central authorities took over the key position in the economic process. This is what happened in the war economies of the twentieth century, in contemporary Russia, and in Germany after 1933. This led to a further growth in cartels, combines, and other such bodies, but under a different economic system these have changed their character (as we showed on p. 108) and have become instruments of the central administration. The plans of consumers have less influence on the economic process the more completely it is administered from the centre. Under rationing and allocation systems consumers' plans are powerless. Whenever central administration of the economy advances, markets disappear or lose all their significance. The consumer has a still less important part. Entrepreneurs and bankers surrender their main functions to the extent that the economic process is controlled by officials "taking over" stocks, releasing them, and issuing their production orders.

The shift in the centre of gravity away from consumers can be traced to a change in the economic system not actuated by economic conditions, which therefore cannot be explained by dynamic economic theories. The theoretical propositions about how the economic process is controlled under perfect competition become less and less adequate for explaining economic changes, the further this type of economic system diverges from that of the real economic world. The propositions lose their relevance, but are not incorrect. The theoretical system needs extending, not replacement by another.

If the anonymous plans of millions of consumers and their purchasing power lose their function of determining what is to be produced and in what way, and this function is partially or mainly taken over by the plans and orders of a central administration, then economic fluctuations alter their entire course and character. Economic actions are no longer directed to meeting consumption. The consumer is no longer an active agent, but a passive member of the community. *When the economy is dominated by a central administration fluctuations take the form of shifts in consumption, not in employment.* To initiate investment projects, the central administration can force down consumption by directing labour and other means of production away from producing houses, foodstuffs, and other consumers' goods, and into the building of canals, machinery factories, and other parts of the productive apparatus. Depression and unemployment need no longer appear, because every worker can be employed by an order from the central administration without reference to the values he produces. In a centrally administered economy disproportionate production results mainly in a shortage of consumers' goods and in fluctuations in their supply.

In accordance with their reactions to fluctuations three types of economic system can be distinguished ("real" types such as commonly exist, not "ideal" types).

In economic systems consisting mainly of independent economic units, such as have existed throughout long periods of history, investment usually proceeds only at a very moderate rate. The construction of large buildings or the use of machinery is impossible within so small an economic world. Fluctuations in investment are of little importance. Of course, there are changes in everyday economic life owing to variations in population and climate and the rapid and radical alterations caused by wars.

In the *second* type of economic system, in which exchange predominates, the economic process is much more extensive and the division of labour is developed very much further. In this case, as we know, the individual plans and actions of many firms and households are brought into mutual adjustment by means of prices. How far this is successfully achieved depends on the forms of market and the monetary system. There are "stable" and "unstable" systems of this type. Those are "unstable" in which the prevailing forms of market are without a determinate equilibrium, such as bilateral monopoly, or bilateral partial monopoly, and monetary systems in which marked contractions or expansions in the volume of credit are possible. Again, severe disproportions in production can occur if much investment is taking place. Above all such economic systems lack a mechanism for effectively smoothing out disproportionate developments. An example is the world economic crisis of 1929–32. The market forms then prevailing were unable to overcome the disproportions that had been created, and this was the main cause of the severity and length of this depression. Economic fluctuations take a different course in stable systems of the exchange type, in which the banking system is not inclined to violent expansions or contractions and where perfect competition prevails. Such systems are regulated by the well-known mechanism of competitive price formation, and under them there is a tendency for complete equilibrium to be brought about.

In the *third* type of system, dominated by central administration of the economy, the picture is again completely different. If the administration wishes, it can force up the rate of investment. It can also carry out long-term investment without important fluctuations. Investment activity is only limited by the impossibility of forcing the supply of goods for current consumption below a certain minimum, without altering the effectiveness of the labour supply. Since there is no possibility of accounting in any objective units, or of any reliable calculation of costs, there is large-scale mal-distribution of labour and other means of production. But lack of equilibrium in this particular sense takes quite a different form from that which occurs in systems based predominantly on exchange, since it finds expression in the current supplies of consumers' goods.

The value of a scheme of types of this kind must not be overemphasised. It may, when completed, help the study of problems of fluctuations, but it must not mislead one into neglecting the special characteristics of each particular economic system which give it an individuality of its own, and which it derives especially from the nature and extent of the many supplementary formal elements it contains. Only the morphological analysis of actual economic systems can clear the way to a solution of the problem of the trade cycle.

V. ECONOMIC POWER

(1) "In the Middle Ages", Jacob Burckhardt said, "the two sides of man's consciousness—that turned outwards on the world and that looking inwards at himself—lay, so to speak, behind a veil, dreaming and half awake. The veil was woven from beliefs, delusions, and childish imaginings." This veil disappeared with the Renaissance. The modern purely secular state with its far-reaching claims to power at home and abroad, with its principle of "reasons of state", and its ruthless struggles for power, swept through history like a powerful wind. But however much the Renaissance marks a break with the Middle Ages, the latter also were full of struggles for power. It would be a misunderstanding of Burckhardt to interpret him as not being aware of this fact. Not only was there a clash between the powers of church and state, but bitter struggles for power occurred elsewhere: the towns against the clerical and secular landlords, the towns amongst themselves, the nobility against the craftsmen, among the different guilds and the ruling classes in the cities, the landlords among themselves. What was at stake was not simply the spiritual independence of the church or political power, but often interwoven with these political and religious struggles there was the desire to conquer or destroy economic power. Concentrations of economic power are not peculiar to the period since the Renaissance, or to the era of "capitalism". They existed to an even greater extent in the Middle Ages and in other periods of history. To understand economic reality past, present, and probably throughout the future, it will be necessary to understand economic power and to perceive the striking uniformities in the method of groups struggling for power. How are we to do this?

(2) This is a question of the greatest importance. Historians and economists are always in danger of missing the significance of struggles for power, their fury and brutality. Particularly during periods of peace or of a belief in progress, as towards the end of the nineteenth and the beginning of the twentieth centuries, there is a tendency to take the sting out of history, and especially out of economic history. Even to-day many

economists still seem unable to appreciate how full economic history is of brutal struggles for power. As a result they are apt to smooth away the sharp edges of economic life and so fail to understand it.

It took Taine twelve years to write his *History of the French Revolution.* Those long years left an impression on him which he has described most vividly. He quotes Clement of Alexandria, the authority on ecclesiastical law, as saying: "In the Egyptian temples the holy of holies is veiled by mysterious gold-embroidered curtains. If you approach with the intention of looking at the image of the god, the priest stops you, sings a hymn in the Egyptian language, and pulls back the curtain as though he were going to show you the god. What you see is a crocodile, a large snake, or some other dangerous reptile. That is the Egyptian idol, some fearsome creature moving around on its purple covering." Taine continues: "There is no need to journey to Egypt and return to the ancient world. For my part I wanted to see these things at close quarters. I set myself in the second half of the last century and have lived there for twelve years. Like Clement of Alexandria, I have looked at the temple and then at the idol from near at hand." We economists too must pull back the curtain with which partisan ideologies have veiled the concentrations of, and struggles for, economic power. We too must look at them from close at hand, and what we shall then see will often resemble what Clement of Alexandria saw behind the curtain. Economics is, or more correctly ought to be, a completely dispassionate science. How then can we obtain through it an understanding of economic power?

In the *first* place, the economist must have first-hand experience of economic power and of struggles for economic power. If, for example, Schmoller had had personal experience of struggles between cartels and outsiders, and not simply come by his knowledge of cartels and cartel policy through books, enquiries, and interviews with industrialists and senior officials, he would have realised that what happens is not as he soothingly suggests "a victory for certain common interests over greedy, short-sighted selfishness", but that what is victorious is a form of group selfishness. He would also have been careful not to characterise the self-interest which the cartels represented, as a form of common partnership. In short, he would have understood what economic power was.

What applies to Schmoller applies also to many economists of his day and ours. They lack simple everyday acquaintance with economic struggles and the trickery, subterfuge, and brutality with which they are waged. We must first understand contemporary economic life before we can properly understand the economic struggles of past periods, as, for example, those of the guilds and their policies in the Middle Ages, which many historians and economists represent as so ideally harmless. The schooling and disillusionment of personal experiences is the best guide to the struggles for power of the past.

Secondly, the scheme of morphological and theoretical propositions must be applied to a concrete historical situation. There is no fundamental inapplicability of economic theory to the phenomenon of economic power. It is only inadequate or doctrinaire theory not derived from the analysis of historical conditions that is bound to fail. Correctly worked out, economic theory is not only reconcilable with the phenomenon of economic power, but, together with the morphological apparatus, it is an indispensable means for understanding it. By applying our morphology we can characterise any existing power conditions (*v.* para 3 below), and by applying economic theory we can determine more closely its extent and its economic effects (*v.* para 4 below).

(3) We have already shown (*v.* p. 120) that the totally centralised economy represents the maximum concentration of power in the central authority, which alone formulates economic plans and controls the actions of all the members of the community, who for their part are left without power or freedom. The typical condition of labour in the centrally administered economy is slavery and bondage. Thus it was in the Inca state between 1450 and 1525, where the conquered tribes were held down not only by the military organisation of the Incas, but by the rigid central administration of the economy. Similar concentrations of power existed in the great temple economies of the Pharaohs, where the individual was to a large extent deprived of his freedom of movement, though some characteristics of an exchange economy were present. It

would be a mistake to look for economic power only in large communities. It exists also in smaller social units with a centrally directed economy; that is, where a "simple" centrally directed economy or independent economy (or economic unit) exists, or a centrally directed economy without a central administration. When a Greek of the fifth century B.C. had ten slaves working in his house he had far-reaching economic power over them, as did the controller of a manor in the early Middle Ages over his slaves or tied tenants. In the centrally administered economy economic power is public, in the simple centrally directed economy it is private.

Wherever the system is fundamentally that of an exchange economy, where, that is, individual economic units depend on the market and adjust their plans and actions accordingly, economic power asserts itself in another way. Very powerful economic positions can be built up here as well. These are often supported by the state and through them political power is exercised. In the exchange economy economic struggles develop between rival powerful groups. After working out our morphological system we can readily understand this. It is clear that the power of an individual economic unit is the greater, the more the form of the market approaches that of a monopoly or monopsony. It holds further that an individual monopoly, other things being equal, is in a stronger position than a collective monopoly, the power of which is often weakened by internal conflict. *Thirdly*, positions of power are much more easily built up on either side of markets if they are closed, or if one side is closed, than in open markets. *Fourthly*, the power of an economic position varies with the importance of the market. A monopoly of wheat in a country eating wheat bread is in a position of much greater power than the monopolist of sewing cotton in the same country.

Let us take some examples from history. At the turn of the thirteenth and fourteenth centuries, the long-distance traders and ship-owners of Lübeck and of the so-called "Wendish" towns of the Baltic, by combining closely together, managed to obtain a dominating economic position in Norway. The Hansa headquarters in Bergen was in a tremendously strong economic position: it had a monopoly of imported corn, flour, and beer for Norway, and, as sole purchaser, a monopsony of cod and other fish which, when prepared, were sold monopolistically, or partially so, throughout Europe. Also, as the control of the entire shipping traffic with Norway was in the hands of the Lübeck ship-owners and their friends, it had a further monopoly. "The way in which the German merchant succeeded in tying the northern fishermen of Lofoten to his branch in Bergen by means of a permanent indebtedness of the fishermen to the Bergen merchant, is one of those facts of medieval economic life which simply cannot be made compatible with certain irrepressibly romantic conceptions of it" (Rorig).

We have here a case of concentration of power, the peculiarity of which was that three monopolies were linked together in mutual support in a special way. The supply monopoly of certain important foodstuffs in Norway, the demand monopoly (monopsony) for Norwegian fish, the main product of the country, and a partial supply monopoly for Europe of an important food. The demand monopoly was to a large extent, though not legally, "closed" by the indebtedness of the fishermen, so that a competitor was unable to enter. By applying the the theory of monopoly we can explain the effects of the economic power of Lübeck and her allies in Norway and the European market on the distribution of income and property in Lübeck and the other Hansa towns.

The economic power of the great Ravensburg Trade Association and the other associations of the Lake Constance area in the late Middle Ages has been described by Aloys Schulte: "About 1400 the many linen weavers of Constance and other towns on the lake were selling their linen to large numbers of competing traders who were active throughout the western world. When partially monopsonistic trade associations began to be formed, conflicts broke out between the associates and the linen weavers' guild." The revolution of 1429 and the period of tension preceding it were partly due to economic factors. The weavers of Constance saw the enormous profits made by the Muntprats company and believed that they could circumvent it. So long as they had a large number of merchants as customers this calculation was correct, but as competition decreased with the formation of associations, until in the end there was just the one purchasing association covering many towns, they found that they were unable to do so. We do not know how the Muntprats did their buying, but it is clear that here was the first open struggle between a German guild and a trade association building up a monopoly position for itself. The weavers were defeated and the Muntprats and many other firms joined the Ravensburg Association, which now brought together in one association traders from all over the area north of Lake Constance, and controlled the imports and exports of the whole territory for about a century, possessing, of course, great political influence. Our classification of market forms enables us not only to describe the historical facts more precisely, but also to appreciate better the concentration of power on the one side and the loss of power and independence on the other.

The power of the Fuggers and other Augsburg houses in the sixteenth and seventeenth centuries had a different basis and different effects. The absolutist princes needed a lot of money to carry on their wars, and could get it only from a few houses which were in the position of oligopolists, or of partial or even complete monopolists in the loan market. The princes themselves, being oligopsonists, offered the financial houses what princes alone could offer, that is, exclusive rights of wholesale trade or trading privileges. That is how the notorious copper and silver purchases of 1514 and 1515 in the Tyrol came about, and how many other temporary and permanent monopolies were obtained with state support.

The power of the Fuggers rested on an unique concentration of the monopoly power as moneylenders with closed monopolies both of supply and demand in many branches of wholesale trade and partly in mining. We can only understand the differences between the economic power of the Fuggers, that of the Ravensburg Trade Association, and that of the Hansa merchants in Norway, if we use the tool provided by our classification of the forms of market. These uses make it particularly clear how necessary this morphological analysis is for understanding economic history.

The position of a European central bank of issue in 1910 was different again. Here was a case of a simple closed supply monopoly of bank notes in a country. The position was significant because it covered a good which was of great importance in everyday economic life at that time.

We may define the power of the German trade unions in 1927 or that of the employers' associations of the period, in the same way. In the labour market, bilateral partial monopoly or similar forms existed. Struggles broke out in the course of which the power of one group was weakened by another. How far this could go, and how far in this case an equilibrium was reached, can only be discovered by using the theory of bilateral monopoly. Similarly, the struggles between two or three shipping lines serving a particular port as oligopolists can be understood, as can the campaign of the German cement syndicate against outsiders and those sheltering or seeking shelter behind it, against whom the partially monopolist syndicate was often able successfully to wield monopoly power.

Only in one form of market does economic power disappear completely, that is, under conditions of perfect competition. Let us take, for example, the German market for knitted goods in 1925, or the rye market of eastern Germany in about 1880. No supplier or demander influenced supply, demand or price by his actions to the extent that he took account of the reactions to his purchases or sales in the market. In his economic plan price was a datum. No supplier of knitted goods or of rye was dependent on a special customer. It was the same in the labour markets in which approximately perfect competition reigned, for example, the Berlin labour market for domestic servants in 1924. No employee was dependent on a particular employer or association of employers, and *vice versa*.

Some may wonder whether, under perfect competition, the comparatively large fortunes that some individuals have at their disposal might not put them in positions of greater power. The big industrial or manufacturing firm has considerably greater power *vis-à-vis* its customers and its workers than has the small firm. Might not this show that the power of the individual firm does not depend only on its position in the market, but on its size ? The answer is : no. The big agricultural unit which sells its own corn or cattle under competitive conditions does not possess any considerable economic power. It only does so if in consequence of its size it has certain markets partially or entirely under its control; that is, where it is not subject to competitive conditions but to some other form of market. The big agricultural unit may, for example, have a monopsony or partial monopsony of the labour supply of a village, giving it economic power over the inhabitants who are all dependent on the big firm. This ceases to be so when other sources of demand for labour appear. Therefore, the size of the firm does not alone indicate its economic power, but only makes for economic power, or a position of power, if it leads to monopoly, oligopoly, or forms of market other than perfect competition. The larger the firm, the greater the chance that it is buying or selling in such a form of market and thus exercising economic power, but nothing further can be concluded. In the exchange economy it is the market position which decides the extent of economic power, with the result that under perfect competition even large firms are to a considerable extent powerless.

Under perfect competition the individual unit is almost powerless, but not completely so. The participants in a perfectly competitive market are not so powerless as those members of a totally centralised economy who do not belong to the controlling authority. There is a distinction here of great practical importance. An economy of perfect competition in all markets and a centrally administered economy are two extreme limiting cases at opposite poles to one another. With competition approximately perfect every supplier or demander does exert some small influence. Without individuals being conscious of it, all together determine prices and therefore the whole economic process. As there are no concentrations of power, there are no relations of personal economic dependence, though certainly there is dependence on an anonymous market. If perfect competition existed in all markets in a country, all firms, households, and the entire population would be to a large extent without economic power, or rather each would have a very small share of power. Economic power would not present any considerable problem in such a country.

(4) After applying our morphological analysis and determining the degree of economic power in a particular case, the propositions of theory can be used for a more precise description of its extent and for understanding its effect.

For example, the power of a coal syndicate might be studied. The basis for the analysis of its power would be the fact that it had the position of a supply monopolist, not of a partial monopolist or oligopolist, and that the supply was closed and the monopoly a collective one. The power of the syndicate may vary within this form of market. To fix it more precisely, the results of theoretical analysis must be used. These show, among other things, that the greater the elasticity of demand the less powerful is the position of the supplier. The elasticity of demand for coal may be large because such substitutes as oil and lignite are available. This would limit the power of the syndicate. Any rise in price could easily be evaded by consumers using other kinds of fuel. If such substitutes disappear and the elasticity of demand declines, the power of the syndicate would increase. In the second place, if the demand curve is raised to the right the power of the supplier increases, while it decreases if the curve is lowered to the left. If, say, as a result of an expansion of credit, more coal was demanded at the same price, the power of the coal syndicate would increase. In the reverse cases, if with the price of coal remaining the same less coal is demanded because of deflation, then the power of the syndicate would decline. These relations can easily be ascertained for other forms of market.

The corresponding propositions for the supply side have the same validity, though obviously in the reverse sense. The less elastic supply is, the more limited the power of the supplier. If with a fall in wages the supply of labour on a labour market remains the same or even increases (*v.* p. 155), then the power of a monopsonist firm over its workers is much stronger than in the case where with a small fall in wages the supply of labour declines sharply. Finally, if the supply curve shifts to the right with demand remaining the same, the power of the workers is reduced, and if it shifts to the left it is increased.

(5) "Power" is simply a word, and unless we make some reference to its wide significance in economics, as in politics,

we shall not get very far. Mysterious talk about the power of "capitalists" and its obscure effects does not tell us much, so that it is important to make clear the essential characteristics of economic power.

Our short sketch shows that this word "power" has covered throughout the centuries, and in different parts of the world, widely varying facts, as has also the term "struggles for power". The economist's task is to get to grips with these facts, to distinguish them from one another, and to bring to light their economic and political effects. If that is done, some real content can be put into the concept of economic and political power. Economic power is not something irrational or mystical, but is comprehensible and accessible to rational analysis. It is the same with the opposite of power—economic dependency and lack of freedom. Because of the variety in the facts this is a difficult task to face. None of the positions of power that we discussed resembles another, whether it is that of the Egyptian temple administration, that of the Bergen branch of the Hansa in the fourteenth century, that of the guilds of Flemish traders, that of the Silesian merchants of the middle of the nineteenth century, or those of modern central banks of issue, railway administrations, and heads of central administrative authorities. None of them is like one another.

A special scientific method is necessary if we are to penetrate into the phenomenon of economic power and understand the relations between economic and political power, usually to be found in mutual support of one another. How the problem can be dealt with has been briefly described. An eye for historical fact and historical perspective must be combined with use of the morphological and theoretical apparatus. Here the classification of economic systems, from the centrally directed economy to the many forms of exchange economy, can be of important assistance in understanding the multiformity and variety of history. It is not sufficient, for example, to explain that before 1914 in Germany the Reichsbank, certain cartels, employers' associations, trade unions, and railway administrations held positions of great economic power. When applying the scheme of market forms and monetary systems one must also describe the sources and effects of the different positions of economic power, define their place in the existing economic system, indicate the concentrations and coalitions of economic power, and account for the areas occupied by comparatively powerless individual economic units. Only in this way can struggles for power really be understood, as also the entirely different significance they have according to whether it is a struggle between single large suppliers, or a case of bilateral monopoly. Or one might take the case of the German economic system in 1939, where the power of the central administrative authorities was pitted against powerful private groups such as cartels or large partially monopolistic enterprises. Then there are the many varieties of struggles for economic power throughout the world economy, in the markets for nitrogen and electric bulbs.

Not only is there a vast variety of ever-changing phenomena. In the many forms of power to-day and in the past, and in the confusing variety of economic struggles, certain basic forms of organisation and certain parallel relationships between facts will be found to repeat themselves. The deeper the analysis of individual cases is carried, the more plainly a certain uniformity in the phenomena of economic power emerges. Economic power and the struggles over it, as well as economic dependence and bondage, in spite of all their multiformity, show the same kind of general unvarying form which we have already discovered in the structure of economic systems and in everyday economic activities.[59]

Chapter V

MAN IN HIS ECONOMIC LIFE

WE HAVE DEMONSTRATED that the apparently unlimited range of economic forms which history has to show can be reduced to a limited number of typical economic systems, each with its particular variants, and that this provides a basis for understanding economic reality.

It may be objected that even though the variety of *institutions* can be reduced to order, *the individual man* is always changing. Was he not quite different in the Middle Ages from what he is to-day, acting economically in quite a different spirit? Surely there are great differences between the attitude to economic life of men of different cultures, between the European, the Chinese, the Indian, and the South American? Nineteenth-century science has taught us to see man not as a fixed constant, but as continually changing in the course of history. If this is true, how can an attempt to work out a *single* apparatus of economic theory for the whole of history be successful? It would be so only if man showed a certain constancy in his economic plans and actions. His behaviour differs at different times and in different countries, and thus the main question is: *How do these human differences affect the course of economic events?*

I

Before we can answer this important question we need first to consider some of the prevailing views on the subject. These being generally familiar, there is no need to do more than briefly sketch them here.

The question derives from the conception of economic history prevalent in the late nineteenth and the beginning of the twentieth centuries, that, in his economic life, man behaves differently from age to age. The changes in man's economic life are best expressed by saying that whereas he used to act on the principle of meeting his needs (*Bedarfsdeckungsprinzip*), he now acts according to that of acquisitiveness. Prevailing theories of economic motivation are mainly based on contrasting these two principles and their alternating predominance. "Differences", Sombart wrote once, "arise originally out of the varying goals the economic subjects set themselves." Men either strive to provide themselves with supplies of consumers' goods limited in quantity and kind, that is, they try to cover their natural requirements, or they strive after profits, that is, to gain by their economic activity the maximum quantity of money.

In the first case we describe their economic actions as coming under the principle of meeting their needs, and in the second under the acquisitive principle. Sombart holds that all economic life before capitalism was for meeting needs. This was the case with the early independent economies of primitive tribes, the household economies of the ancient world, and the craft industries of the Middle Ages. He and his followers laid special stress on the spirit which characterised medieval economic life. In the Middle Ages, in Europe, the peasant, the landlord, the craftsman, and the trader acted on the principle of meeting their own needs. They were dominated by the idea of subsistence, and all they wanted, apart from the exceptions which proved the rule, was to satisfy a need given in nature and extent. Capitalism with its desire for profit diverges strongly from this attitude. However, capitalism is now passing and the post-capitalist socialist economic systems will victoriously reintroduce the principle of meeting needs (or "production for use"). Then production will not be for monetary gain, but to provide consumers' goods. That is Sombart's argument which we present here as representative of the whole trend of thought. It is no mere accident that such views have found wide public acceptance.

Wishing to understand correctly men's economic behaviour in the past and in the present, we are merely interested in the antithesis of the principle of meeting needs and that of seeking profit. If the antithesis holds, then two theoretical systems are necessary, one in which needs, and another in which the profit motive, is taken as given.

There are two ideas contained in this antithesis. It is stated as a basic principle. Then, secondly, it is held that at some periods the one, and in other periods the other, principle has been realised. It therefore contains both a philosophical thesis and an historical thesis.

A. Let us take the second statement first and assume that the antithesis is logically sound. We have to ask first whether economic life before the so-called capitalist period really was carried on according to the principle of meeting needs.

The question hardly requires a negative answer, for it has already received one. Take first the Middle Ages. So long as the earlier picture of medieval economic life as one of small "bourgeois" town economies was accepted, it was easy to assume that the idea of subsistence was the prevailing one. The more modern picture, with its extensive division of labour between localities, with long-distance trade holding an important position, and with a variety of highly developed forms of trade and credit, makes it possible to see in what spirit men carried on their economic life in the Middle Ages. It was in no uniform spirit. There was first of all the long-distance trader moved by a strong profit instinct. Nor was it the case that "he sought to satisfy all his greed for profit and money outside the region of the production and transport of goods, and partly even of the trading of them" (Sombart). Quite the opposite. The long-distance traders of Cologne, Lübeck, Nuremberg, Bruges, Venice, and many other great cities were really the organisers of the economic life of the Middle Ages. In its central and later periods, it was their bold spirit of enterprise driven on by their desire for profit and power, which created and upheld the whole economy of Europe.

Of course, there were many differences even in the same city. The Lübeck merchant aristocrats of the late fifteenth century had no longer anything approaching the daring and enterprise of their forefathers of the beginning of the fourteenth century. Such differences in the economic spirit of the ruling class are also important as between different cities at the same period, for example, between Bruges and Antwerp around 1500. However important the differences were, these traders and merchants were all dominated by a powerful striving after profit.

This was not always by any means so cynical and brutal as it was in the case of the Flemish cloth-trader and aristocrat Jehan Boine Broke, of whom Espinas has given a terrible picture. But what moved these traders was always the striving after profit. Medieval trade gave expression to a vigorous lust for power to which the notion of subsistence was completely foreign.

Certainly a different spirit often prevailed among the craftsmen, where the idea of subsistence had a certain importance. The craftsmen in their dealings with merchants demanded at least a customary subsistence, while at the same time fighting for an improvement. The history of most towns is full of such struggles. "*Mutatis mutandi* the member of the guild may well be compared with the organised worker in Europe of recent decades" (Gunnar Mickwitz). There is no trace of what is called the principle of meeting needs among this class of craftsmen, who were not usually of the ruling class. Their notion of subsistence was something different from what the older generation of historians held it to be.

The position of the economy of the ancient world was very similar. There is no need to occupy ourselves with the false picture of economic life in ancient times which the constructors of "stages" and "styles" of economic development have drawn, nor with the variety of different economic forms actually realised. We want now to consider the so-called household economy,* which was by no means typical of the economy of the ancient world, but which existed in certain countries and periods, in Homeric Greece and in Rome in the second century A.D.

It is thoroughly false to suppose that there was no "striving after profit" in such a "household" economy. There was, often to a very high degree. The slaves were often most ruthlessly exploited and their labour used to enrich their master. Descriptions of the big estates of later Roman times, on which hundreds and thousands of ill-nourished slaves laboured in chains at their heavy tasks for the sake of the almost unlimited greed for profit of their masters, make the idyllic accounts of "production for use", or the principle of meeting

* Oikenwirtschaft.

needs, supposed then to be prevailing, sound extremely peculiar. A very serious error is being committed when people believe that in such "household" economies only the claims to subsistence of the participants were satisfied, or *that in a centrally directed economy only the principle of meeting needs could be realised.* History shows just how false this is. Where the centrally directed type of economy, or something approximating to it, has existed, it has often been that people not only "strove after profit", but did so to excess and with appalling brutality. The great oriental empires of antiquity, the big estates in India where immense riches were amassed, or the Incas who used their centrally administered economy to enrich themselves with gold and treasure, are forceful examples. This "striving after profit" has not *necessarily* been a feature of predominantly centrally directed economics. It was not general in the "household" economies of the ancient world, nor in the family economies of Europe in the nineteenth century, nor yet in certain Christian communities in America which had a communal economic system. It has depended on the moral and religious standing of the leaders. History shows that very often this unscrupulous striving after profit flourished strongest where the majority of the community was more or less completely powerless.

This contradicts the view of Aristotle and many modern writers that the pursuit of profit developed first with the introduction of money and an exchange economy, and that it cannot express itself in a centrally directed economy. The idea that subsistence "characterises all pre-capitalist economic life" finds no confirmation in history. Economists should free themselves once and for all from such dangerous and unreal conceptions about the economic life of the past.

B. This only answers the historical question. The question of principle remains. Is this antithesis applicable?

We hold that it is not. It does contain some truth and if necessary can be used provisionally, but if pressed deeper it fails.

(1) It is false to contrast antithetically the pursuit of monetary gain and the meeting of needs. For monetary profit or gain is always pursued in order to satisfy needs. It is only

necessary to look at the facts and ask why the modern worker or employee seeks money. It is to satisfy his needs, money being only a means to an end or a means of exchange. For the modern entrepreneur monetary gain is never an end in itself. Small entrepreneurs who are a large majority, need money to meet their daily needs, whether they are retailers, small industrialists, or farmers. The entrepreneur with a big income is also moved by the desire for self-expression and power. These also are needs, often felt with the greatest intensity, and they motivate economic action in the same way as other needs. The concept of needs must not be drawn too narrowly. Men will always make use of the money they earn. The maximum possible quantity of money is never the final goal of economic activity. Even for the neurotic miser money meets the need for a feeling of security against his fears for the future.

(2) The antithesis includes the implication, sometimes expressly stated, sometimes tacit, that the principle on which the centrally directed economy is based is that of meeting needs, while in the exchange economy it is that of profit. It is taken for granted, notably by Marx and his disciples, that with the disappearance of the exchange economy the principle of meeting needs will prevail. Sombart simply contrasts the economy based on exchange and the economy based on meeting needs. Nowadays the opposite would be more correct. In particular, the centrally administered economy is not based on meeting needs. In economic systems in which centrally administered methods of control predominate, it is the central administrators who decide about the economic process. How far they consider the meeting of consumers' needs depends on their particular judgments. They can, for example, undertake a huge investment or armament programme, and limit the supply of consumers' goods to the minimum. We know from history how often this happens. In so far as the authorities may wish to meet the consumers' needs, the very variety of these makes it extremely difficult for them to determine what they are and how to direct the productive process so as to meet them. In the exchange economy the influence of consumers is always greater, though it varies with the form of the market.

It is at its greatest under perfect competition, and much more limited under monopoly, which is placed in this respect between perfect competition at one extreme and the centrally administered economy at the other.

(3) It might be objected that our argument is not fully convincing. For example, there have been farmers who have wanted simply to satisfy their traditionally given needs, who, when these are satisfied, disregard any opportunities for making more money. In contrast with these there are others who exploit to the full every opportunity of monetary profit. Whether they do the one or the other has an important influence on the course of economic events, and this contrast is what the antithesis of meeting needs and striving after profit is aiming at expressing.

To this the answer is that the distinction is essential, though it is very imprecisely described in ordinary language. The economist must take account of it and formulate it precisely. We shall discuss this presently. But the antithesis of "meeting needs" and "striving after profit" is not an adequate description. A farmer who only cultivates and sells sufficient to meet his limited traditional needs is also striving for monetary gain. Often the monetary gain is bound up with the intention of satisfying only limited traditional needs. On the other hand, men who exploit every chance of earning more, and who act, that is, on the principle of monetary gain, are satisfying their very extensive "needs".

On the whole this contrasting of the principles of meeting needs and striving after profit must be avoided. It is appreciated that there is and has always been a certain variety in men's economic behaviour, and that this behaviour alters, but one cannot describe its variety in these terms; in fact, this antithesis obscures rather than expresses it.[60]

II

We must formulate afresh the question of how the differences in human beings and in their behaviour which we find in history, influence the course of economic events.

If we investigate a manor of the early Middle Ages and compare it with an English ironworks of the present day, and then ask how the attitudes of those directing these two economic units differs, and how their special characteristics affect the course of economic events in the two cases, we are confronted first with the preliminary question of how far the behaviour is in each case uniform or varied. This is a question of great importance.

We shall show that in both cases their economic behaviour is at the same time constant and varying, *constant* at one level and *varying* at another.

A. *Constant:* everywhere and at all times man finds himself in the daily situation of having to adjust his needs to the means at his disposal for satisfying them, and *vice versa.* In this respect nothing has altered fundamentally since the beginning of history. Not only is the human situation always basically the same, but also the actions intended to overcome the problem remain in essentials constant. Everywhere men try in their economic plans and resulting actions to attain a certain end with as small an expenditure of means as possible. They always follow the economic principle.

Perhaps it was ignorance of what the economic principle means, or ignorance of history, but in the main probably a combination of both, that has misled people into thinking that men have only acted in accordance with the economic principle in what is called the "capitalist" era, and that previously and in other cultures it has been otherwise. There is nothing whatever in history to support that view. Let us consider the Chinese peasant of the late nineteenth and early twentieth centuries. He lives in a family economy enlarged to include all his kinsmen. His everyday life is dominated by a belief in spirits and a worship of his ancestors. But however much he is bound by beliefs, superstitions, customs, and traditions, within this framework (or it might be said, with these data as a framework), he acts in accordance with the economic principle. He makes sacrifices partly from an ethical and religious sense of duty: to that extent the sacrifices are an end in themselves. Or he makes sacrifices in order to ward off a threatened crop failure: then they are a means to an end. In both cases he is acting according to the economic principle. In the one case by making the sacrifice, he seeks to gain his end with the minimum possible expenditure of values, and, in the other, the sacrifice is itself a means for obtaining as large a harvest as possible.

During most of human history magic has been an important factor in man's thoughts and actions, but it is not to be supposed that the economic principle has therefore not been followed. If the Roman peasant under the Empire sacrificed to Saturn the god of sowing, as well as to other gods, and generally held to the old surviving primitive techniques, he was acting entirely in accordance with the economic principle. He expected a service from the gods in return, so the sacrifice represented a part of his economic expenditure. Similarly with the Roman ship-owner the prow of whose ship was exquisitely carved in order to please the god of winds and calm the waves. Travellers report that even to-day in certain villages in New Guinea, when houses are being built, a magician is commissioned for a fairly high fee to cast a spell on the beams. To us such expenditure seems an uneconomic and useless expense at variance with the economic principle, but to the people of this New Guinea tribe it is a necessary cost, and follows from the economic principle. Without it, according to what they believe, the purpose, that is, the building of the house, would not be carried out at the lowest cost. The house would be destroyed by floods and storms and further heavy but avoidable expenditure would be necessary.

It would be easy to add to these examples. Saints living in the desert on locusts and wild honey acted according to the economic principle, as do children influenced by ideas of magic. It is not to be confused with the striving for maximum profits or with the principles of "capitalism". Planning and acting on the basis of the economic principle is not simply a peculiarity of "the trader" or of the modern European and American trader. "It is the maxim of all action based on human reason" (*v.* Zwiedineck-Südenhorst).

It does seem, however, that in certain periods a fundamental change has taken place, for example, since the Renaissance, with the much more precise fixing of weights and measures, with the business of firms and households accounted for in writing, with simple and double-entry book-keeping, balance sheets, profit and loss accounts, and exact budgeting. Surely this means that a spirit previously unknown has been introduced into economic life? Historians have shown how gradual this development was and how the constant refinement of economic calculation altered the character of business management, which, in turn, influenced economic development. The knowledge of double-entry book-keeping was a precondition for the south German expansion of the beginning of the sixteenth century. Where this knowledge was lacking or slow to penetrate, as in the Hansa towns, economic development was delayed. It would seem that the conclusion must be that, as the methods of economic calculation improved, a complete transformation occurred in men's attitude to economic life.

Doubtless the difference exists and is important. Between the Black Forest peasant of to-day, who at the most makes a few disconnected jottings about purchases and sales, and a commercial enterprise using the latest procedures in business administration, or between a manufacturer of vases in the later Roman period and a modern American factory, the difference is vast and expresses itself in their economic actions. But this difference does not consist in the modern firm's acting according to the economic principle, while the older one did not. Rather the purpose of all these refinements of economic calculation is to carry out the economic principle with greater precision. That and nothing else is the intention behind them. The Black Forest peasant who has no notion of book-keeping and the manager of a vase-making business in the ancient world, both plan and act according to the economic principle. They do not achieve this as successfully as those who have mastered the completely rational techniques of business management. They can only make very imprecise estimates of values, which the others can make much more exactly. That is the difference between them.

Systematic fixing of weights and money, book-keeping, accounting, and other discoveries do not mean that men have introduced a new economic principle as their norm of action. They have rather wanted to find a means of keeping more effectively to the one fundamental principle of economic life which they have tried to follow from the beginning. Homo

Sapiens everywhere and at all times acts according to the economic principle, even if one thinks with Bergson and other philosophers that Homo Faber is his correct name. He is no longer Homo Faber if he does not follow the economic principle. To this extent, mankind in its economic life shows a certain general unvarying style.[61]

B. Along with this unity and constancy in man's economic behaviour there is the immense variety of ways in which the economic principle is carried out. The constancy of the economic principle provides the foundation for elaborating and applying an apparatus of theoretical analysis for explaining economic relationships. But the variety of economic behaviour, all covered by the economic principle, makes it necessary to supplement this apparatus at different points and to proceed carefully when applying it.

Where and in what way, it may be asked, do the differences in men's attitude to economic life express themselves, and how do these differences affect its actual course?

(1) *Subjectively* men always act in accordance with the economic principle, even those peasants who in Germany to-day still hold to the three-field system in agriculture. They do this because the old traditional technique seems to them the best, and because all the innovations of the last hundred and fifty years, in so far as they are aware of them at all, seem too risky. *Objectively* these peasants are acting contrary to the economic principle. To-day it is generally known that it is uneconomic to leave a third of the land fallow each year. In the Middle Ages, when the three-field system was the only one known and practised in many parts of Europe, such a peasant was *objectively* acting in accordance with the economic principle. After the profound transformation in agricultural technique he no longer does so.

Economic theory assumes that the manager of a firm always looks for that use of the means of production which, under all the given conditions, is the most favourable. It assumes, therefore, objective and not merely subjective obedience to the economic principle. This assumption over long periods of history is in complete accordance with the facts. It is immediately applicable to the case of medieval agriculture which was carried on in accordance with the existing state of technical knowledge—the three-field system. But there are also important exceptions, and particularly at the present time, when technical knowledge and other data are changing rapidly. Economic theory takes no account of the fact that many farmers to-day do not use that combination of the means of production, or employ their fields in that way, which would be the most favourable under existing conditions of technical knowledge and prices. One of the conditions postulated by economic theory is not completely realised and this fact must be remembered when the theory is applied.[62]

At the present time this divergence between the subjective and objective realisation of the economic principle is of relevance and importance in another connection, that is, in the centrally administered economy, which is a form of economic organisation of considerable importance to-day. In the centrally administered economy it is a question of how the central administration or its organs can select that economic plan which best satisfies the given needs with the given means and technical knowledge at its disposal. For instance, is the building of a railway or of a power station more useful for satisfying the requirements laid down by the central administration? Where and by what technical methods shall the power station be built?

The centrally administered economy has no instrument for selecting the most favourable plan from the huge number of possible plans. It is without a measure of scarcity necessary for objective application of the economic principle. The rough *in natura* valuations which can be carried out by a small independent economic unit, lead in a centrally administered economy to miscalculations, because of the sheer size of the system. Similarly it is impossible to fix prices that express rightly the scarcity relationships of goods. The central administration chooses to some extent arbitrarily the plan to be carried out and cuts the knots it cannot untie. Where are the five thousand workers needed for clearing the site for a power station to be taken from? The central administration conscripts them from the neighbouring agricultural workers, quite unable to calculate whether the loss of goods is smallest or not at this point, that is, whether its action is objectively in accord with the economic principle or not.

In a centrally administered economy the authorities want to formulate their plans and direct the economy in accordance with the economic principle. They want to fulfil their ends with the minimum expenditure of values. But it is accidental whether they choose plans which approximate more or less—or possibly hardly at all—to what would be the optimum plan. Economic systems dominated by a central administration, for example, the war economies of the twentieth century, are examples of how far actual plans diverge from the economic principle and how serious the problem is. It follows for the economist that theoretical propositions obtained from the analysis of a model of a centrally administered economy must be applied with great care to the economic process in any actual case of a mainly centrally administered system. It must be remenbered that this form of control of the economic process is characterised in reality by central planning of all economic activities, *combined with an element of chance.*

(2) When one remembers the extent to which men's needs for material goods are generally flexible, it is clear that they will usually act in accordance with either of two principles. Either their level of needs is regarded as alterable, or as approximately stable over shorter or longer periods. (We are not concerned here with changes in the needs for particular goods.) The two kinds of behaviour merge into one another. The same man acts sometimes in one way and sometimes in another. But the difference exists. It is expressed in men's economic plans and actions and is economically important.

Action according to the first principle means that the manager of the firm reacts to a rise in price with an expansion of demand, as, for example, a large farmer might. Better agricultural prices cause him to intensify cultivation, to use inferior land, to employ more labour, and so increase his income and satisfy his needs more completely. If prices fall his actions are reversed. Cultivation is less intensive, production and supply fall off, and fewer of his needs are satisfied.

If the manager of the firm acts according to the second principle, he acts so that a rise in the price of his product is not followed by his expanding production. To satisfy his needs to the same extent the same real income is required, so he cuts down production as the price rises. Doubtless such cases often occurred in nineteenth- and twentieth-century agriculture particularly in peasant economies. The handworkers of whom Goethe tells, who "had mostly the good sense to do no more work than was necessary for a happy existence", also acted in this way. With higher prices they did less work. They earned their living with less expenditure of effort. They were not offending against the economic principle, as has falsely been supposed, for they tried to obtain the same standard of living for themselves with as small an outlay as possible.

Managers of firms react in the opposite way if in the main they seek to maintain the same standard of living, after a fall in the price of their product. Thus in the middle of the nineteenth century many home weavers increased their supply as, with the progress of industrialisation, the price received for woven goods fell. In the severe world agricultural crisis which broke out in 1927 many farmers tried to counter falling prices for agricultural goods with an increased effort by existing labour supplies and an expansion of production, so that the income and standard of living of their families would not fall below a certain level. There are certain limits to this kind of behaviour. If prices fall further and further under the pressure of additional supplies, their reserves of labour will be exhausted and it will be impossible for such firms in the long run to approach their former standard of living by working more.

In the household the difference between the two principles is expressed thus: where living standards are flexible, when wages rise the worker may work more or get other members of the family to work who did not do so before, because it is worth more to work. The standard of living of his household rises as a result both of the higher wage rate and of the extra work done. With higher wages more labour is supplied by the household, and if the wage rate falls, less.

If the head of a household follows the second principle, he will react differently. With a fall in wages supply increases in order to maintain the standard of living. The worker and his family look for more work. The same effect is obtained when the prices of important consumer goods rise. With money wages constant real wages fall. The worker then tries to prevent a fall in his standard of living by working more.

This example shows that the same household may at some periods act according to the second principle and at others according to the first. A fall in wages may first of all lead to a reduction in the supply of labour from that household. If the wage continues to fall the reaction may after a certain point change. The supply of labour will be increased again in order to maintain a certain minimum standard of living.

The difference between these two principles also appears in economies dominated by a central administration. A technical discovery, for example, may result in a higher standard of living when plans and actions follow the first principle. The authorities may alternatively take the needs of the community for material goods as given, and use the discovery for shortening hours of work.

In any case, both kinds of behaviour are always present in the real economic world. Economists must not just regard simply the one principle, that of an alterable standard of living, as the general rule, when they are making a theoretical study of supply in an exchange economy, but they must also consider economic behaviour in accordance with the second principle. Otherwise their theory will fail in some of the cases in which it is applied to concrete problems, such as, for example, that of the last world crisis in agriculture.

Why men have flexible or fixed levels of material needs can only be answered for individual peoples, classes, and periods, and in particular historical situations.[63]

(3) There is another distinction no less important. The head of a community with an economy mainly under central direction, or the head of a firm, is *either* aiming at maximum net receipts for himself, *or* at the optimum output for those working with him or whom he is supplying. He acts either according to the principle of maximum net receipts or of optimum output. In practice a middle way is often sought between these two principles. (We need hardly emphasise again that both cases are ones of needs being met.)

A community whose economy is mainly of the centrally

directed type, such as a medieval manor, can be organised in either of two ways. Its economic leaders can either aim at meeting the needs of the lord of the manor or his household, or they can consider rather the serfs, semi-serfs, and free peasants. Here, and in any centrally directed economy, the economic leadership has a certain freedom in fixing its objectives. Of course, the leaders have to allocate to those subject to them at least sufficient to maintain productive efficiency. But they may often exceed this lower limit to a considerable extent with more generous allocations. The selection of crops to cultivate and the whole economic plan will look different according to whether the principle of maximum net receipts or of optimum output is being followed. From the history of Egypt, or of ancient Rome, or of the early Middle Ages, we know how very closely dependent the fellah, slave, or statute labourer, was on his master and on the extent of his claims.

The difference between these two principles appears in another form in the exchange economy. Here its effects depend on the form of market, and the distinction between perfect competition and monopoly is of the first importance. Let us take a firm all of whose markets are perfect, and which therefore regards the price of all its factors and products as given. It will then produce up to the point where marginal cost equals price, and in producing this output it will be acting according to the principle of maximum net receipts. But what is important is that it is also producing its optimum output with the given productive equipment. If it produced more, the cost of the additional units would exceed the price received, more values would be consumed than produced, and the economic principle would be violated. Under perfect competition it makes no difference whether the principle of maximum net receipts or of optimum output is followed. Under the pressure of perfect competition the same amount is produced and sold in both cases. If the market is monopolistic on the supply side the discrepancy between the consequences and actions of of the two principles can be considerable. This distinction between competition and monopoly is important both theoretically as well as for economic policy.

We saw that the monopolist in his plan takes as given the

reactions to his policy he expects from the other side of the market. If he follows the principle of maximum net receipts, with given productive equipment he produces up to what has been called "Cournot's point". The actual market price enforced is always higher than marginal cost, and the supply to customers is always smaller than it *could* be without any violation of the economic principle. If the principle of optimum output is followed, then the monopolist fixes the price so low that it equals marginal cost, and the supply to consumers is larger than if the other principle is followed. Whether, for example, a gas-works with a monopoly of the supply of gas to a town follows the principle of maximum net receipts or, either voluntarily or under compulsion, that of optimum output, obviously makes a vast difference. The price of gas in the latter case is lower, and the town is better supplied with gas, a point of importance for economy policy and a country's economic constitution.

This distinction is also relevant under conditions of monopoly on the demand side (monopsony). The management of a factory making optical instruments may be in a monopsonistic position in relation to labour in a small town. By following the principle of maximum net receipts he can force down wages to a level not precisely determinable. But the firm *need* not do this. It can also follow what is the optimum policy from the point of view of the workers, paying wages equal to the marginal product of labour. Under certain circumstances, particularly if this factory also has a monopoly in the market for optical instruments, the difference may be considerable, which leaves an important field for the social policy of the firm or the state.[64]

It is now possible, and necessary, to look back at the antithesis between the principle of meeting needs and that of profit-making. It is clear that the facts and differences of human behaviour which it vainly attempts to summarise are describable by the two comparisons we have just been discussing under (2) and (3) above.

(4) In the late nineteenth century and at the beginning of the twentieth century men made their economic plans for long periods, even decades ahead. They saved for the future and even in their youth were thinking of their needs in old age, and

planned and acted accordingly. The economic behaviour of the early Christians was different. Believing in the early coming of the Kingdom of God they took no thought for the morrow. In the language of economics, their economic plans were for the short term and took no account of the needs of the more distant future. From this point of view two economic types of men can be distinguished throughout history, those who plan for the long term and those who plan for the short.

At all times both types have occurred. Side by side with the middle class at the end of the nineteenth century with their long-term economic plans, there were bohemians and scroungers who planned only for a day or two ahead. But at some periods either the one type or the other has predominated.

We have already found at different points in our studies how markedly dependent the everyday economic process is on whether men simply consider their present needs or whether to a greater or lesser extent they consider their needs in the nearer or remoter future. It is on this that the structure of production and the distribution of goods in the present and future depends.

The Berber of Tunis, for example, makes as a rule very short-term plans. He only works sufficiently to earn his living for a few days ahead. He saves and invests almost nothing, and only begins to work again when he has spent everything. If everyone's plans were of such a "short-term" kind only a constantly shrinking apparatus of production would remain, and the supply of goods would be very small. On the other hand, the managers of firms and households in Europe and America invest, save, and plan for a very long time ahead. That is what enabled the modern apparatus of production to come into existence. The authorities of a central administration as a rule work on the basis of very long-term plans. That was so in the Inca empire. It is also the case with the central administrations of modern economic systems of this type, which plan and carry out vast investment projects like power stations and blast furnaces, while current supplies of goods to consumers fall off.

The temporal range of economic plans, on which the size of investments depends, is of great importance for the actual course of economic life and for the supply of goods. This fact must be remembered whatever economic problems are being studied, and we have taken account of it in the theoretical apparatus we have worked out.

(5) The German peasant at the beginning of this century remained on his farm even when agricultural prices fell and his economic position deteriorated. He accepted a fall in his income and tried to counter it by working more. Only when the contrast between earnings possible in agriculture and manufacture became very marked, did he turn his back on agriculture. Most farmers in the United States behaved quite differently. As soon as prices were unfavourable, and the farm no longer remunerative, they moved off either to look for other better land to farm, or else to enter industry.

Strong traditional ties bind the German peasant to his farm, while the American farmer still has something of the unsettled mobility of the first white settlers on the North American continent. This difference in attitude is of great importance in economic life, and must be appreciated if the differences in agriculture and in the flow of goods in Germany and America are to be understood.

It is imponderable factors of this kind that shape the economic life of nations, and they must be fully considered by the economist. We do this by regarding them as a given element in the structure of the economic system. For the purposes of theoretical analysis they belong with the sixth datum in our list, that covering legal and social organisation.

C. Our conclusion is that, as in the study of the many different forms of economic organisation, so in studying man in his economic life, one must put on one side obsolete classifications and look at him as he is and has been: the merchant of Ypres or Florence in the late thirteenth century, or of Nuremberg in the fifteenth century, or the member of a German guild in the eighteenth century, or the Prussian peasant of the same period who differed so much from his successor of the nineteenth century, or the North American nonconformist, or the Japanese peasant of to-day. Their economic behaviour must be understood in their special intellectual, geographical, and political surroundings, and we must guard against making ourselves puppets in the form of hastily constructed "real" types, such as, for example, "the medieval man" acting on the principle of meeting his needs, or "capitalist man" governed by the profit principle. Here too, as Rüstow has said, "all 'monist' explanations of a historical period must be deliberately avoided".

If we look closely at men as they have been in history, we realise that the more clearly we see the uniqueness of each individual, *the plainer it is that men's economic behaviour, that is, their actions and plans, are both uniform and varied.* Any description is false which neglects either the one aspect or the other, and the economist must clearly bring out both. He can do this by showing that all normal men everywhere and at all times act in accordance with the economic principle. This is the element of constancy. (The point of view of the historical school that men change completely in the course of history is contradicted by the facts.) On the other hand, we can ascertain the characteristics of the differences in man's economic behaviour by working out five pairs of contrasts. If we set these out together they ought to suffice in characterising the economically relevant behaviour of mankind.

Let us take a few examples. With the passing of the ancient world, as is well known, a change in men's religious and intellectual attitude took place, in fact one of the great religious and spiritual revolutions of world history. In contrast with the previous epoch many men no longer wished for unlimited gain, but only to satisfy a constant modest level of needs, in order to have the time to serve God and prepare for His Kingdom (that is, a change in the *second* of our five points above). Connected with this was the *third* point, that it was no longer "maximum net receipts" that should be the aim of economic life but "optimum output". At the same time, and this is covered by our *fourth* point, economic plans did not reach so far into the future. Imponderable factors were controlling men more closely than before, and only in respect of our *first* point did men's behaviour scarcely alter, that is, they acted unchangingly in accordance with the economic principle.

Here is a second example. Let us consider how a modern American entrepreneur A differs from B, a French peasant. (*a*) A acts objectively in accordance with the economic principle; (*b*) he has a flexible and unlimited standard of needs; (*c*) he acts according to the principle of maximum net revenue; (*d*) he makes long-term economic plans; (*e*) he is generally little bound by traditional ties. (*a*) B, the French peasant, only acts subjectively in accordance with the economic principle; (*b*) he has a constant level of needs; (*c*) he manages to satisfy these needs by acting in accordance with the principle of maximum net receipts; (*d*) he provides for the distant future though in a different, more cautious way; (*e*) he is generally strongly influenced by imponderable traditional factors.

We do not imagine that by this kind of schematised description we can "cut and dry" all history; that would be a complete misunderstanding of the economist's task. We are not, by such descriptions as these, trying to portray the full extent of the great spiritual and intellectual change that took place in later classical times: that would be an absurd claim. Nor is the second example intended to account for the difference between the French and American character with its many different historical origins. What we want to achieve is something different. We want to understand the effects which the spiritual and intellectual characteristics of individual men in different periods, classes, or nations, exercise on actual economic events.

Now we see how that is possible. The *constancy* of economic plans and actions, which at all times and among all peoples follow the economic principle, makes it possible and necessary to construct a single theoretical apparatus. The *variety* apparent in economic behaviour requires the construction of this theoretical apparatus (which we discussed under headings B. (2)–(5) above), but also cautiousness in its application (as was clear from B. (1)). While the very great variety of actual economic forms is made manageable by the morphological system, the variety in human behaviour can be grasped by working out pairs of contrasting characteristics as above.

It becomes possible in this way to understand the religious, spiritual, political, and moral changes of periods like that in which Christianity arose, and to link this up with an accurate insight into the effects of such changes on the daily economic process.[65]

Chapter VI

CONCLUSION

MANY AUTHORS CONCLUDE their books with a summary. I am not going to do that, as I cannot set out the main ideas of this book more briefly than in book form. Schopenhauer said of his main work that he only wanted to express in it a single idea, "but in spite of all my efforts I could find no shorter way of communicating it than this whole book". I should like to repeat that with all respect. I am afraid I must disappoint anyone who hopes to find a summary or recapitulation which will give him the main content in a quarter of an hour, without his having to read the whole book.

It is, however, necessary to add some further points which may help to exclude misunderstandings. At the same time we may draw some further conclusions from the arguments of this book which have already been indicated in outline, but which may need further clarification and expansion.

(1) A lengthy discussion has taken place around the question whether economics can be made quantitative. The argument against this is that economic life does not consist of quantities, but of various kinds of purposive activities. An economist who thinks in quantities is said to be thinking "like a natural scientist", or "materialist", and to be failing to understand the historical aspect of economic life and that economics is a "moral"* science.

To this the answer must be that the nature of economics not only does not exclude quantitative thinking, but even requires it.

No final decision in this dispute will ever be reached, if one starts from concepts, axioms, definitions, or analytical schemes of any kind. A decision cannot be reached by logical deduction from any particular premises, but only by considering the

* Geisteswissenschaft.

subject-matter itself. In other words, it is the character of the problems thrown up by the real economic world as we meet them that decides this question.

It is clear that the problem of the structure of the economic system is not a quantitative one. The problem of the organisation of the contemporary German monetary system or of German agriculture does not require a quantitative answer, nor do questions about economic systems or the partial systems they contain. On the other hand, only someone quite remote from the real economic world could hold that other central problems in economics are *not* quantitative. Every worker knows better. His wage is a quantity and he gives out sums of money, or quantities, for food, accommodation, and clothing. He knows that all economic planning and action is related to quantities; similarly every manager with his cost accounting, book-keeping, balance sheets, profit and loss calculations, financial, marketing, and production plans. At other periods calculations have been less precise, but all economic systems have always dealt in quantities. The Russian peasant of the eighteenth century, who sought to provide for his family under a form of centrally directed economy, knew very well that it was *quantities* of bread, meat, clothing, etc. which were needed and which had to be obtained to satisfy their needs. Every centrally directed economy reckons quantitatively. The economist, therefore, has to ask why particular quantities are produced, how the stream of goods is distributed quantitatively between consumers and consuming groups, why particular investments have been made, and what determines the spatial distribution of goods.

In all sciences the solutions to their problems must do full justice to the problems themselves; so, in economics, quantitative questions must get quantitative answers. Although the question of the structure of the contemporary American banking system does not require a quantitative answer, that of how money is created under this system, and how the whole contemporary American economic process is affected, certainly *does*.

Theoretical economists who refuse to formulate quantitative questions about everyday economic life are blind to the facts of everyday experience. They must have observed that their own incomes are quantitatively limited, that the prices they pay daily are quantities, and that they are constantly comparing the sizes of their receipts and expenditure. The discussion of such an unrealistic thesis as this shows particularly clearly the sterility of a formalist economics concerned only with concepts, and the need for constantly returning to a simple direct regard for the facts.

(2) Relationships in economic life can only be discovered if the right questions are asked. Such questions are seldom asked before scientific study. Most men are only interested in their immediate surroundings, their horizon reaching no further. They therefore see no reason to ask questions about the economic system or about how the economic process fits together, the questions with which economists have to start.

What is the right way of formulating economic questions? The questions grow out of everyday life and might seem simply to depend on what people want. "We can ask what we like, and we shall ask those questions that interest us" (A. Amonn). Does not the history of all sciences demonstrate that what questions are formulated depends on what is of practical moment, and on the shifting currents of intellectual interests? It is not so much that economic life forces certain problems on our attention, but that *we* approach *it* with our problems. Thus the questions express our personal view.

If this opinion was correct, then since it started from subjectively determined questions and subjective considerations, a science would inevitably end in a chaos of different lines of research. The history of science shows that the questions that are asked are suggested by the practical demands and ruling tendencies of the day. This can be proved particularly easily about the origin of economists' questions. Up to this point there is agreement. But this is not the end of the argument. It is also true that only those questions are persisted with which show themselves fruitful. It is certainly clear how the question of the interdependence of the economic system, which the classical economists asked, arose out of the entire intellectual, political, and economic situation of the eighteenth century. But the question proved itself justified. It has been clear that an answer to it was required if economic life was to be explained. However much the intellectual, political, and economic situations to-day differ from those of the late eighteenth century, economists have to keep pressing this question and making efforts to answer it. To drop it would be to give up the attempt to understand the economic process. The same is true of the other central problem which economists have to answer, that about the economic system. Whatever it may be that gives rise to this question, it remains a valuable and indispensable one, and yields so much that it has to be formulated.

There are two main problems in economics, that of the forms in which economic life is carried on, and that of the course of the daily economic process within these forms. The differing structure of these central problems determines the character of economics.

A long series of particular problems follows from the two essential central problems. For example, the question of the interdependence of the system as a whole, or of how it fits together, leads on of necessity to the problem of the great antinomy and how it can be overcome. Every step towards resolving this antinomy leads on to new problems. The solutions of further problems lead on to further tasks. Only when the morphological system and the propositions of economic theory are applied to actual cases, does this long chain of questions, answers, and further questions find its conclusion. Finally, the formulation of the main and subsidiary problems of economics is not subjective or arbitrary, but results from a logical approach to the subject-matter. As in any other science, it is not permissible to ask what questions we like. Problems shown to be pseudo-problems must be excluded. We must only put and persist with those questions which justify themselves under investigation, and which help us in penetrating into the real economic world.

(3) The two central problems around which everything turns arise out of everyday experience. But they cannot be solved by means of everyday experience alone (apart from the fact that industrialists, farmers, merchants, and workers in the everyday world never ask these questions). This is the central

task of economists: to distil scientific experience from the contradictory *pointilliste* experience of everyday life.

It might be questioned whether economics ever can arrive at scientific experience, whether, that is, it can constitute a science.

Our answer is positive. But the way by which we reach a positive conclusion is a special one. The unwillingness of many economists to look inside the individual economic unit must be overcome. Often this disinclination is to be explained by their fear of losing the view of the whole, of which the individual household or firm is only a very small part. This anxiety is unfounded. Rather it is only by studying the structure of actual individual units that we can work out ideal types which, when applied, enable us to understand the structure of economic systems, and also provide a basis for theoretical propositions and for understanding the course of economic activities.

The combining and harnessing together of history and theoretical analysis is not achieved by obscuring our view of historical events and limiting the application of our theories to particular historical periods. To do that would be to sacrifice both history and theory. The path to our objective is in the opposite direction. *The economist who wants to understand the interdependence of economic life by theoretical analysis must also pursue to the fullest extent his observation of actual economic events.*

(4) It is of decisive importance in carrying out this methodological procedure and for arriving at scientific experience that the right method of abstraction is adopted and rightly applied. Abstraction must be primarily by distinguishing the significant characteristics, as in studies of single economic units, thus enabling the real economic world to be grasped and understood. (Neglect of this method of abstraction has contributed considerably to the lack of realism in economics.) "Generalising" abstraction involving withdrawal from actual economic phenomena must take second place. It has a certain part to play in the scientific definition of economic systems and in discovering the dominant and supplementary elements in their structure.

By abstracting their salient characteristics from economic phenomena the economist constructs "ideal" types, which are quite different from the usual "real" types.[66] This procedure is to derive from economic life the basic forms of which it is made up. These basic forms are and always have been strictly limited in number, making possible a simplification which reduces the unlimited multiformity of economic systems and processes to comprehensible proportions. "To construct theories for every possible combination of conditions would be a gigantic Utopian enterprise like printing a book with a special alphabet for every different word. A morphological system is equivalent to an alphabet of individual letters, combinations of which can without great difficulty be made as needed for concrete problems" (F. W. Meyer).

(5) The morphology and theory are created out of the analysis of the real economic world and are tools for obtaining scientific experience and for achieving a scientific and penetrating understanding of economic phenomena. In this way they solve what is the central problem of a science, to reveal necessary relationships and unity where the naïve thinker sees only chance and arbitrariness.

People of a purely empirical attitude of mind usually view theoretical work unfavourably and are not prepared or able to appreciate its importance. They ought to realise clearly that they are denying themselves an understanding of economic life. This would do away with many of the misunderstandings as to the task and the logical character of economic theory which are widely held even among theoretical economists, for example, the view that theory consists of formulae that describe actual events, or that it represents a complete summary of experience, that its place comes at the end of a science, that experience is to be contrasted with theory, and that there are "theories" which do not agree with experience or "practice". Nor can theories be deduced out of definitions, nor is a theory some kind of nebulous generalised ideology. Genuine theories arise out of the application of reason to the study of the facts for the purpose of the scientific explanation of the real economic world. Ideologies being expressions of men's desires are frequently used as weapons in economic warfare, but simply obscure the view of the economic world. Finally, theory is not a system of concepts or definitions that has to be set out in advance of the study of the facts, without any basis in or relation with the real world. Theory properly understood does not come either at the beginning of economic studies, as the formalist economist believes, nor at the end, as the empiricist holds, nor separately and parallel, as the extreme dualists would have it, but is methodologically at the centre throughout. It is an instrument for enabling us to obtain scientific experience.

The claim we are making for economic theory and for morphological systems is both modest and extensive. It is modest in so far as it only pretends to be an instrument of knowledge, not its object. It is extensive in that it claims to be an intellectual instrument of universal applicability. All economic reality can be scientifically understood by using this instrument. It is not that the same pure forms, of which our morphology is made up, or the same theoretical propositions, are always relevant, but that a particular part of the analytical apparatus is always applicable for explaining the structure and course of economic phenomena at any particular place and time.[67]

(6) In building up a scientific picture of the economic world definitions play an important part. They summarise the results of factual analysis, and make it possible to use these results for further studies. The substitution step by step of scientifically defined concepts for the imprecise concepts of everyday language with which the economist has to start, is made possible by progressive analysis of the facts. At the same time it helps this analysis forward.

If we take a concept such as "price" we find it impossible, to start with, to define it scientifically. The economist's knowledge about price is, at the outset, no greater than everyday knowledge. But when in the course of analysing the facts he constructs the different types of economic systems, the economist is faced with his own problem of defining price, and must give a precise delimitation of the concept. It then becomes clear that "price" means something quite different in the exchange economy from what it does in the centrally directed economy. In the exchange economy, with its many firms and households, individual plans have to be co-ordinated, and this is achieved by prices. The formation of prices is the central process in the economic system, and has far-reaching but precise functions. All economic actions have to be adapted to prices. It is quite otherwise in the centrally directed economy in which the plans of a single authority control economic events, and where prices, in so far as they exist at all (and this, as we have shown, is not always the case in this type of system), represent something quite different from those in the exchange economy. At this stage of the analysis of the facts it is possible and necessary to define the concept of price, and at the next stage those of the different forms of market, "monopoly price", and "competitive price" can be defined.

The definitions always summarise step by step the knowledge which has been gained. The concept of price now gets real content and a precise definition. With other concepts, such as those of an "economic system", "firm", "value", "capital", "money", etc., the same transformation takes place. To begin with, the imprecise language of everyday life is used, and as the analysis advances, well-defined scientifically serviceable concepts are gradually worked out. The succession of definitions shows the way the science advances from everyday experience.

Often definitions are assigned a different place in economics. They are often put at the beginning, and the work of many economists is characterised by the fact that it starts with definitions of basic concepts. The motives for this procedure vary.

Some hold that the economist has to begin with definitions of "economy", "production", "price", etc., because from the start he is working with concepts which have to be clear before they can be used. It is, of course, true that we always do work with concepts. The economist needs them as soon as he starts working on his subject-matter and putting his first questions. There is no doubt on this point. But it must not be concluded that the economist must or can *begin* with definitions. How can he say, before studying the facts, what an economic system, a firm, price, value, or capital is? If he tries to do so, scientifically unfounded notions will be absorbed into the definitions and so into the science. By this path, too, biased views and confused ideologies creep into economics.

Other economists start with definitions mainly in order to define the subject-matter with which they are subsequently to concern themselves. They try to define the concept of "economy", for example, right at the beginning, in order thus to define the subject-matter of economics. But this kind of delimitation by definitions is impracticable and also unnecessary. A science cannot successfully define its territory until it has a knowledge of it. It is unnecessary because the limits of the subject-matter appear from the problems which arise for solution. Particular problems and the specific instruments required for their solution limit the field of each science, as Max Weber pointed out. All sciences, including economics, grow up not by discovering a subject that has first to be delimited by definitions, and then more closely described, but by the emergence of their problems and the development of the methods of solving them.

Finally, there is a third reason of a different kind why definitions are sometimes given first place. Many approach economics with points of view of which they are already convinced from the start, and economic science for them is simply the elaboration of these theses. The definitions with which the reasoning begins serve in such cases to try to introduce prescientifically fixed arguments into scientific economics. That is the approach of the "formalist" "conceptual" economists with whom we are already so familiar.[68]

(7) In his efforts to open up a way to the solution of his problems the economist is confronted by the important fact that men everywhere and at all times act on the basis of economic plans for overcoming their shortages of goods. This fact makes it necessary, if one is studying either the structure of any actual economic system or of everyday economic processes, first to turn to the economic plans and the planning data. This is the point of entry into the real economic world. This is where the treatment of both our problems has to begin, and this beginning decides the rest of the path.

(8) The science of economics must be systematic. "This is not simply in order to give expression to the æsthetic element in our nature. The subject-matter of science is not the material for an architectural game. The systematic character of a science, if genuine, is not something invented, but lies in the facts, and its existence therein has to be discovered. A science must be the means by which the realm of truth is extended, and this realm is no disordered chaos but governed by uniformity and regularity."[69]

As every household and firm is part of a complete system, and every single economic action part of a complete process, it is necessary to understand the system and the process in their entirety. We do not impose the system on the facts, but find it in the facts. As we have repeatedly shown in this book, because economic events make up an interdependent whole, economics itself must form an interconnected body of knowledge. It does this by developing a morphological scheme and a systematic theory. The structure and interrelationships of events, and the way they all fit together, has to be matched by the interrelationships in the system of our scientific knowledge. Otherwise scientific knowledge is incomplete. To be systematic it must be organised as an interrelated unity.

The demand that every particular problem in economics must be seen as part of a system and within the framework of a whole economy, conflicts with *two* contemporary tendencies. The more refined theoretical methods become, the more theoretical economists prefer to engage in detailed studies of certain particular relationships. The opinion gains ground that economics is dissolving into a number of detailed theories. Against this we want to maintain the unity of the main theoretical problem. All particular questions of the control of production, the fixing of wages, the effects of saving, etc., are aspects of the one main question of the interrelationships running through the whole of our interdependent everyday economic life in a social economy. From this arises the necessity for a systematic theory doing justice to the interdependence of the whole economic system.

Secondly, we are opposed to the general view, also held outside our subject, that any sort of systematic analysis is harmful.

Life, so it is argued, cannot be confined in any system. The most powerful expression of the opposition between life and reason is best seen in the systematising efforts of the latter. Historically this modern rejection of systematic analysis is easily explained. It is a product of the modern trend towards irrationalism and voluntarism. This kind of criticism of system-building in economics and other sciences, and particularly in philosophy, would be justified if the systems were based on unrealistic postulates. Then the danger is certainly very great that the system will blind one to reality and lead to a doctrinaire attitude. But the critics of systematic science go wrong when they themselves become doctrinaire and fail to understand that systems have to be constructed where the interrelations in the facts demand them. To abandon systematic analysis would be to abandon the attempt to understand economic life altogether.

(9) We saw it as an essential task of economics to rid itself of the tendentious ideologies of vested interests. Only those solutions of the two main problems have scientific value which eliminate these. Only a science resting on precise observation of the facts, advancing its analysis lucidly step by step, can get clear of the confusion of everyday experience. At the same time a scientist must hold strongly to the idea of truth, otherwise he will be in danger of surrendering to the ideologies of vested interests.

From what we have said it is clear why economists often fail to appreciate their great task. They often lack a method of getting hold of and looking at the real economic facts, and often depend in this respect on practical experts. They often fail to understand how economic life fits together, which they can only do with the help of theory. For example, no one not firmly grounded in the theory of money can form an independent judgment about monetary events, such as, for example, devaluations. He has to rely on the opinions of banking experts who are mostly interested parties. Economics suffered from the relativist conception of truth brought about by the historical school, pragmatism, positivism, and other intellectual movements of the previous century, which obscured the great decisive gap between everyday experience and scientific experience. Perhaps no other science has suffered so seriously from this as has economics.[70]

(10) The rapid changes history has brought in recent times have put economics in a serious position. If economic systems change as rapidly as they have in many countries during the last decade or so, economic knowledge seems condemned to a high rate of obsolescence. What is the use of studies of competitive price, it might be asked, if competition disappears and monopoly or direct state control takes its place? What is the use of monetary theories worked out ten years ago, when the monetary systems were quite different from those of to-day? Economists try as far as possible to keep up with the current situation and work out theories corresponding with it. Here again there seems to be a paradox. The more exclusively economists devote themselves to the current situation, the more they may be inclined to propound as "absolute" generalisations which are based simply on the momentarily existing system in their own country. The more strenuously modern they want them to be, the more rapidly their judgments become obsolete. Any shift in economic policy—say, any major change in the law regarding competition, or the constitution of the monetary system—upsets their theoretical structure. The former analysis dealt with a state of affairs now transformed, with a previous economic system, and economists now have to struggle with new theories also limited in application, which in their turn remain valid only until some further move in economic policy is made. And so the changes go on. Thus economics is without a firm basis, always trying to catch up with events and always moving from one crisis to another.

On the other hand, a morphological and theoretical system, built up by extracting the significant characteristics from economic phenomena, survives historical changes. Such a system must certainly be sufficiently comprehensive and not be based only on contemporary facts. It is not enough to say with Carl Menger that one is concerned only with events in the present. The economic life of all times and of all peoples is important for the economist. The historical horizon of economists must be broader. Only by studying different sorts of economic systems can a comprehensive serviceable morphology and theory be built up. The further we look back into the past, and the more we look at other economic cultures, the better equipped will be our morphological and theoretical systems for surviving future changes in events. *Secondly,* the logical character of economic theory must be understood, and the fundamental distinction between "truth" and "relevance" must be recognised. As institutions change, it is only the relevance of particular parts of the theory that changes, and nothing more. Theoretical propositions irrelevant to-day can in a few years become relevant again.

Certainly it will often happen with the appearance of new and previously unknown monetary systems that certain additions to the morphological scheme or to some other aspect of the analytical apparatus, will be necessary. The apparatus will never be finished. In applying it one is constantly faced with new problems. This does not alter the fact that the economist can never be completely surprised by events if his analysis is derived from comprehensive historical experience, as well as from intensive study of detailed phenomena. He can face the changes history brings with assurance and is more secure against its crises.

(11) Understanding economic events as they really are presupposes that economic problems can be segregated, yet at the same time seen in the general context of history as a whole. For example, German economic life to-day can only be understood, not merely when the specifically economic questions of the structure of the German economy and the interrelations in the everyday economic process are answered, but when also it is clear how economic events are bound up with the life of the nation, with political and social events and with intellectual movements.

One-sidedness in either direction is dangerous. To segregate one-sidedly economic questions leads to a neglect of their connections with other departments of life and fails to do justice to the facts. This is shown by the "stages" of economic development and by most trade cycle theories. On the other hand, exclusively to concentrate on the general historical interconnectedness of all aspects of life, and to say that economic questions cannot be separated and studied by themselves, is to admit oneself unable to analyse the economic world. One is bound to remain a dilettante with a confused picture of economic events, unable to see the connections between them. This is what happened with the "romantic" economists both of former and more recent times.

A certain conflict exists between the striving of economics to solve its own problems, and its striving after general historical understanding. This conflict is continuously met with in economic studies. It is fruitful and necessary and not to be eliminated.[71]

(12) At the beginning, in formulating our problems, we criticised such existing constructions as the "stages" and "styles" of economic development. In conclusion we now ask whether the results we have reached are at all near to these "stages" and "styles"; whether, that is, (*a*) our picture of actual economic systems, or (*b*) the construction of our morphological system of pure types, can be regarded as a continuation of the theory of "stages" and "styles" of development, and of "real" types of economic systems. Our answer is no.

(*a*) The classification of economic systems bears no relation to the economic stages and economic styles. They are something entirely different.

First, the economic system is an individual thing, the economic stage or style (of development) a type. When we want to study, say, the economic system of the age of Pericles, or the quite different system of Italy in the first century, or the large number of other economic systems of classical times, we do not try to capture this multiformity in a number of stages or styles such as that of "Household Economy". For example, there was an economic system in eastern Germany in the thirteenth century, and another sort of system in the Flemish towns around 1270, and another Flemish economic system around 1350 (*v.* p. 237 ff.). These are all individual things. On the other hand, the doctrine of stages and styles of development brings them together as "city economies" or even "Early Capitalism". A particular German economic system existed in 1940 essentially different from that in 1900. The doctrine of "stages" attempts to represent these and many other historical situations under the designation of "national economy".

There is a *second* difference closely connected with this. The construction of "stages" and "styles" of development is quite a different process from understanding the different economic systems. The former are built up out of a characteristic or a series of characteristics. That is how "real" types like "Capitalism", "City Economy", and "Household Economy" are created. It is quite different with the various economic systems. When seeking to understand these one starts with a single question, that of the structure of the system. What is the economic structure of contemporary Germany? Or what was that of the United States in 1800? It was shown that this question cannot be answered directly, but that considerable further analysis must be undertaken in order to work out a morphology of the ideal types of economic systems, the different varieties of centrally directed economy, different forms of market, the main forms of monetary economy and monetary system. This is how our aim of understanding the economic systems existing to-day or in 1800 can be realised. This form of question and this procedure have nothing in common with the theory of "stages" and "styles".

Thirdly, the economic "stages" and "styles" of development are meant to serve as the basis for theoretical studies, but not so the economic systems. We know, of course, that theories limited in application to single stages or styles, say for the City Economy or for Capitalism, have neither ever been constructed nor ever can be. But that is the intention, and it is an essential motive for the construction of these styles and stages. This is not the purpose for which we seek an understanding of the different economic systems. Such attempts must clearly fail. For the number of forms of organisation realised in one economic system is too large and blended together in too unique a combination for them to serve as sets of conditions descriptive of an economic system of which theoretical analysis would be possible. It would be a vain undertaking, for example, to work out special theories for the German economic system in 1900 and for that in 1940 for the purpose of explaining the economic process in Germany at those two dates. (The theories are constructed rather on the basis of the pure forms, the different ideal pure types of economic systems, and their variants.) Certainly in order to apply the theoretical apparatus to the actual course of economic events, it is necessary to know what were the actual economic systems and their dominant elementary forms. There is no such possible application for the "stages" and "styles" of development.

(*b*) Our different *types* of economic system, the forms of centrally directed economy and of markets, the monetary systems and the whole morphological system for the study of economic facts, have no more connection with the "stages" and "styles" of development than have our economic systems themselves. These are pure ideal types or forms which are not intended to give a cross-section or summarised picture of real economic systems. They have another purpose, are derived in another way, and have a different logical character. It is, therefore, dangerous to make comparisons between particular characteristics of the series of various styles or stages that have been constructed and the descriptions of the ideal types of economic systems. It is too easily forgotten that stages and styles and a morphological system are on two quite different levels. In addition it must be realised that theories, according to whether they follow the one procedure or the other, have an entirely different significance, limited in application to a particular period in the case of the stages and styles, and with the other procedure not limited in their *truth* but only in their *relevance*. This gives some impression of the magnitude of the contrast.

This is not a case of different houses being built of the same sorts of stone. The stones themselves are different. There is a different kind of relationship with the historical facts, present and past, about men in their economic life, and about economic institutions. There is also a different use of analysis. All this is not said in order to claim originality. Science and its tasks are too great for such claims to be anything but absurd. The distinction has to be drawn thus firmly so as to prevent further work on a house which economists have already spent too long in trying to build, and which is neither habitable nor ever can be made so in the future.[72]

(13) The different individual sciences are often arranged under certain classifications on the basis of which particular methods are ascribed to them. Economics is often included under the so-called "moral" sciences,* as contrasted with the natural sciences, and what is called the method of the moral sciences is supposed to be applied when pursuing them. By others again, economics is sometimes put nearer the natural sciences and an attempt made to apply in them the methods of physics. In either case this procedure is not permissible. Every science must develop its own method and character out of the special nature of the problems of its subject-matter and by working out these problems. It is the problems of the subject thrown up by reality and needing a solution that shape the procedure. The nature of its two main problems calls for historical and theoretical treatment of a unique kind. This is what fixes the position of economics in the scientific cosmos.

Economics must maintain its independence of all other sciences, for they have different problems to solve. It will fail in its task if it is dominated by methods of investigation taken over from the history of the natural sciences which have not arisen out of the problem of the great antinomy in economics. As no other science has the same conflicting problems to overcome, any simple transfer to economics of methods derived from other sciences would be inapposite and misleading.

It is just when the special characteristics of economics are fully worked out, and our understanding of economic reality pushed as far as possible, that points of contact with other sciences are found. The isolation of individual sciences, so rightly complained of, cannot be removed from above by some superficial classification, but only from below by each working at the problems of its subject-matter. First to occur are many points of contact with economic history. There are also very close connections with other historical sciences when these are each regarded as parts of universal history. We have already discussed this at length.

(14) It follows that the theory of business administration†

* Geisteswissenschaften. † Betriebswirtschaftslehre.

cannot be kept separate from the rest of economics. Separation would only be justified if a special group of problems existed. The independence of its problems is the only basis for the independence of a science. The problems of economics and of business administration belong together. Firm and household are parts of the whole economy and the course of economic events in them is part of the course of events in the whole of society. The two central problems of economics are also the two central problems of business administration. The structure and management of firms and households can only be understood in the framework of the whole economy and as parts of the whole course of economic events in which they belong. Therefore, all scientific students of business administration necessarily find themselves also studying the different economic systems and the interrelations in an exchange economy. There is no ground whatsoever for one science, that of business administration, confining itself to the conditions of the individual economic unit, while the other, economics, ignores them. Because of the size of the problem it is right and understandable that the student of business administration studies more the relations *within* the firms and households, and the economist more the relations *between* economic units. But the difference in emphasis should not lead to a separation into two separate sciences.

As with the separation between historical and theoretical economics, it is true in this case also, that splitting up the science leads to its problems being left unsolved. If the economist studies the economy as a whole and its processes without a knowledge of the responsible agents in the economy, that is, the firms and households, his work must be unrealistic. How can the structure of a modern agricultural economy be understood without a thorough knowledge of the structure of its farms of all sizes? How can all the economic relationships of a contemporary monetary system be understood without a knowledge of modern banking technique and the ability to read the precise meaning of the banks' balance sheets?

On the other hand, a student of business administration who stops short at the individual firm can never grasp the meaning of its structure and activities, nor of its balance sheets and cost calculations. His horizon is too narrow and his treatment of the problems insufficiently co-ordinated (*v.* p. 87 ff.). If the economist *overlooks* the individual economic unit, while the student of business administration *confines himself* to the individual unit, the two will not approach what can be achieved by starting from the structure, plans, and actions of the individual firm and household, and advancing to conditions in the economy as a whole; that is, proceeding from the individual unit to an understanding of the whole economy. An understanding of the whole economy makes possible a scientific understanding of the individual unit and its activities, an example of Böckh's well-known saying that "those who want a thorough knowledge of the individual part must understand the whole". The unity of the problem becomes particularly clear where, as in the centrally administered economy, or independent economy, one authority controls the whole economic process; that is, where the entire process is comprised in a single economic unit.

The separation between business administration and economics was in particular the result of the attempts of many economists to solve problems of the whole economy, while disregarding the individual units of which it is made up. Where the views of this school predominated a vacuum resulted. The structure and behaviour of the individual unit was left unexplained. Students of business administration tried to fill the vacuum. As soon as it is recognised that it is necessary to discover the interrelationships in the economy as a whole through a study of the structure and of the activities of the individual unit, the vacuum disappears, as does the separation of business administration from economics.[73]

(15) The economist, by gaining an understanding of different economies and their structure, and of the course taken by the economic process, is then able to advance to a further big complex of problems, that of economic policy.

This is its background. More and more countries are being industrialised and those that already have been, are going through new stages of industrialism which is everywhere destroying the old economic systems. Simultaneously great intellectual and political revolutions have changed and dissolved the old systems. The numerous and rapidly changing economic systems of the age of industrialism have mostly been dominated by the exchange form of economy, and lately also by the centrally administered form. These changes have led to many upheavals in the course of the economic process, to concentrations of and struggles for power, and to social tensions, and have hastened the spread of mass civilisation.

One of the great tasks of the present age is to find an effective and lasting system, which does justice to the dignity of man, for this new industrialised economy with its far-reaching division of labour. This means that the shortages of goods pressing every day on nearly all households must as far as possible, and for as long as possible, be relieved. At the same time a life of individual freedom must be possible. A solution of this task, on which so much depends (not only men's economic existence), requires the elaboration of a practicable economic constitution (*v.* p. 82) which satisfies certain basic principles. The problem will not solve itself simply by our letting economic systems grow up spontaneously. The history of the last century has shown this plainly enough. The economic system has to be consciously shaped. The detailed problems of economic policy, whether of agricultural policy, trade policy, credit, monopoly, or tax policy, or of company or bankruptcy law, are part of the great problem of how the whole economy, national and international, and its rules, are to be shaped.

For many decades men have been accustomed to turn to particular problems of economic policy case by case. But the interdependence of all economic life demands that they all be seen and treated together interdependently. If economic policy neglects to do this the results are painfully clear, as in the case of states which tried to pursue an autonomous trade cycle policy and also remain on the gold standard, or which tried by their company law to obstruct the formation of joint stock companies, but countered the effect of their legislation by their tax policy.

These problems are vast and difficult and can only be solved if use is made of the fruits of the scientific study of economics. Every single measure of economic policy affects the whole economy and the whole economic process. Of this interdependence, which must radically influence all decisions of policy, economic science alone provides an understanding, by the application of its morphology and theory. The economist must do the preliminary thinking for an economic constitution for the whole modern economy. It is not a task of discussing doctrines or ideologies but of concrete organisation. This further great complex of economic tasks is not discussed in this book. The statement must suffice that the understanding of economic life, present and past, with which alone we have been concerned, is also a preparation for the work of shaping the economic constitutions of the future.[74]

(16) Legal and economic thought in the course of the nineteenth century and at the beginning of the twentieth century went their separate ways and have seldom been in contact. In this period the conviction predominated that although a legal system had to be established and built up, an efficient "natural" economic system would develop spontaneously. It was not necessary consciously to create an economic system. It arose of its own accord. Consequently the legal system contained no principles by which the contracts, business agreements, company promotions, etc., of everyday life were to be linked together in an effective unified economic process.

Meanwhile it has become obvious that the modern industrialised world does not of itself produce an effective economic system, but requires certain controlling constitutional principles as a foundation. This change alters the relation between legal thought and practice on the one hand, and economic life and thought on the other. Legal thought and practice will to an increasing extent have the task of co-operating in the building and establishing of this economic constitution. The different branches of law—for example, those concerned with companies, taxation, monopolies, labour, patents, and branded goods—will depend for their content and interpretation on the decisions about the economic constitution as a whole, and will be very different according to whether the controlling principles of perfect competition, or of some other form of market, or those of a centrally administered economy, predominate.

Here are some examples. In the administration of justice

and in legal science the problem has often arisen whether price undercutting is permissible or not. In the administration of justice the case is probably decided by the "fairness" or "unfairness" of the undercutting. But there is no firm basis here for a judgment to rest on. For whether there is "unfairness" or not is usually decided according to the very nebulous notions of the judge about the "fairness" of prices, and about the economy in general. But when the judge starts from the intentions of the economic constitution—say the maintenance of competition—and applies this controlling principle, then, when he distinguishes between the different forms of market, especially between oligopoly and monopoly and perfect competition, he is able to distinguish between the undercutting of prices which is compatible with these principles and that—such as occurs in monopolistic warfare—which is not. Similarly legal science and the administration of justice can only understand the meaning of freedom of occupation, or of unlimited liability, when they are seen as principles of the economic constitution. The purpose of the unlimited liability of the entrepreneur in a competitive economy is to make him careful in the disposition of his resources, and in investing and producing, and automatically to eliminate him if unsuccessful. Unlimited liability is part of a competitive system, and its destruction by legal policy endangers the functioning of this system. Unlimited liability has no function in the centrally administered economy, for the control of the economic process and the selection of the leadership proceed differently. The treatment of particular problems by legal policy gets a meaning, and single measures are successfully co-ordinated, if legal policy follows the controlling principles that are to be carried out in practice.

Economists to-day are working on the practical controlling principles by which effective economic constitutions, national and international, can be built up, and which will be fruitful in all fields of economic policy. Here economic and legal thought can work together, whether it is on the treatment of cartels or on general business law, on questions of the international monetary system, or on other questions of economic and legal policy.[75]

(17) The conflicts in the claims of reason and perception, the concrete and the abstract, synthesis and analysis, must not be removed but made fruitful. These contrasting partners must be fully brought to bear, in their purest and most complete forms, on our problems. Economics lives by such conflicts and through them reaches a scientific understanding of economic life.

The unity of its theoretical system enables it to comprehend the multiformity and variety in history. The genuine and in no way speculative intellectual analysis that economics has developed does not conflict with, but serves to illuminate, those living facts which surround us and which have been lived through by us and our predecessors.

NOTES

Note 1. Failure to start from the facts and from factual problems is the original sin of all empirical sciences. Words and concepts usurp the place of the analysis of facts and conditions. Many are those who blind themselves to the facts by words, definitions, false abstractions, slogans, and prejudices. There were, for example, the notorious opponents of Galileo, who refused to make use of a telescope to look at the moon of Jupiter, because according to their theory and definitions Jupiter could have no moon, and therefore any further study of the heavens was superfluous. "This kind of person", Galileo said, "believes that truth is not to be found in the world or in nature, but in the comparison of texts". To-day such blindness to, or fear of, the real world can be laughed at. But such laughter is hardly justified. Economists are especially apt to suffer from a failure to see the true point of departure of their subject in everyday experience and its problems.

Max Weber said at the first Congress of German Sociologists in the course of a discussion of the concept of "economy": "In my opinion, we have generally to start from the fact that sciences, and what they are concerned with, come into being when problems of a particular kind appear, and when specific means for dealing with those problems are demanded. 'Economy', then, is something we select from out of the variety of our experience when we are faced with particular sorts of problems" (*Schriften der deutscher Gesellschaft für Soziologie*, I. Bd., 1911, p. 267). For further criticism of basic concepts see H. Dietzel: *Theoretische Sozialökonomik*, 1895, pp. 149 ff., and below pp. 50, 301.

Our formulation of the question of the interrelations of the economic process has met with some objections. It has been complained that this question, that is, our first main problem, has not arisen from a study of the real economic world, and that I am only deluding myself in thinking that it has. It has been taken over from the classical economists (Amonn, in *Jahrb. f. Nat.*, Bd. 153, 1941, pp. 15 ff; Ruppin, in the same journal, Bd. 156, 1942, p. 106; Weippert in the *Zeitschrift für die ges. Staatswiss.*, Bd. 102, 1941, pp. 1 ff).

This is a strange but not uninteresting objection. I have emphasised at length that the classical economists asked this question (see pp. 18, 26, 47) and it was superfluous to point this out. But this objection does show how difficult it is for some economists to face up to the unavoidable task of turning their attention to the real economic world as we see it in firms and households. Economists, in Galileo's words, are still comparing texts and thinking that their problems can be solved in this way. So they never emerge from the paper world of models and threadbare controversies. The task is to get a really spontaneous and immediate grasp of economic problems and their full relevance. The great service of the classical economists, which I was particularly concerned to emphasise, and which must never be underestimated, was that they formulated the problem and dealt with it by new methods. What is important is that we see the reality of the problem. We have to deal with it, not because the classical economists did so, but because it is a fruitful one to raise for the study of the real economic world (see p. 297). That is the essential point. The second main problem, that of the nature of the economic system, is also essential, although the classics never raised it in this form. Faced with the problems of the real world everyone has to formulate these questions for himself, whether tohers have done so before or not.

Note 2. On the threefold or fourfold division of theoretical economics, see J. B. Say: *Cours complet d'économie politique*, 1828; more recently, Karl Diehl: *Theoretische Nationalökonomie*, Band II bis IV, 1924–33; H. Dietzel: *op. cit.*, pp. 128 ff., who gives a detailed survey of the development of the threefold, fourfold, or twofold division of economic theory. In this connection Dietzel's statement that "Economic life is an organic whole", is certainly true, and just for that very reason we must abandon the attempt to formulate independent theories of production, exchange, distribution, and consumption. For further criticism see Carl Menger: *Grundsätze der Volkswirtschaftslehre*, 2nd Ed., 1923, Chap. 4, para. 1.

Note 3. The problem of the time structure of economic activity is often not fully understood and so a further example may be provided here. Let us imagine the mines, machinery, factories, textile works, canals, farms, and land, in fact the whole gigantic productive apparatus of England, as it is to-day. Add to this the working population and the stocks of raw materials and semi-finished goods. Faced with these quantities of labour, natural resources, and produced means of production, the following great question, among others, arises: what to-day shall be the time structure of production in England? Obviously there is an infinite range of possibilities which fall between two limiting cases. The one limiting case is that the entire means of production of every kind, including labour, should be used for extending the productive apparatus. Agriculture would concentrate on adding to livestock and the output of the iron and steel industry would be devoted to making new blast furnaces and machinery factories. Provision for the present and near future would be cut down as far as possible in favour of investment and provision for the more distant future. Supplies available in the present would be very small in order to make possible greater supplies in the future. The other limiting case would be if the greater part of the means of production and of the services of labour were used so as to increase final consumption as rapidly as possible. There would be no expansion of the productive apparatus at all, which would rather be reduced and gradually used up in the interests of larger present consumption, livestock being slaughtered, and machinery and houses no longer maintained and replaced. In this limiting case provision for the present would be much larger, but at the expense of the future. In actual fact, one of the many possible intermediate courses would be adopted. The question is, *what determines the decision*? It is obviously impossible to explain the productive activities of the English people without putting and answering this question of the time structure of production, a problem which includes that of savings and investment.

For criticism of Walras and Pareto on this subject see Wicksell; "Pareto's Manuel d'economie politique", *Zeitschrift für Volkswirtschaft*, 1913.

Note 4. The economist has the task, in dealing with the opinions and ideologies of everyday life, of uncovering them and seeing through their influence, of freeing himself from them, and arriving at objectively valid conclusions. Whether and how far this latter objective is possible is studied at length in this book.

We lack a psychological or sociological study of the ideologies of vested interests. For ideologies of the sixteenth century see Strieder: *Studium zur Geschichte kapitalistischer Organisationsformen*, 2. Aufl., 1925, especially Book 2; J. Höffner: *Wirtschaftsethik und Monopole im fünfzehnten und sechzehnten Jahrhundert*, 1941.

It would also be necessary to study historically how economic theory, in the course of its development, has faced up to this double task of understanding and seeing through popular opinions and ideologies. It would emerge from this that the older thinkers were mostly more aware of the problem than many more recent writers. The passage quoted from Foster (1697) is taken from Schulze-Gävernitz: *Der Grossbetrieb*, 1892, p. 7. Quesnay (*Maximes Generales du Gouvernement économique, ca.* 1748) says in his discussion of monopolies, privileges, etc.: "What shines out amid darkness is often false and deceptive. The natural order is often upset by special interests which are always pursued in secret or disguised as the general welfare". On the influence of vested interests and their ideologies on Mercantilism and on economic policy, see the severe but relevant criticisms c.f. Adam Smith: *Wealth of Nations*, Book 4, Chapters 3 and 8; E. F. Hecksher; *Mercantilism*; and C. J. Kraus: *Staatswirtschaft*, 1808–11, 2 Bd., I, pp. 243 ff.

Not only economists are apt to be careless and unsuspecting of the ideologies of vested interests, but often students and practitioners of law do not show the necessary caution when faced with "interested" interpretations and claims in cartel law, company law, general business law, and the law of fair competition, etc. It is in this way that the influence of economic pressure groups in public life spreads. See, for example, the judgment of the Reich High Court of 4 February, 1897 (RGZ.38, S.155 ff), which has been of fundamental importance for the legal and economic treatment of cartels, and which was quite uncritically used in the arguments and propaganda of vested interests. (For a criticism of this decision see Franz Böhm: *Ordnung der Wirtschaft als geschichtliche Aufgabe und rechtsschöpferische Leistung*, 1937, pp. 150 ff.) A study of all the legal pronouncements of the Reich High Court in civil cases from this point of view is very badly needed.

On the methodological task here "the question how confused naïve experience can become scientific experience and how objectively valid empirical conclusions can be arrived at is the principle methodological problem of every empirical science" (E. Husserl: "Philosophie als strenge Wissenschaft", *Logos*, 1911, and *Logische Untersuchungen*, 4. Aufl., 1928, I, 1).

"The everyday experience from which our theories start is naturally the common starting point for all the empirical sciences. All of them have to aim at getting beyond this, for only to that extent is their existence as separate sciences justified. Each science has to rise above or overcome everyday experience in one way or another" (Max Weber: *Gesammelte Aufsätze zur Wissenschaftslehre*, 1922, p. 269).

Finally, here are some words of Schopenhauer from the introduction to the second edition of *The World as Will and Idea.* He describes there the common activities, writings, and speeches of everyday life and says that these activities are guided by one's interests rather than by insight ("Absicht nicht Einsicht"), the truth being certainly the last thing which is being cared about: "Or is it really believed that in all this striving and turmoil, where it is in no way the aim of it all, truth can be arrived at *incidentally*?"

In starting out, not *tabula rasa,* but from a quantity of pre-scientific prejudices, the economist suffers the same lot as all other empirical scientists, from the political historian to the astronomer. But few empirical sciences have more pre-scientific prejudice to reckon with, more vigorously supported by the vested interests of individuals and groups. For this reason especially there is in economics a specially marked discrepancy between the everyday nature of its problems and the quite uncommon effort that is necessary in order to deal with them scientifically. This is one of the reasons for the unpopularity of economics; it demands that one frees oneself from carefully cherished errors, which is a feat only few men can manage. On this subject Kant at the beginning of his treatise *Was ist Aufklärung?* of 1784 has said all that is necessary.

On this fundamental problem for the study of economics, see also pages 52, 53, 265.

Note 5. The term "history" is often used to cover both *the historical events* themselves as well as *the writing of history* (on this see Hegel's *Lectures on the History of Philosophy*). From this common ambiguity many avoidable confusions have resulted. I understand by "history" only the historical events themselves and refer to the science of history as "historical writing". In this book when we say that "the history of the Middle Ages teaches us that . . ." I mean that the actual events of the Middle Ages teach us that, and not historical writings about the Middle Ages.

Further, history consists not only of the events of the past but also of the most recent times, of the present, and of to-day. In this sense we are living through history every day.

Finally, "History refuses to interest itself in the details of family life, the daily round and daily events of the individual" (E. Bernheim: *Lehrbuch der historischen Methode*, 4. Aufl., 1903, p. 3). This is simply describing what the usual emphasis of the historian is. Economic everyday life nevertheless remains an essential part of history.

Note 6. On the task of theoretical studies in economics see also my work "Was leistet die nationalökonomische Theorie?" in *Kapitaltheoretische Untersuchungen*, 1934. See also pp. 56, 60, 222,

Note 7. On the subject of the "unchanging general style or form" ("invarianten Gesamtstil"), see also pp. 240, 273, 295,

Note 8. On the attitude to history of the writers of "the Age of Reason" and their allegedly unhistorical ways of thought, see A. Sorel: *Montesquieu*, 1887; W. Dilthey: "Das 18. Jahrhundert und die geschichtliche Welt" (*Ges. Schriften*, Bd. 3); E. Cassirer: *Die Philosophie der Aufklärung*, 1932, pp. 263 ff.

It is not enough to treat the historical thinkers of the Age of Reason mainly as the forerunners of the still influential nineteenth-century school of historical writing dominated by the idea of development, as Meinecke does in the first volume of his *Entstehung des Historismus* (1936). They were historians who started from different problems and had quite a different attitude to history and reason. (On these two attitudes to history see also my article "Wissenschaft im Stile Schmollers", *Weltwirtschaftliches Archiv*, 52, 1940, pp. 468 ff.

Against the usual criticism of the classical economists from the point of view of the historical school, see Schüller: *Die Klassische Nationalökonomie und ihre Gegner*, 1895; and H. Dietzel: *op. cit.*, pp. 103 ff.

For criticisms of the theoretical system of classical economics see Wicksell: *Vorlesungen über Nationalökonomie*, 1913, Vol. I, pp. 61 and 77; Böhm-Bawerk: *Grundzüge der Theorie des wirtschaftlichen Güterwerts*, 1932, pp. 130 ff., and *Gesammelte Aufsätze*, 1924, pp. 481 ff.; L. Walras: *Éléments d'économie politique pure*, 1926, Leçons 38–40; G. Cassel: *Theoretische Sozialökonomie*, 5. Aufl. para. 32.

By "classical theory" I understand the theory of the classical economists, that is the economists from Quesnay to John S. Mill and Von Mangoldt, *not*, as is often the case recently, *also* the modern theoretical economists. It is surely showing a complete disregard of the basic notions of their systems to neglect the differences between the classical theory and the modern systems as created by Gossen, Menger, Walras, Jevons, Marshall, Wieser, Böhm-Bawerk, and others. This difference is fundamental. To refer only to two points: while the modern theories try to understand the entire economic process as arising out of human needs, this is not the case with the classics. And *secondly*, a phenomenon of central importance like that of costs receives in the classical and modern theories an entirely different explanation, and is given quite a different significance for the economy as a whole. The theoretical picture of the course of economic life is to-day quite a different one from that of the classical economists, and this must not be disregarded.

Note 9. As regards the procedure of "conceptualist" economists, it may be pointed out that other sciences have overcome " conceptualism" earlier than has economics. " 'Sizi' despises", wrote Kepler once to Galileo, "the world as we perceive it and does not see it himself. He disbelieves those who know about it and plays about with childish conclusions like one of the peripatetic philosophers in a paper world". This is a severe, but even to-day a relevant, judgment. For criticism of the method in the empirical sciences which begins with definitions, see J. F. Fries: *System der Logik*, 3. Aufl., 1937, pp. 298 ff.; and A. Trendelenburg: *Historische Beiträge zur Philosophie*, Bd. 3, 1867, pp. 61 f., where he says among other things: "In contrast to the old methodological rule which begins the study of a subject with a definition, Campanella once said that a definition comes at the end of a science. It is certainly not a prologue, but rather an epilogue to our knowledge. For the definition contains in summary and in the shortest form the essence of our knowledge and its conclusions. Only *after* our investigations can the correct relations be brought together in a definition. For further criticism of "conceptual" economics see also pp. 24, 94, 301.

Note 10. The dualism of theoretical and historical economics was defended by, among others, Carl Menger in his *Untersuchungen über die Methode der Sozialwissenschaften*, 1883, and H. Rickett in *Die Grenzen der Naturwissenschaflichen Begriffsbildung*, 3, Aufl., 1921. Carl Menger, incidentally, did mention that theory can be of service in understanding the real economic world. But its application is a task "for the historian, for whom the theoretical social sciences are in this respect auxiliary". Such remarks as these tend to blunt the sharpness of Menger's dualism but do not remove it, since he calls for two different sciences with two different intellectual objectives and two different ways of thinking. Furthermore, it is a mistake to assume that the purely historical economist can apply economic theory. Rather it is only the economist who understands how to work with theory from the start, and how to construct the theoretical tools, who can apply it in understanding the real world. The failure of methodological dualism does not detract from the great achievements of Carl Menger as a theoretical economist. For an extreme dualist point of view see A. Ammon: *Objekt und Grundbegriffe der theoretischen Nationalökonomie*, 1927, and other works by Ammon, for example his book on Ricardo (1923), where in the introduction he distinguishes between a "formal" and a "real" problem of economic distribution, the latter lying quite beyond theoretical treatment. See also his recent work, "Nationalökonomie und wirtschaftliche Wirklichkeit", *Jahrb. f. Nationalök.*, 1941, Bd. 153, pp. 1 ff. and 130 ff.

On the origin and rise of modern economic theory see Fr. Wieser: *Gesammelte Abhandlungen*, 1929, pp. 35 ff. and 110 ff.; J. M. Keynes, in *Memorials of Alfred Marshall*, 1925; J. Schumpeter: *Grundriss der Sozialökonomik*, I, 1924, pp. 113 ff.; L. Robbins' introduction to the new edition of Wicksteed's *Commonsense of Political Economy*, 1933; Hayek's introduction to the reprint of Menger's *Grundsätze*, London, 1934; W. S. Jevons' preface to the 2nd edition of his *Theory of Political Economy*, 1879.

Note 11. For the purely empirical point of view see Schmoller's criticism of Menger (*Zur Literaturgeschichte der Staats- und Sozialwissenschaft*, 1888, pp. 175 ff), Schmoller's Berliner Rektoratsrede *Wechselnde Theorien und feststehende Wahrheiten*, 1897, his article "Volkswirtschaft, Volkswirtschaftslehre und ihre Methode" in the *Hdw. d. Staatswissenschaften*, 3. Aufl., and his *Grundriss*. In the great debate between Menger and Schmoller both parties were wrong, nor was the truth somewhere in the middle between the two. Neither Menger's dualism, of which Schmoller perceived the danger, nor Schmoller's pure empiricism, the failure of which Menger foresaw, does justice to economic reality. A new start is necessary.

Within the German Historical School there were various men at work who, in their attitude to economic theory and in formulating their problems, tried to avoid the mistakes of the pure empiricists. (Among others M. Sering, on whom see Dietze in the *Jahrb. für Nat. v. Stat.*, 1940, Bd. 151, pp. 1 ff.) For criticism of the common statistical brand of pure empiricism see W. Lexis: *Abhandlungen zur Theorie der Bevölkerungs- und Moralstatistik*, 1903, pp. 240 ff.; Fr. Lutz: *Das Konjunkturproblem in der Nationalökonomie*, 1932, pp. 128 ff.

Note 12. The beginnings of theories of "stages" or "steps" of social and economic development can already be found in the writers of ancient Greece, particularly in Aristotle. In the eighteenth century there was much discussion of the different forms of society, of the different peoples, of hunters, shepherds, agriculturists, etc. (e.g. Adam Smith: *Wealth of Nations*, Book V). But the theory of stages of development first really came to the forefront in the nineteenth century. This was not only because of the rapid changes in economic life in the nineteenth century, which must have suggested the construction of such a theory of stages, but also because of two other intellectual developments which both, independently of one another, influenced scientific thought in the direction of such a theory. The dawn of a new consciousness of history and the trend towards an "individualising" approach to history which took place at the end of the eighteenth and nineteenth centuries demanded a much closer observation and study of the different forms of economic life. Another important stimulus came from quite another direction: the victory of the idea of evolutionary development in the natural sciences. This victory was so complete that it spread to all other sciences. This was the period when a legal thinker such as Ihering could summarise the entire conclusions of his studies in the history of law by saying that they completely confirmed Darwin's theory (see *Zweck im Recht*, 1868, I, Bd., IX). On the history of the idea of development and its various forms, and for criticism of it, see Rudolf Eucken: *Geistige Strömungen der Gegenwart*, 6. Aufl., 1920, pp. 132 ff. and 206 ff.). The victory in the field of Social Science of the idea of evolution as developed by the Natural Sciences is often attributed to Comte and the great influence he exercised on European thinking (*Cours de Philosophie positive*, 1830–42). Comte explained very forcefully how the individual facts of state and society follow as parts of the general and necessary laws of development. His important theory of the three stages of development has had an immense influence. Partly directly, and partly via Spencer, Comte has influenced economics in Germany in the direction of evolutionary ideas, and in this way has assisted the construction of theories of economic stages of development. That holds also for Schmoller, on whom, as on Spencer and Comte, the influence of Darwin was decisive (see K. Diehl: *Theoretische Nationalökonomie*, I. Bd., 1. Aufl., 1922; W. Mitscherlich: *Die Lehre von den beweglichen und starren Begriffen*, 1936, pp. 142 ff.; and the Freiburg dissertation of Diehl's pupil Franz Raab: *Die Fortschrittsidee bei Gustav Schmoller*, 1934). On the invasion of the social sciences by ideas derived from the natural sciences see Hayek: "Scientism and the Study of Society", *Economica*, 1942–44.

On the theory of economic "stages" see any standard German textbook: e.g. K. Knies: *Die politische Ökonomie vom geschichtlichen Standpunkte*, 1883, pp. 351 ff.; K. Bücher: *Die Entstehung der Volkswirtschaft*, 8. Aufl., 1911; Sombart, whose work *Modern Capitalism* is based on the nineteenth-century idea of economic development, and whose short work *Ordnung des Wirtschaftslebens*, 2. Aufl., 1927, may be consulted; J. Plenge: *Stammformen der vergleichenden Wirtschaftstheorie*, 1919; A. Spiethoff: *Die allgemeine Volkswirtschaftslehre als geschichtliche Theorie*; "Die Wirtschaftsstile", in *Schmollers Jahrbuch*, 56, 1932, p. 891. On "intuitive" empirical theory ("anschauliche Theorie") see E. Salin: "Hochkapitalismus", *Weltwirtschaftliches Archiv*, Bd. 25, 1927, p. 314; A. Spiethoff: "Schmoller und die anschauliche Theorie der

Volkswirtschaftslehre", *Weltwirtschaftliches Archiv*, 62, 1938, p. 400; W. Vleugels: "Leistung, Schwächen und tatsächliche Bedeutung der deutschen Nutzwertlehre", *Weltwirtschaftliches Archiv*, 61, 1937, p. 275. The works of Keynes are a clear example of how modern theoretical economics may be based on contemporary economic phenomena. On the attitude of C. Menger see p. 305.

Note 13. "Stages" and "styles" of economic development, different "types" of economic system, and all other such "*real*" types have quite a different significance from *ideal* types and are obtained in quite a different way, that is, by *generalising* abstraction. On the other hand, ideal types are created by *isolating* abstraction or the abstraction of specially significant characteristics (see pp. 105, 109, 173, 223, 300).

Karl Menger already made use of the term "real" types (*Untersuchungen über die Methode der Sozialwissenschaften*, 1883). Schmoller had the right intuition in seeing that the "ideal types" as defined by Weber did not apply to his and Bücher's "stages of economic development", but he did not follow up this idea. For further remarks on the differences between these two kinds of types see also Notes 24 and 66.

Note 14. For the latest extension of the boundaries of history back into pre-history see Schmidt-Koppers: *Völker und Kulturen*, I, 1924; Menghin: *Weltgeschichte der Steinzeit*, 1931; F. Heichelheim: *Wirtschaftsgeschichte des Altertums*, 1938; as an introduction see F. Kern: *Anfänge der Weltgeschichte*, 1933.

Note 15. On the gradual regression to more primitive conditions, interrupted by isolated periods of prosperity, of the economic life of the ancient world in its later stages see M. Rostovtzeff: *Gesellschaft und Wirtschaft im römischen Kaiserreich*; F. Heichelheim: *op. cit.*, Chapters 7 and 8.

Note 16. For the new picture of the economy of the Middle Ages at their height and in their later stages, and for the supersession of the theory of the "city economy" see A. Schulte: *Geschichte der grossen Ravensburger Handelsgesellschaft*, 1923; J. Strieder: *Studien zur Geschichte Kapitalistischer Organisationsformen*, 2. Aufl., 1925; F. Rörig: *Die europäischer Stadt*, in the Propyläen *Weltgeschichte*, 1922, Bd. 4; also Rörig's lecture, *Mittelalterliche Weltwirtschaft*, 1933; J. Kulischer: *Allgemeine Wirtschaftsgeschichte*, Bd. I, 1928; Clemens Bauer: *Unternehmung und Unternehmungsform im Spätmittelalter und in der beginnenden Neuzeit*, 1932, and *Venezianische Salzhandelspolitik bis zum Ende des 14. Jahrh.*; *Viertel-Jahrschr. f. Soz. v. Wirtsch-Gesch.*, Bd. 23, 1930, pp. 273 ff.; W. Abel: *Agrarkrisen und Agrarkonjunktur vom 13. bis zum 19. Jahrh.*, 1935; B. Kuske: "Die Entstehung der Kreditwirtschaft und des Kapitalverkehrs" in *Kreditwirtschaft* (Kölner Vorträge), 1927; H. Sieveking: *Wirtschaftsgeschichte*, 1935, p. 63. Of older works critical of the theory of the "city" economy we may mention Stieda: *Hansisch-venetianische Handelsbeziehungen im 15. Jahrhundert*, 1894.

I am very grateful to Clemens Bauer for numerous suggestions and references to problems of medieval economic life, and concerning general problems of the different kinds of economic system.

The question remains as to how it was possible that economic historians and economists, like Below, Bücher, Sombart, and many others, could so completely misunderstand an epoch of history, near to our own time, for which many clear sources were at hand; how they could see as a number of independent city economies what in fact was an extensive economic area with considerable division of labour; and how they could completely miss the existence and central importance of long-distance trade in the Middle Ages. There are other factors responsible besides the dominant ideology of "development" and progress which encouraged the overlooking of periods of regression, such as took place after the sixteenth century. The dislike of Thomas Aquinas and many of the other social and ethical thinkers of the Middle Ages for long-distance trade was misunderstood, in that the great discrepancy between the standards of the philosophers and the actual reality of economic life was missed. Furthermore, it was the towns which were mainly responsible for economic *policy* in the Middle Ages, not the state. Therefore the towns and their immediate surroundings were wrongly regarded as closed economic areas, the range of validity of their legal decisions being confused with the range of their economic relations.

Note 17. On the much controverted problems of the economic history of the ancient world, see Max Weber's article "Agrargeschichte", in the *Handwörterbuch der Staatswissenschaften*, 3. Aufl.: F. Oertel's appendix to Pöhlmann's *Geschichte der sozialen Frage and des Sozialismus in der antiken Welt*, 3. Aufl., 1925; I. Hasebroek: *Griechische Wirtschafts- und Gesellschaftsgeschichte*, 1931, Foreword.

Because only partially satisfactory answers have been given to the question of the economic systems of the ancient world in the original sources, there is a wide field for the constructive activities of researchers. One sort of attempt made is to project into the ancient world the economic conditions and economic and social contrasts of to-day, and from the course of the ancient struggles to find support for a particular point of view in contemporary controversies. This is what Edward Meyer, Pöhlmann, and, recently and much more carefully, Rostovtzeff have done. Or, on the other hand, the ancient world is seen as the direct, contrast of the modern economic world, as with Rodbertus, Bücher, and recently, Hasebroek. There is either a modernising or anti-modernising error. The conditions looked for are either the same or similar, or else entirely the opposite to those of the present day. But each period must be understood for itself.

Note 18. Economic and historical works about the medieval economy suffer from not putting in the forefront the question of the framework of the economic system. It is quite inadequate, for example, to ask how far a barter economy and how far a monetary economy existed in the Middle Ages, because, under the term "barter economy" completely different economic systems may be understood (see Note 35).

In addition to the works mentioned in Note 16 on medieval economics, we may mention, L. M. Hartmann: *Zur Wirtschaftsgeschichte Italiens im frühen Mittelalter*, 1904; A. Dopsch: *Wirtschaftliche und soziale Grundlagen der europäischen Kulturentwicklung*, 2. Aufl., 1924; F. Lütge: *Agrarverfassung des frühen Mittelalters im Mitteldeutschen Raum*, 1937; R. Passow: "Die grundherrschaftlichen Wirtschaftsverhältnisse in den Lehren von den Wirtschaftssystemen", *Jahrb. f. Nat., Bd.*, 112, 1919; E. Kelter: *Geschichte der obrigkeitlichen Preisregelung*, Bd. I, 1935; G. Mickwitz: *Die Kartellfunktionen der Zünfte*, 1936; J. Höffner: *op. cit.*

Note 19. On the problems of the different modern economic systems see Franz Böhm: *Wettbewerb und Monopolkampf*, 1933, and "Ordnung der Wirtschaft als geschichtliche Aufgabe und rechtschöpferische Leistung", 1937 (an introduction to the series *Ordnung der Wirtschaft* by Franz Böhm, Walter Eucken, and Hans Grossmann-Doerth); Fr. Lutz: *Das Grundproblem der Geldverfassung*, 1936 (see here the account of the British monetary constitution, and the actual monetary system in Britain which we touch on briefly in the text). Fr. Lutz: "Goldwährung und Wirtschaftsordnung", *Weltwirtschaftliches Archiv*, 1935; H. Gestrich; *Neue Kreditpolitik*, 1936, and *Kredit und Sparen*, 2. Aufl., 1947; H. Grossmann-Doerth: *Selbstgeschaffenes Recht der Wirtschaft und staatliches Recht*, 1933; W. Eucken: "Staatliche Strukturwandlungen und die Krisis des Kapitalismus", *Weltwirtschaftliche Archiv*, 1932, and "Wettbewerb als Grundprinzip der Wirtschaftsverfassung", in *Schrift der Ak. f. d. Recht*, Gruppe Wirtschaftswiss., Bd. 6, 1942; A. Rüstow in *Schriften des Vereins für Sozialpolitik*, Bd. 187, 1932, S. 60 ff.; W. Röpke: *The Social Crisis of Our Time*, 1950, *Civitas Humana*, 1944, and *Die internationale Ordnung*, 1945; F. A. Hayek: *The Road to Serfdom*, 1944; W. Lippmann: *Principles of the Good Society*, 1937; C. von Dietze: "Landwirtschaft und Wettbewerbsordnung", *Schmollers Jahrbuch*, 66. Bd., 1942, S. 120 ff.; L. Miksch: *Wettbewerb als Aufgabe*, 2. Aufl., 1947; and the publication *Ordo*, edited by Eucken and Böhm, first number 1948.

The economies of modern nations, in which many millions of individual economic units are bound up together by a thorough-going division of labour, as in a single giant factory, require, if they are to function, a system based on definite fundamental principles. Allowing an economic system uncontrolled growth, with unsystematic intervention by the economic policies of the state, leads, in the long run, as the experience of the last half-century convincingly shows, to economic systems in which the economic process only operates with severe disruptions and which finally, as in the later phases of the ancient world, must lead back to a primitive economy. Modern economic life, that is, demands an *economic constitution*. The works we have just mentioned have the aim of preparing the intellectual path for such an economic constitution (see also page 313).

Note 20. For the scientific understanding of the different kinds of economic system, see especially Part III, Chapter 4, page 255. On the legal order and the economic order see page 275, and also M. Weber: *Wirtschaft und Gesellschaft*, 1922, pp. 368 ff., as also Weber's important contribution to the discussion in *Schriften der Deutschen Gesellschaft für Sociologie*, 1. Bd., 1911, pp. 265 ff.; further, R. Stammler: *Wirtschaft und Recht*, 5. Aufl., 1924, especially pp. 177 ff.

Note 21. On the unhistorical over-simplifications of the theories of "stages" and "styles" of development see M. Weber: *Gesammelte Aufsätze zur Wissenschaftslehre*, 1922, p. 195. Max Weber certainly did not draw the necessary conclusions from his very able criticism (see Note 66). For criticism of the theory of "stages" of development see Bechtel: *Der Wirtschaftsstil des deutschen Spätmittelalters*, 1930, pp. 3 ff. It would be a misunderstanding of our point of view to represent it as opposed to the grouping of economic systems into larger categories or classifications. To keep close to reality, however, this kind of grouping or classification must be in accordance with the basic structure of the different economies. We can speak of a particular type of economic system such as that of the Greek city state in antiquity, in so far as a uniform structure was realised there. But it is illegitimate to include under a single "style" of economic development two entirely different economic systems, such as that in Italy, and that in Egypt at the time of Augustus.

The tendency to over-simplification in economics is shown not only in descriptions of the different forms of economic life, but also in the accounts of the course of everyday economic life, for example, in studies of the trade cycle. The attempt is made to represent the changes in everyday economic activity as following a single uniform type of cycle or normal cycle, and then a single theory is created to explain this normal cycle. Much too little attention is then paid to the different trade cycles, to the influence of non-economic and particularly political events on economic life, and, as a result, the facts of the real economic world are disregarded. There is no single, normal trade cycle. (See Lutz: *Das Konjunkturproblem in der Nationalökonomie*, 1932; the contributions of Stucken, Neisser, Lutz, and myself to the Spiethoff Festschrift, *Stand und nächste Zukunft der Konjunkturforschung*, 1933; Tintner: *Prices in the Trade Cycle*, Vienna, 1935; Hayek: "Price Expectations", "Monetary Disturbances", etc., in *Readings in Business Cycle Theory*, Blakiston; also Chapter IV.)

Note 22. It is significant that the same economists who emphasised in their programme the role of "understanding" ("Verstehen") in economics (see, for example, Sombart's book *Die Drei Nationalökonomien*, 1930) have done everything possible to hinder the understanding of economic history by basing their work on these "stages" or "styles" or "real types" of economic system. Here is a case, not rare in the history of science, where there is a fundamental contrast between programme and performance in a particularly blatant form. The separation of economic history from the rest of history, and the illegitimate over-simplification involved in forming such "typical" cross-sections of economic life, make historical understanding impossible.

Some authors such as Bechtel (*op. cit.*) and Müller-Armack (*Genealogie der Wirtschaftsstile*, 1941) use the concept of a "style" of economy in quite a different sense from that of, for example, Spiethoff. They aim, with the help of their concept, at understanding the connections between the different aspects of the life of a period, for example, religion and art, and how they are bound up with economic life. The "style" characterises the whole life of a period; it is not intended to help overcome the Great Antimony, that is, not to solve the problem of the co-operation of history and theory in economics. It is, therefore, not relevant for us to comment further on this concept here. The first question to ask about such a concept as this would be whether it is suitable for explaining the connections between economic events and other branches of life. For criticism of the theories of stages and styles of economic development, and for the relations between economic theory and history, see particularly A. Rüstow: "Zu den Grundlagen der Wirtschaftswissenschaft", in *Revue de la faculté des sciences économiques*, Istanbul, Vol. II, No. 2, 1941, pp. 105 ff.

Note 23. The hypostasising of general concepts has often played an important role in European intellectual history. One group of radical conceptual-realists in the Middle Ages saw in general concepts, such as warmth, or cold, or colour, real things like other particular things and ascribed to them a special kind of reality. They held that universals were substances which produced and determined particulars. Similarly we find to-day radical conceptual-realists, who, albeit unconsciously, in the way they use the concept of capitalism, are ascribing to it a higher reality beyond the particular individual facts of economic history, seeing it as determining these facts. They see capitalism as the *causa efficiens* not only of economic, but of all historical events. This magical or mystical treatment of the concept of capitalism dominates a considerable part of recent sociology and economics.

A conspicuous example is the book by Schumpeter: *Capitalism, Socialism and Democracy*. This book not only relates the achievements of "capitalism" or the capitalist process in technology and economic life as though "capitalism" were a person or real substance. We hear, too, of the rise of capitalism, which created modern science, which shaped the development of painting after Giotto, which created modern pacificism and modern international morality, but which has brought about a general hostility to itself which threatens the collapse of the foundations on which it is built. Schumpeter is a positivist. His aim is to portray the facts without taking up an attitude towards them. He aims, like Comte, the St. Simonians, and many other positivists, at describing laws of development as they are to be found in history. He rejects the use of such terms as "force" or "cause" since these are metaphysical. The result, however, is that he introduces an anthropomorphic supernatural force, capitalism, which becomes *the* operating force in history. It is capitalism which is the source of the ideas of legislatures, of the scientists' discoveries, of the moral philosophers' ideas of value, and which even gives the painters their paint-brushes. It is as though one was reading a story about some all-powerful creature and its activities. Since Comte, positivists have been proclaiming the supersession of theological and metaphysical ways of thought by the third stage of human intellectual history—that is, the positivist stage. Like Comte and many other positivists, Schumpeter does not notice how far he is diverging from his own programme and falling back into magical or mystical thinking. Few metaphysicians have so unconcernedly worked with what is really only a personified substance and so confidently believed that in it they have found the effective agent in all history.

Modern conceptual realists could learn much from the medieval debate over universals and from the failure in it of conceptual realism. The course of that debate ought to be a warning to them. See B. Geyer: "Die patristische und scholastische Philosophie", Ueberweg's *Grundriss*, 2. Teil, II. Aufl., 1928, pp. 205 ff.; Windelband-Heimsoeth: *Lehrbuch der Geschichte der Philosophie*, 1935, pp. 241 ff., and the literature mentioned there. For a thorough criticism see Lotze: *Logik*, 1874, para. 340 ff.; Husserl: *Logische Untersuchungen*, 2. Aufl. 1914, 2. Bd., pp. 106 ff. and 121 ff. On "conceptual" or "formalist" economics see above pp. 50 ff.

Concepts like "capitalism" or "socialism" are no substitute for the morphological study of the real economic world.

Note 24. The attempt to summarise economic reality in "stages" or "styles" of economic development (which resulted only in this development being lost sight of) is to be explained partly by lack of clarity about the logical character of the types which were being worked with.

While they are being constructed, a certain amount of freedom is claimed for them as being "ideal" pictures or "ideal" types. Actual historical facts are to some extent disregarded, since it is only a question of an "ideal" picture. But after their construction it is explained that *real economic conditions* are actually summarised, reproduced, or portrayed. At first it is maintained that such a type as the "city economy" represents an ideal picture, and the facts which do not correspond with this picture can be disregarded. Later it is held that the "city economy" should be recognised as a representation of the actual economy of the Middle Ages after the twelfth century. In this way a subjective and arbitrary picture of economic history is created.

There are two errors in logical or scientific method here. *First*, the *ideal* type, which always simply selects one aspect of economic reality, is not distinguished from a *real* type which has to portray the real economic world. *Secondly*, it is forgotten that in working out ideal types, as in working out real types, a definite and strict procedure must be adhered to which excludes or limits subjectivity. So long as types are worked with carelessly, the harm they cause will be serious. But worked out and applied in the right way, they are an extremely effective scientific tool.

Note 25. On the relations between classical political economy and the actual economic world, and in particular the economy of its time, see p. 47.

On the logical character and the validity of economic theory see pp. 39, 173, 229, 248, 300, and Notes 54 and 67.

Note 26. All particular economic problems are part problems of the two *main* economic problems. If the question is one of the organisation of a chemical concern, or of the structure of an agricultural co-operative, or about the formation of cartels in the German agricultural machinery industry, or about the structure of the German credit banks, then these are all sub-questions of the main problem of the German economic system, and they must always be approached as such. Similarly, if the question is one of the economic position of the chemical industry, or of the situation of the milk industry, or of the development of output and prices in the agricultural machinery industry, or of the liquidity of the German credit banks, these are all sub-questions of the main question of the economic process in contemporary Germany. These examples themselves show how closely the two main problems hang together.

We may already here give a warning about the complete impracticability of one way of attempting to solve this problem. The construction of particular theories and explanation of the economic process for each single system, would be quite impracticable. It would be to disregard the complexity of any actual economic system, to try to make it serve as a basis for theoretical analysis. A picture of any actual economic system does not provide the simple limited sets of conditions on which alone theories can be constructed. It is impossible to construct two special theories for the contemporary German or American economic systems in order to explain everyday economic life in Germany or

America. Quite another way must be sought. We shall return to this subject in Chapter IV of Part III.

Note 27. The whole of Part III is a unity and like the whole of this book can only be understood as such. For readers who would like help in keeping this unity constantly before them, I would advise the use of the opening sections of each chapter and particularly of Chapter IV.

The objection might be made to the argument in the text that in referring back to the simple phenomena of economic life we do not find complex concepts like that of a peasant holding, or a household, or a shoe-factory, etc. The elementary data are much simpler than this. It is only after severe theoretical work that concepts like those of "a peasant holding" or "household" are created. Two points should be made here. *First,* this objection confuses two different levels of scientific study. The question of how experience comes to exist in the first place, and of how any concepts are formed at all, is not one for the student of a particular science. It is a problem for the philosopher. The scientist in a particular field starts from everyday experience and tries to develop his scientific experience from that, and so to arrive at objectively valid conclusions, In order to understand the economic life of a village "A" economists have not got to ponder over the original sense data which constitute their experience. They rather start from everyday experience and use everyday concepts to study the farms, etc., which they find in the village. *Secondly,* the objection overlooks the reason why it is necessary to-day to lay such special emphasis on a direct approach to the economic facts. This is because so many fail to look at the facts, but put concepts like that of "capitalism", etc., in the forefront and make deductions from these concepts. The actual world in front of them, which it is their task to understand scientifically, remains unexplored.

Note 28. On the two forms of abstraction, "generalising" abstraction and "abstraction of significant salient characteristics", see Lotze: *Logik,* 1874, pp. 40 f., 169 ff., and 176; W. Wundt: *Logik,* 1906, II, pp. 11 ff.; and especially E. Husserl: *Logische Untersuchungen,* 2. Bd., I. Teil, 2. Aufl., pp. 106 ff. and 216 f.; and also Cournot: *Essai sur le fondement de nos connaissances,* 3rd Ed., 1922, pp. 230 ff.

In the abstraction of significant characteristics, a procedure which was first brought fully to development by modern science, the single aspects of any actual conditions are emphasised. In this way pure forms worked out, as is shown in the text, for a single household, a single firm, a single farm, or a single manor. "Generalising" abstraction, on the other hand, proceeds by surveying many facts and summarising the common characteristics of these facts in concepts. By surveying a large number of estates the concept and real type of a "household economy" is created, and from a large number of medieval cities the real type of "city economy". See also pages 221, 226, 300, and Note 13.

Note 29. On the monastery of Bobbio and other medieval manors of the early Middle Ages see L. M. Hartmann: *op. cit.*; H. Bickel: *Die Wirtschaftsverhältnisse des Klosters St. Gallen,* 1914; A. Dopsch: *Wirtschaftsentwicklung der Karolingerzeit,* 1913.

Note 30. On the productive system in the Middle Ages see the works mentioned in Notes 16 and 18 and, for the first centuries after the Renaissance, G. Aubin and A. Kunze: *Leinenerzeugung und Leine-*

nabsatz im östlichen Mitteldeutschland zur Zeit der Zunftkaüfe, 1940. The bilateral monopoly in the amber goods industry in Lübeck in the fifteenth century must be understood in connection with the amber raw material monopoly. (On this see *Lübeckisches Urkundenbuch*, I, 6, 1881, N. 448 and 586; W. Stieda in *Mitteilungen des Vereins für Lübeckische Geschichte*, 1886, pp. 97 ff.; W. Tesdorpf: *Gewinnung, Verarbeitung, und Handel des Bernsteins in Preussen*, 1887, pp. 6 ff.) A study of the important and peculiar system of amber production in the Middle Ages, making use of a scheme of different market forms, would be very fruitful.

Note 31. A bibliography of the economic history of the earliest historical times and of the ancient world in the Mediterranean is to be found in the second volume of Heichelheim's *Wirtschaftsgeschichte des Altertums*, 1938 (see also Note 14). In the Inca empire the economic system was mainly that of a totally centralised economy (see H. Cunow: *Geschichte und Kultur des Inkareiches*, 1937; L. Baudoin: *L'Empire socialiste des Inka*, 1928, and the literature mentioned there; see also the articles "Inca" and "South America" in the *Encyclopœdia Britannica*).

Note 32. On the problems of the direction of a centrally administered economy see *Collectivist Economic Planning*, edited by Hayek, London, 1935, and L. Mises: *Socialism*. The attempts of recent decades to solve these problems practically in many industrialised countries has brought them to a new stage. For example, German experience in this field has been very extensive. In Germany, after 1936, various methods were used for overcoming the problem. But it was found impossible to construct a satisfactory machinery for economic calculation in the centrally administered economy, in so far as this type of economy was realised. (See also my articles in the *Jahrbuch für Nationalökonomie*, Bd. 159, 1944, pp. 176 ff., and in *Economica*, 1948.)

The extensive English and American literature of Taylor, Schumpeter, Lange, Lerner, and others is based on Barone's well-known article of 1908 (see Note 40). Barone seeks to prove that the Ministry of Production in a collectivist state must and can act as though perfect competition existed. It would first distribute claims to consumers' goods, and then so direct the factors of production as to satisfy consumers' demands, as would happen under perfect competition according to the cost principle. Economic calculation in the two cases would be essentially similar. This line of argument follows from the old (but still widely held) point of view that the "fundamental logic of economic behaviour is the same in an exchange economy as it is in a socialist economy, and that the solution in the one case holds for the other" (Schumpeter).

But this thesis can neither be proved nor maintained. Barone and his followers start from the following initial conditions: the consumers make their own economic plans and the central administration so directs the entire process of production that the demands of consumers are met. It is not the plans of the central administration that are finally decisive as to the use of consumers' goods, labour, and factors of production, but the plans and demands of consumers. The following criticism may be made of this peculiar model. In the real world this case has never occurred and most probably never will occur. A state will not collectivise the means of production in order straight away to hand the control over them to consumers. It is entirely unrealistic to assume that the methods of a centrally administered economy would be used to transfer the control of the economic process from the officials to consumers. This model is not in fact one of a centrally administered economy, but is a special kind of exchange economy in which, incidentally, the principle of optimum output is upheld (see pp. 126, 288). The theoretical analysis of such a model cannot legitimately be used in dealing with contemporary problems of "collectivist" economic systems.

If *real* centrally administered economies are studied, and not this model, it will be seen that their working is quite different from that of the exchange economy, particularly in the case of perfect competition. Economic calculation (see page 284), investment, saving, economic fluctuations (see page 259), the distribution of economic power (see page 264), and international trade, to refer only to a few groups of problems, are in the two cases completely different. It is impossible to understand the real economic world, past or present, without understanding this fundamental difference, which expresses itself in all the events of everyday economic life.

The magnitude of the task which the directors of a centrally administered economy of an entire nation have to solve results usually in independent authorities being entrusted with particular branches of the economy, for example coal, iron, timber, cement, etc. To reconcile the economic plans of all these authorities is extremely difficult, because a satisfactory means of economic calculation is lacking, as well as for other reasons. If the attempt at reconciliation is unsuccessful, then a kind of group anarchy will result with a number of central authorities, and only nominally a centrally administered economy. Usually none of these difficulties appear in the simple centrally directed economy or the independent economic unit.

Note 33. On a scale of reckoning as a necessary condition for the functioning of an exchange economy see G. Cassel: *Theoretische Sozialökonomie*, para. 40.

Note 34. The theory of the different forms of market is old and was founded already by the Mercantilists, although they hardly got beyond an outline.

The classical economists, because they aimed at studying and discovering the natural course of the economy under natural conditions (see page 48), were not much interested in the different forms of market in the real world. Because of this, and later because of the division between historical and theoretical studies, the whole theory was dropped. Isolated attempts were made by Cournot (*Recherches sur les Principes Mathematiques de la Theorie des Richesses*, 1838), Carl Menger (*Grundsätze der Volkswirtschaftslehre*, 1871, pp. 175 ff.), and others, but were not enough to bring about a change.

This may explain why, up till now, there is not much clarity or agreement among economists, or in public discussion, as to what the important forms of market really are; for example, what perfect competition is. Perfect competition has been, and is still, often confused with "open markets", although all forms of market can be and often have been "open". But worst of all has been the confusion of "laissez-faire" with perfect competition. This can perhaps be understood for the beginning of the nineteenth century. It was then believed that by abolishing public monopolies, privileges, vetoes, etc., the condition of perfect competition could be produced. But it is inexcusable that this error was not recognised later in the nineteenth century and that still to-day "laissez-faire" is often identified with perfect competition. It could be easily shown that a policy of "laissez-faire" by no means results in perfect competition but in monopolies, partial monopolies, oligopolies, etc. This confusion is still to-day one of the most lasting of economic errors and particularly dangerous for those engaged in working out economic constitutions.

Modern research has aimed at defining the forms of market precisely. We have referred in the text to the dangers. Often a system of market forms is constructed *a priori* instead of being obtained from economic reality and found in it. Systems of market forms of this kind do not reproduce the forms in the actual economic world. For example, perfect competition is described as that form of market in which the influence of the individual is non-existent, which obviously is only the case when there is an infinite number of suppliers or demanders. Monopoly is defined as the opposite of this. That is, when a firm supplies the whole market and all possibilities of substitutes are excluded, so that only one firm can be supplying all goods for the whole world. Both cases are unrealistic and the real world lies in between them. Such definitions of competition and monopoly as these are of no help in getting to understand the variety of forms in the real economic world. They are useless for defining actual conditions. Working out the different forms of markets must start with the real phenomena. And these are to be found in the same way as the other ideal types of economic system. They have to be discovered. This can be done by studying the economic plans of actual economic units; for the planning data on which those taking part in a market construct their plans can be precisely ascertained. It is from these plans and not from the behaviour of economic units, a concept which can be given varying content, that the forms of market can be discovered. Forms of market obtained in this way, by studying economic reality, can solve the double problem with which they are faced, that is the understanding of actual economic systems (see pp. 222, 308) and the provision of a basis for theoretical analysis to be applied to the economic process and its inter-connections (see also page 227).

Of the extensive recent literature see Böhm-Bawerk: *Kapital und Kapitalzins*, Vol. 2, 3rd Ed., 1912, pp. 357 ff.; Wicksell: *Lectures on Political Economy*, Vol. I; Pareto: *Manuel d'économie politique*, 2nd Ed., 1927, Ch. III, 40; Sraffa in *Economic Journal*, 1926; Chamberlin: *Theory of Monopolistic Competition*; E. Schneider: *Reine Theorie monopolistischer Wirtschaftsformen*, 1932; J. Robinson: *The Economics of Imperfect Competition*, 1933, and her article, "What is Perfect Competition?" in *Economic Journal*, 1935; R. Frisch: "Monopole-Polypole—La notion de force dans l'économie", *Festschrift für Westergaard*, 1935; H. Stackelberg: *Marktform und Gleichgewicht*, 1934; also "Probleme der unvollkommenen Konkurrenz, *Weltwirtschaftliches Archiv*, 48, 1938, and "Grundlagen der Nationalökonomie", *Weltwirtschaftliches Archiv*, 51, 1940; L. Miksch: *Wettbewerb als Aufgabe*, 2. Aufl., 1947; E. Liefmann-Keil: *Organisierte Konkurrenz-Preisbildung*, 1936; Hans Möller: *Kalkulation, Absatzpolitik und Preisbildung*, 1941; for a tabular scheme of market forms see Stackelberg: *Marktform und Gleichgewicht*, p. 3, and Miksch: *op. cit.*, pp. 307 ff. On forms of market and economic power see p. 265 above.

Note 35. For the barter economy see Wicksell: *Lectures on Political Economy*, and C. Menger: *Grundsätze*, 2nd ed., 1923, Chapter 9.

Note 36. The analysis of monetary history is often made more difficult by the questions which are taken as the starting point. Usually monetary history is treated as a history of coinage or, especially under the influence of Knapp, from the point of view of legal history. It is only if *economic* questions are put as to the origin of money, as to the forms of market in which it originates, and as to the relationship between the unit of account and money, that theoretical treatment becomes possible.

For the monetary history of the ancient world see Ebert's article "Geld" in *Reallexikon der Vorgeschichte*, and numerous articles in Pauly-Wissowas. *Real-encycl. d. Klass. Altert. Wiss.* 4. Aufl.; Heichelheim: *op. cit.* The descriptions of medieval monetary systems usually deal primarily with the history of coinage. Hence they overlook the great significance of the notes of indebtedness of private people and of city and state authorities in the medieval economy. The difference between the unit of account and the means of exchange, such as existed on a considerable scale in the Middle Ages, is underestimated, and even the coined money is not really studied as an economic phenomenon. Of more recent works on medieval economic history we might particularly mention in this connection: Kuske: *op. cit.*; G. Mickwitz: *Aus Revaler Handelsbüchern*, 1938; M. M. Postan: "Private Financial Instruments in Medieval England" (*Vierteljahrsschrift f. Soz. v. Wirtschaftsgeschichte*, Bd. 23, 1930; M. Chiaudano; "Contratti di cambio, etc". (*Veröffentlichungen der Kgl. Ak. d. Wiss. von Turin*, 1931); H. Laurent: *La loi de Gresham au moyen âge*, 1933; I. Wackernagel: *Städtische Schuldscheine als Zahlungsmitted im 13. Jahrhundert*, 1942.

On the modern development of money and monetary systems see K. Helfferich: *Das Geld*, 6th Ed., 1923; E. Lukas: *Aufgaben des Geldes*, 1937; R. Stucken: *Deutsche Geld- und Kreditpolitik*, 1937; and F. Lutz: "Neue Goldwährung", *Weltwirtschaftliches Archiv.*, 46, 1937. A large part of the investment, and therefore of the industrialisation, of the late nineteenth and early twentieth centuries would not have taken place if money in the form of notes and bank money had not been created by the granting of credit by the banks. By this union of the granting of credit and the creation of money (or the repayment of credit and the cancellation of money), the whole relationship between investment and savings has been fundamentally altered. See A. Hahn: *Volkswirtschaftliche Theorie des Bankkredits*, 3rd Ed., 1930; H. Gestrich: *Kredit und Sparen*, 2nd Ed., 1947.

Note 37. On the subject of exchange economies with different forms of market, see Stackelberg: *Marktform und Gleichgewicht*, pp. 29 ff. and the literature mentioned there.

Note 38. An error made by some of the older monetary theorists was that of starting from the concept of the general price level, an average quantity and a theoretical construction with which the economic subject, confronted simply with *particular* prices, never reckons. From the concept of a price level nothing further can be deduced. Such an average quantity as the price level "can only be used, if necessary, at the end of an analysis to summarise a result and express in a single word or figure a total situation" (K. F. Maier: *op. cit.*, p. 18). See also Hayek: *Prices and Production*, 1931, pp. 3 ff.; Haberler: *Der Sinn der Indexzahlen*, 1927, pp. 70 f.; and from another point of view, A. Lösch: *Die räumliche Ordnung der Wirtschaft*, 2. Aufl., 1944.

Note 39. The classical economists often studied a form of exchange economy in which perfect competition was taken to hold in all markets, and in which at the same time a metal currency was in circulation. They were dealing with an extremely interesting combination of a form of market and monetary system, but simply with a *single* particular combination—a limiting case. Certainly the later classical economists went further than this when they recognised the importance for the whole economic process of the creation of paper money, an important step in which connection the works of Overstone (*Tracts and other Publications*, 1857, page 411) are particularly interesting.

The transition to a new way of formulating the problem was first made in Wicksell's *Interest and Prices*, 1898.

Note 40. Most accounts of the course of events in a centrally directed economy start as a rule from the question of how the economic process develops in such an economy, which is contrasted with a market economy, or "free" or capitalist economy (see Pareto: *Manuel*, Chapter 6, pp. 52 ff.; E. Barone: "The Ministry of Production in a Socialist State", *Collectivist Economic Planning*; Wieser: *Natural Value*, 1893; and the works mentioned in Note 32). Collectivism and a centrally directed economy are not the same thing. Collectivism describes an actual condition completely absent at some times but realised at others. Central direction of the economy occurs at all times and among all peoples. It has always been there and always is there. Certainly often there are only traces of central direction, but it has also often been the dominant element in an economic system, mostly in the simple form of the independent economy. Collectivism is an imprecise term for a number of different sorts of economic system in which elements of a centrally administered economy predominate. These elements of a centrally directed economy are always to be found in the real world and we extract them in order to discover an ideal type of economic system which we may use as an important model. This model is that of the centrally directed economy with its two forms, the simple centrally directed economy, and the centrally administered economy, each with its variants (see p. 119). In this way, as contrasted with other procedures, it is possible to understand the multiformity in economic history on the one hand, and on the other to construct models which represent precisely defined sets of conditions on the basis of which theories can be worked out.

A theory of the centrally directed economy which has to explain the economic process and its relationships in this economic system is both necessary and possible. It is necessary because the economic process in a centralised economy takes a different course from what it does in an exchange economy, and therefore actual economic systems which are predominantly under central direction take a different course from systems in which elements of an exchange economy are predominant. For example, the relation between production and distribution in the two cases is very different and the process of investment also. The influence of the tastes of individual consumers is much weaker, or completely excluded, in the centrally directed economy, consumers being quite powerless, particularly in the centrally administered economy, which is, however, able to concentrate much more easily on meeting a particular complex of requirements, for example, armaments. Money plays an entirely different role in the two systems and economic power has a completely different significance. These differences have emerged especially prominently in recent years, and theoretical analysis has to study them precisely. A theory of the centrally directed economy is perfectly possible, as our outline has tried to show, because the economic plans of the leaders, and therefore their actions, result from particular data and empirical rules, which makes it possible for the economic process and all its problems to be defined and described. One contemporary theoretical economist holds the view "that with the exchange economy that field of study is disappearing in which alone, throughout the whole field of social science, regular objective relationships can be ascertained". If he is right, then economics will have to abandon the understanding of a considerable part of economic reality. But he is wrong. Economists must not withdraw from an area where important knowledge is to be, and must be, obtained.

Note 41. On the need for a twofold treatment of stocks resulting from past production (partly as an economic problem and partly as an economic datum) see Eucken: *Kapitaltheoretische Untersuchungen*, 1934, and "Hauptproblem der Kapitaltheorie", *Jahrbuch für Nat.*, 1937. On the problems of capital, which we can only touch upon in this book, see the recent works of R. Strigl: *Kapital und Produktion*, 1934; v. Stackelberg: "Kapital und Zins in der stationären Verkehrswirtschaft", *Zeitschrift für Nationalök.*, Bd. X, 1941; E. Lindahl: *Studies in the Theory of Money and Capital*, 1939; J. R. Hicks: *Value and Capital*; F. A. Hayek: *Pure Theory of Capital*, 1941.

Note 42. For the first empirical rule (Gossen's first law) see Gossen: *Entwicklung der Gesetze des menschlichen Verkehrs*, 1854, and the articles cited in the article "Bedürfnis" (in *Handw. d. Staatsw.*, 4th Ed.) by H. Mayer. For the transformation of Gossen's law into the law of diminishing marginal rate of substitution see J. R. Hicks: *op. cit.*, p. 11, and Stackelberg: "Entwicklungsstufen der Werttheorie", *Schweiz. Zeitschrift f. Volksw.*, 1947.

Note 43. For the second empirical rule see T. N. Carver: *The Distribution of Wealth*, 1921, Chapter 2; Edgeworth: *Papers*, 1925, Vol. I; A. Mitscherlich: *Die Bestimmung des Düngerbedürfnisses des Bodens*, 1924; E. Schneider: *Theorie der Produktion*, 1934; see also Morgenstern's bibliography in the *Zeitschrift für Nationalök.*, 1931, No. 4.

For the third empirical rule, see E. v. Böhm-Bawerk: *Kapital und Kapitalzins*, 4th Ed., 1921; Burchardt in *Weltwirtschaftliches Archiv.*, 1931–32; N. Kaldor in *Econometrica*, 1937, pp. 201 ff.; Strigl: *Kapital und Produktion*, 1934; E. Schneider in *Jahrb. f. Nat.*, 1938; Eucken in *Jahrb. f. Nat.*, 1940, pp. 113 ff.

Note 44. On the problem of risk see Böhm-Bawerk: *op. cit.*, Book 4, Section 1; Knight: *Risk, Uncertainty and Profit*; H. Marquardt: *Die Ausrichtung der landwirtschaftlichen Produktion an den Preisen*, 1934; Marquardt writes (pp. 128–29): "The problem of risk must be treated as an independent theoretical problem. It is impossible to disregard the element of risk without the practical man shrugging his shoulders and saying, 'All this is quite different in practice from what it is in theory'. Our investigation as it has developed, has shown more and more clearly that realistic theory must take account in its analysis of the element of risk if it is not to remain helpless in face of the facts".

On the problem of expectations see C. Menger: *Grundsätze der Volkswirtschaftslehre*, 2nd Ed., 1923, p. 149; Pigou: *Industrial Fluctuations*, 2nd Ed., 1929; G. Myrdal: *Monetary Equilibrium*; Keynes: *General Theory*, 1936, Chapter 22.

Note 45. There is a considerable unity in modern economic theory, in the formulation of its problems, in its methods of thought, and in its principal results. It is by no means simply a disconnected series of propositions. For an introduction to modern economic theory we may refer readers to W. Röpke: *Die Lehre von der Wirtschaft*, 4th Ed., 1946; R. Strigl: *Einführung in die Grundlagen der Nationalökonomie*, 2nd Ed., 1935; Stackelberg: *Grundzüge der theoretischen Volkswirtschaftslehre*, 1943; E. von Böhm-Bawerk: *Kapital und Kapitalzins*, 4th Ed., 1921. See also Notes 8 and 10.

The approach to problems of monetary theory by way of an analysis of the individual economic unit is to be found among the older writers in C. Menger: *Grundsätze der Volkswirtschaftslehre*, 2nd Ed., 1923, pp. 325 ff.; L. Walras: *Élements*, 1926, pp. 320 ff.; A. Marshall: *Money, Credit and Commerce*, 1923, pp. 282 ff.; for more recent works see K. F. Maier: *Goldwanderungen*, 1935; H. Gestrich: *Kredit und Sparen*, 2nd Ed., 1947; J. R. Hicks: "A Suggestion for Simplifying the Theory of Money", *Economica*, 1935.

Note 46. On the concept of the static State and for criticism of this concept see Chapter 4 and the works mentioned in Note 58.

It must be specially emphasised that the constancy of data necessary for a static State must be completely adhered to, that is, tastes or needs in the present and future must remain constant. For a static State it is necessary that in formulating this year's economic plans the requirements for the following year must be foreseen to be the same as this year. Correspondingly replacements must be provided for, so that the stocks of goods produced, particularly stocks of durable means of production, are held at the same level. Otherwise the apparatus of production will be expanding or contracting. On the method of variations see also page 253.

Note 47. The following criticism has been made of Robinson Crusoe analysis: "To try and conceive of a number of Crusoes living together in a community is as confusing as trying to imagine a complete bowl as the fragments into which one is only subsequently going to smash it" (Gottl: *Bedarf und Deckung*, 1928, p. 70; for further criticism see Diehl: *Theoretische Nationalökonomie*, I, 2nd Ed., 1922, p. 4; Cassel: *Grundgedanken der Theoretischen Nationalökonomie*, 1926, pp. 10 f.; Sombart: *Die drei Nationalökonomien*, 1930, p. 176). Certainly such an idea would be fantastic, but no one holds it. The purpose of Crusoe analysis is quite different. If we are to continue to use this rather unfortunate comparison we may say that there is no need to fear that the bowl will be smashed. What we do is simply, first, to study a small bowl, the construction of which is relatively simple to understand. Then we turn to a number of larger bowls of more complicated construction, that is, the different forms of social economy, of which the structure and interrelationships can be more easily understood when we have first made a study of the smaller bowl. "It is for very good reasons", said Böhm-Bawerk, "that we take a look for a time at Robinson Crusoe before we venture to approach the complex picture presented by the real economic world. But the proper field for our theory is the social economy". On the great heuristic value of Crusoe analysis see M. Weber: *Gesammelte Aufsätze zur Wissenschaftslehre*, 1922, p. 196; H. Dietzel in *Jahrb. f. Nat.*, 1890, Vol. 54; Böhm-Bawerk in the same journal, 1892, Vol. 58; G. Sulzer: *Die Wirtschaftlichen Grundgesetze*, 1895, pp. 80 ff.; J. B. Clark: *Distribution of Wealth*, 1902, pp. 40 ff. For the Robinson Crusoe stories of the eighteenth century, which have no connection with modern theoretical economics, see H. Hettner: *Geschichte der deutschen Literatur im* 18. *Jahrhundert*, 6th Ed., 1912.

For the great heuristic value of the concept of a barter economy, in spite of the contrasts between a barter economy and a money economy see the conclusive arguments in Wicksell's *Interest and Prices.* For an examination of Say's law for a barter economy and for a monetary economy see L. Micksch: *Gibt es eine allgemeine Überproduktion?* 1929.

Note 48. Cassel's work *The Theory of Social Economy* is the best known of the modern attempts of theoretical economists to construct a unified theory of the exchange economy while disregarding the different forms of particular markets and giving only a subsidiary treatment of the socialist economy. Cassel's intention is to study an exchange economy, leaving aside competition and monopoly, in which the quantities of goods are distributed for the whole economy in the most rational way. As the formation of prices is strictly according to the principles of cost, this one case alone is given exclusive study. The theory thereby attains great formal unity, but is less suited for the explanation of the real economic world. (See W. Kromphardt: *Die Systemidee im Aufbau der Casselschen Theorie*, 1927, and Schumpeter in *Schmollers Jahrbuch*, 1927, pp. 241 ff.)

Some historical economists, partly with a view to bringing historical and theoretical economics closer together, have tried to begin with a "timeless" theory and then go on to theories limited in application to a particular period. Spiethoff, for example, talks of a "timeless economy", to the theory of which he gives first place. By a "timeless" economy he understands a social economy directed by a single will, in which there are no independent economic units. This is simply a centrally directed economy like Wieser's "simple economy". Although for theoretical work it may prove convenient to apply the results of the analysis of a centrally directed economy to the analysis of the exchange economy, we are not entitled *a priori* to describe the centrally directed economy as a timeless economy. Which economic phenomena are subject to change and which are not cannot be laid down *a priori* but only *a posteriori*; that is, in the course of analysing the actual historical facts (Spiethoff in *Schmollers Jahrbuch*, 1932, pp. 892 and 918; Vleugels in *Schmollers Jahrbuch*, 1937, pp. 279 f.).

Note 49. Propositions about changes in economic life resulting from changes in data are, when properly arrived at, logically necessary.

But such propositions cannot be made about changes which economic events bring in the data. Such statements are only problematical.

Here are some examples: economic theory can state exactly how certain changes in data can result from a rise in wages. But whether and how far the rise in wages will lead to an increase in the efficiency of the worker (that is, to a change in the datum "labour") cannot be exactly determined. Attempts to do this have usually resulted in failure. Similarly monetary theory helps one to prove precisely what changes in economic life would follow from a policy of deflation. In the real world a lengthy deflationary depression will in a modern state lead to severe political crises, to changes in economic policy, and to changes in the economic system. But whether these reactions in the data follow, and what sort of reactions they will be, depends so very much on the particular structure of the individual states and on many other historical facts, that economic theory must refrain from laying down any certain conclusions.

Note 50. The mistake of treating as data problems which themselves need a solution is often made in the theory of the balance of payments. Imports and exports of a country are regarded as given quantities in the balance of payments and then the relation between the debit and credit side of the balance is treated as explaining the level of the exchange rate and changes in it. But the imports and exports of a country are no more given quantities than the other items in the balance of payments. They depend on the prices in the trading countries as well as on the rates of exchange. The theory of the balance of payments is incomplete and has had harmful effects on exchange-rate policy because it has not correctly described the causes of currency depreciations. (On this see Haberler: *Theory of International Trade*; Eucken: *Kritische Betrachtungen zum deutschen Geldproblem*, 1923, Chapter 1.)

Note 51. Without some dividing line between what is to be taken as data and what not, theoretical study is impossible. All theoretical economists since the beginnings of economic theory work with data. That often these are described not as data but as "given factors" or "basic conditions" or even "productive power" is not important. What is essential is that the data are often incompletely set out.

What Friedrich List called "productive power" belongs really to what we call the economic data. He describes this elsewhere and more extensively as follows: "It is scarcely possible to imagine a law or public regulation which does not exercise a greater or lesser effect on the degree of productive power". We would prefer to say "which does not alter one of the data". It must also be the task of economic policy "to stimulate and preserve the productive power of a country".

So far List is quite right. But he is wrong when he calls for a theory of productive power which he wants to put side by side with the theory of value. By a theory of productive power he understands a theory which is to explain how the economic data in the real world have come into existence. An attempt to create such a theory is bound to fail because the formation of economic data in the real world can only be explained historically. For example, the question why Germany to-day has a particular population of particular abilities and level of education, or why a certain kind of social and legal system exists in Germany, can only be understood and explained historically. "Theoretical explanations can only go as far as the data, to explain which is no longer the task of economic theory", said Böhm-Bawerk in the course of a criticism of Wieser. He continued, "This particular datum is one of the technique of production which permits of no explanation by economic theory, any more than economic theory has the task of explaining, when analysing examples of Robinson Crusoe allocating five sacks of corn between different uses, why Crusoe has particular needs, why he puts them in a particular order, and what importance he attaches to the satisfaction of each one" (*Positive Theory of Capital*, Exkurs VII).

On the subject of economic data see also J. B. Clark: *Essentials of Economic Theory*, 1907; J. Schumpeter: *Theory of Economic Development*, 1934; and *Archiv für Sozialwissenschaft*, 1916–17, pp. 3 ff.; R. Strigl: *Die Ökonomischer Kategorien und die Organisation der Wirtschaft*, 1923; L. Robbins: *An Essay on the Nature and Significance of Economic Science*, 1932; F. Lutz: *Das Konjunkturproblem in der Nationalökonomie*, 1932, pp. 65 ff. and 116 ff.; Ciriocy-Wantrup: *Agrarkrisen und Stockungsspannen*, 1936, pp. 362 ff.; K. F. Maier: *op. cit.*, pp. 56 ff.; F. W. Meyer: *Der Ausgleich der Zahlungsbilanz*, 1938, pp. 14 f. and 159 ff.

The different data need further classification into data from the point of view of the individual economic unit, data from the point of view of the economy as a whole, planning data, and *ex post* data. From our study the conclusion follows that the task of obtaining the data cannot be left to sociology or history, which are not fitted for carrying it out. The economist, when formulating economic problems and abstracting and analysing their significant characteristics, is bound to have to deal with the conditions on which the course of economic events depends. It is these conditions which we are calling data.

Note 52. On the economic system of the Jesuit community in Paraguay see P. Hernández: *Organización sozial de las doctrinas Guaranies*, 1912; M. Fassbinder: *Der* "Jesuitenstaat" *in Paraguay*, 1926.

Note 53. The influence of economics on the study of economic history has often not been favourable because a system of concepts has been applied which does not do justice to historical reality. The very valuable works of Strieder are among those which suffer from a very extensive use of the term "Capitalism".

Heichelheim (*Wirtschaftsgeschichte des Altertums*, 1938) attempts to use Spiethoff's concept of the "style" of economic development. I should like to repeat that the unsatisfactory results of this attempt are not the fault of the historian but of the economist, who ought not to supply such unrealistic constructions as "stages" or "styles" of economic development, but a morphological system built out of historical reality which the economic historian can apply to actual economic systems, and with which he can explain them. (On this see A. Rüstow: *op. cit.*)

Note 54. There are often misunderstandings about the knowledge with which the hypothetical propositions of economic theory provide us. It is held that economic theory consists simply of hypotheses, that is, of provisional conditional assumptions about an explanation, which may fill out a gap in our knowledge. This is a serious mistake from which an incorrect attitude to all theoretical work is apt to result. We are using the term "hypothetical proposition" in the strict logical sense (that is, "*if* a *then* b"). The hypothetical proposition states that a particular conclusion emerges from a particular premise. It is based on the principle of sufficient reason. Hypothetical propositions express logical reasoning and every thinking man is continually making use of them. The contrast to hypothetical propositions is, of course, categorical propositions ("x *is* y"). When rightly arrived at hypothetical propositions are unconditionally and absolutely true and in no sense provisionally so. Any textbook of logic makes this clear and misunderstandings on this point are scarcely excusable.

Note 55. On the methodological problems of applied theory see the works mentioned in Note 51; on the difference between truth and relevance see also my article "Die Überwindung des Historismus", *Schmollers Jahrbuch*, 1938, p. 212; also pp. 227, 306, of this book.

It is easy to understand why the application of theories has been neglected in economics and in scientific method. For the formalist or "conceptual" economist, or for the dualist or purely empirical economist, there is no question of an application of theory. It is useless to want to construct a particular applied theory; the application of abstract theories, if they are to explain actual historical conditions, must proceed from case to case. The distinction between abstract and concrete is confused, if an applied theory is contrasted with a so-called pure theory.

Note 56. On the limits set by insufficient information to the understanding of economic life in ancient times see also pp. 75 ff. Economic history and economics must go as far as they can within these limits. They can only do this if they put first the question of the structure of the system and investigate the sources from this standpoint.

Note 57. On the Great Antimony and its solution see also pp. 34, 304 ff.

Note 58. On the older literature concerning dynamic theories see Schumpeter: *Theory of Economic Development* (on Schumpeter's dynamic theory see E. v. Beckerath in *Schmollers Jahrbuch*, 1929, pp. 1 ff.). Of recent literature we would mention particularly E. Lundberg: *Studies in the Theory of Economic Expansion*, 1937 (on this and on the position of the discussion in general see V. Smith in *Weltwirtschaftliches Archiv*, 1938, pp. 613 ff.); A. C. Pigou: *The Economics of Stationary States*; Keynes: *General Theory of Employment, Interest and Money*; A. H. Hansen: *Economic Stabilisation in an Unbalanced World*. On theories of development in economic history and on their relation with Comte and Positivism, see pp. 64, 70, and on the static State see p. 203.

For accounts of modern trade-cycle analysis see Röpke: *Crises and Cycles* (introductory); G. Haberler: *Prosperity and Depression*, 3rd Ed., 1941. For a fundamental criticism of dynamic and trade-cycle theories see also the works mentioned in Note 21.

Criticism of trade-cycle theories has been met with the argument that it is not only particular trade cycles which have the quality of uniqueness, but *all* economic phenomena, for example, even prices. Therefore it must be equally possible to build not only a theory of prices, but a theory of the trade cycle. But this overlooks an essential distinction. Prices are demanded and paid millions of times every day uniformly. Whereas a single trade cycle, for example, the German depression of 1907–8, or the following boom of 1909–13, are unique phenomena, not uniform and only showing *certain* similarities with other cyclical movements. There is none of the uniformity which is to be found in prices and which is an essential pre-condition for putting general theoretical questions about prices and for constructing a successful theory of prices. (See also my *Kapitaltheoretische Untersuchungen*, 1934, pp. 15 ff., on the uniformity of economic phenomena and on this entire question.)

Note 59. Discussion of the problem of economic power by economists usually revolves around the question whether and how far it is economic law, or political and economic power, that decisively determines the economic process. In contrast with the theoretical economists who maintain that it is the former which is decisive, economic historians emphasise the importance of power though they do not investigate it precisely. This antithesis and this question are not of much help and ought to disappear. The first task of the economist is to ascertain the basic conditions on which economic power rests, and to study the effects of economic power in the real world. (This also leads to highly important conclusions for the problem of framing an economic constitution.) In a period like the present in which great concentrations of economic power are taking place on a large scale this task is an urgent one.

On this question see Böhm-Bawerk: "Macht oder ökonomisches Gesetz?", *Gesammelte Schriften*, 1924, pp. 230 ff.; J. Schumpeter: "Das Grundprinzip der Verteilungstheorie", *Archiv für Sozialwissenschaft*, 1916–17; F. Kestner: *Organisationszwang*, 2nd Ed., 1927. The attitude of the Historical School to modern problems of economic power was clearly expressed in the transactions of the Verein für Sozialpolitik in 1905, which were opened with a paper by Schmoller.

On the ideologies of economic pressure groups see p. 26 ff.

There is no history of economic ideas about power and of the attitude of economists to economic power from the Mercantilists onwards. On the general problems of power in history see Thucydides, Book V, Machiavelli's *Prince*, and Jakob Burkhardt's *Aspects of World History*.

Note 60. On the "principle of meeting needs", or "production for use", as contrasted with the profit principle, see Sombart: *Modern Capitalism*, and *Der Bourgeois*, also his *Ordnung des Wirtschaftslebens*, 2nd Ed., 1927; also Laum: *Allgemeine Geschichte der Wirtschaft*, 1932, pp. 20 f.; Spiethoff in *Schmollers Jahrbuch*, No. 56, p. 911; Rüstow, *op. cit.*, pp. 151 ff. On the economic attitude of mankind in the ancient world and in the Middle Ages see the works mentioned in Notes 16 and 18, also for the Middle Ages: G. Espinas: *Les origines du capitalisme*, I, 1933; Strieder: "Geldwirtschaft und Frühkapitalismus", in Vol. IV of the Propylaen *Weltgeschichte*; Kelter in *Schmollers Jahrbuch*, 1932; Zwiedineck-Südenhorst: *Weltanschauung und Wirtschaft*, 1942; and the works mentioned by Sieveking in his *Wirtschaftsgeschichte*, 1935, p. 79.

Of course, not all the long-distance traders of the fourteenth century were like the Warendorps in Lübeck, or those of the late fifteenth century like the Fuggers in Augsburg. There were many differences and changes in the course of time in one and the same city and family. Very often generations of enterprising and adventurous men were succeeded by generations of rentiers. Such changes have in many cases left profound effects on medieval economic history. The attitude also of peasants and craftsmen has often changed. Often they have been content with a certain standard of nutrition and often not; sometimes they have been peaceful and sometimes aggressive. To characterise the economic attitude of medieval men as one of "meeting needs" and that of modern man as one of profit-seeking is in two respects unhistorical. A single word is being used to obscure the variations in the economic behaviour of different nations, regions, social strata, and periods; and a multiformity is being obscured which can be very easily traced in the medieval sources, and which everyone to-day who is active in the real economic world is aware of for his own time and country. Secondly, the contrast between the modern and medieval attitude to economic life is grossly exaggerated and the human qualities which pervade it not sufficiently regarded. In the text we spoke of the similarities between medieval guildsmen and modern trade-unionists, and between the long-distance traders in the Middle Ages and the modern entrepreneurs. The differences were often not those they are usually imagined to be to-day. "If one has studied profoundly in the sources it becomes quite obvious that the old type of business man often had an economic morality far more disreputable than the contemporary one. He profiteered, cheated, perjured himself, evaded taxes and duties. He borrowed irresponsibly and tried to "do down" his creditors and make excessive profits. Such conduct simply corresponded to his still imperfectly developed economic status and is therefore scarcely to be wondered at" (Kuske).

Note 61. On the economic principle see H. Dietzel: *Theoretische Sozialökonomik*, 1895, pp. 175 f.; O. von Zwiedineck-Südenhorst: *Allgemeine Volkswirtschaftslehre*, 1932, Introduction; H. Möller in *Jahrbuch f. Nat. u. Stat.*, 1942, pp. 241 ff.; A. Fey; *Der homo œconomicus in der Klassischen Nationalökonomie und seine Kritik durch den Historismus*, Marburg, 1936. It is perfectly correct to wish to prove (as recently W. A. Jöhr did in his *Theoretische Grundlagen der Wirtschaftspolitik*, 1943, Vol. I, Chapter 8) that human behaviour is not only to be explained by the striving for the maximum profit, that is, by "capitalistic" motives. Self-preservation, fear, hatred, the lust for power, love, humanitarianism, and other motives, determine in very differing degrees men's actions. But it is not to be concluded from this that because of extra-economic objectives and motives the economic principle is disregarded.

The economic principle has nothing to do with the aims or purposes of human actions. The aims differ greatly and may be egoistic or altruistic, but it will always be according to the economic principle. The head of a monastery may well have no notions of aiming at the maximum profit and act entirely in the service of humanity, but in cultivating his fields, using raw materials, buying goods, and spending charitable gifts, he will be planning and acting in accordance with the economic principle. That is, he will be trying to fulfil a particular purpose with the minimum possible expenditure, in order to maximise the welfare from his fields, raw materials, etc.

Note 62. From what we have said in the text it is clear that the antithesis, so often misapplied, of a "*rational*" as contrasted with a "*traditional*" economic policy must be very carefully handled. Only when an alteration in the level of prices, or in technical knowledge, or in some other datum, makes necessary some new combination of the means of production, but while nevertheless the old obsolescent technique of production is maintained, does a discrepancy arise between rationalist and traditional economic behaviour. Otherwise if technical knowledge and other data remain approximately the same a traditional and a rational economic production policy come to the same thing. See H. Marquardt: *op. cit.*

Note 63. Irving Fisher in his *Elementary Principles of Economics*, 1921, pp. 312 ff. and 137 ff., gives some examples from the labour market of a rise in price being followed by a diminution in supply. "Recent experiments in the coal mines have shown", says Fisher, "that a small rise in the wages of the workers causes them to work longer hours, but that a large rise (60 per cent. above the usual wage) makes for irregular work and a desire to lessen the hours of work". See also Schumpeter's article "Angebot" in *Handwörterbuch der Staatswiss*, 4th Ed.; A. Tschajanow: *Die Lehre von der bäuerlichen Wirtschaft*, 1923; for a mathematical treatment see Stackelberg in *Archiv für mathematische Wirtschafts- und Sozialforschung*, 1938, Vol. IV.

The Mercantilists took it as a general rule that a fall in wages led to an increase in the supply of labour and this strongly influenced Mercantilist wage policy (see E. F. Heckscher: *Mercantilism*). Marshall (*Principles of Economics*, Book 6, Chapters 2 and 12) gave a warning that the number of these cases should not be exaggerated.

When we distinguish between two different kinds of behaviour, according as to whether a man has a changing or a constant level of needs, we are referring to the needs for goods and not to that for leisure. This latter need is not taken account of. The worker who works less when wages are raised is satisfying his needs for other goods and services in the same way as before, but is satisfying more fully than before his need for leisure. This separation between the need for leisure and other needs is legitimate, because as contrasted with the others it is precisely by abstaining from economic activity that the need for leisure is satisfied.

Note 64. The question of how the course of economic events is influenced by action according to the principle of maximum net receipts as contrasted with the principle of optimum output, has never yet been answered in detail. A satisfactory theoretical study must put and answer this problem for the different types of economic system, for the different forms of centrally directed economy, and for the different forms of market and monetary systems.

When the contrast between the profit motive and the principle of "meeting needs", or "production for use" is abandoned, it will be much easier to answer the historical question as to the differences in men's attitudes to economic life and how this affects the course of economic events.

Note 65. At the beginning of the nineteenth and twentieth centuries science was dominated by the desire to study individual phenomena and to get a grasp of the whole variety of human behaviour throughout all the different periods of history. Here lay both its weakness and its strength. Its strength was in stimulating a perception of the multiformity and variety of the historical world. Its weakness was in carrying these efforts too far, and seeing the men of a particular period as constantly changing, not noticing that certain basic characteristics are common to mankind at all times and places. In this way the Historical School forfeited its ability to understand human behaviour. It saw not living human beings, but a scheme of developing "types". It was in this way that such unhistorical and unrealistic contrasts as that between the principle of "meeting needs" (or "production for use") and the principle of the profit motive came to be adopted, and that the attempt was seriously made to try to characterise the whole economic spirit of entire periods of history by the one phrase or the other.

The historians of the nineteenth and the beginning of the twentieth centuries saw as their task that of working out the peculiarities of the different periods of history and of the different particular nations. This was something of a regression as contrasted with that of the seventeenth and eighteenth centuries. Whether we are thinking of Descartes or Kant, or of the economists, the conviction was firmly held that however great the differences between individual men might be, they did not comprise their entire character, but that throughout history there had been common basic qualities. This attitude often led to underestimation of the special characteristics of particular nations, periods, and personalities. Even the economic man was regarded by the classical economists as a constant uniform figure who, so they believed, could be found everywhere and at all times. On the other hand, the economists of that period were not, like their successors, blind to the basic permanent characteristics of human behaviour. Here lay their strength and to this extent their understanding of human beings was the greater.

A correct understanding of men in their economic life would involve a synthesis of these two attitudes.

Note 66. The concept of a type first received a definite scientific content from Plato and, in particular, from Aristotle. Aristotle uses it in all his works in his persistent efforts to combine individual phenomena into wholes. The type stands somewhere between the individual phenomenon and the general. "It aims at discovering the general permanent characteristics of phenomena, and at bringing together what is related in them, and thereby at helping towards a *general* explanation and solution" (Rudolf Eucken: *Die Methode der Aristotelischen Forschung*, 1872, pp. 44 f.). Aristotle's conception of "types" was therefore near that of the real type. "One of the most significant developments in the sciences recently has been the simultaneous appearance of the concept of the type in a number of most widely differing fields, such as zoology, botany, crystallography, chemistry and philology" (W. Wundt: *Logik*, II, 3rd Ed., p. 55). It must be added that the use of the concept of the type was also spreading in history, psychology, and economics (see E. Seiterich: *Die Logische Struktur des Typenbegriffs bei W. Stein, E. Spranger and M. Weber*, 1930). These were mostly cases of the "real" type.

On the building of "ideal" types Max Weber wrote: "They are obtained by a one-sided emphasis on one or more different characteristics, and by bringing together a quantity of different and discreet phenomena which agree in possessing the particular characteristic which has been one-sidedly extracted. These are unified into a single picture. In its full purity this picture is never to be found empirically in the real world. It is "utopian", and the task of the historian is to ascertain in each single case how near or how far the real world approximated to this ideal picture, that is, for example, how far the economic relations in a particular city corresponded to the concept of the 'City Economy' " (*Gesammelte Aufsätze zur Wissenschaftslehre*, 1922, pp. 189 ff., 275 ff., 372 ff.; and *The Theory of Social and Economic Organisation*, Chapter 1). What Weber has to say on the construction of ideal types is not only very incomplete but contains serious defects. He failed to recognise both the fundamental difference between real types and ideal types and their logical character, as well as the differences in the process of abstraction in constructing the two kinds of types. Consequently what he calls an "ideal type" is very vaguely defined. Certainly he criticised the widespread misuse of "real" types (see above, p. 91), but at the same time he accepted Bücher's "stages" of economic development as ideal types (e.g. in *Handwörterbuch der Staatswissenschaften*, 3rd Ed., article "Agrargeschichte des Altertums"). He calls both the medieval "city economy" and the quite differently constructed model of a Crusoe economy "ideal types", thereby contributing to the usual confusion between ideal types and real types which we have already discussed (see Note 24). It is necessary to criticise Max Weber here because his views about the construction of types are still influential to-day, and because it is essential to clear up this important complex of problems. We are not trying to develop a new concept of the ideal type in opposition to Weber's, but simply to define precisely and completely what Weber treated obscurely and incompletely. (On Max Weber see B. Pfister: *Die Entwicklung zum Idealtypus*, 1928; v. Schelting: *Max Webers Wissenschaftslehre*, 1936, pp. 319 ff.) As regards the name itself see Sigwart (*Logik*, II, 2nd Ed., 1893, pp. 240 f.), who spoke of "types which we regard as ideal or perfect for the purpose of comparing particular examples with them". Perhaps Max Weber was influenced by Sigwart's theory. The influence of Weber's theory of types has been strange. Not only was it taken over with all its considerable defects, but it was even believed that Weber had discovered the ideal type. For this latter misunderstanding Weber himself was in no way responsible. Theoretical studies had already long before made use of ideal types, as Weber himself emphasised. The classical economists used such intellectual models. Thünen, for example, did so too, and made some brilliant remarks about their logical character (preface to the 2nd Ed. of his *Isolated State*, also N. Senior: *Lectures on Political Economy*, 1852; J. S. Mill: *Logic*, 5th Ed., Book 6, Chapter 9, para. 3). It is hardly necessary to refer to the use of types in modern theoretical studies, although their logical character has often not been clearly understood.

On the difference between real types and ideal types we may point out that the "household economy" of Bücher is a real type. The concept of a household economy is intended to explain or represent economic reality in the ancient world and in the early Middle Ages. On the other hand, the isolated state of Thünen is an ideal type which is used as an intellectual model. It is a state with a large town lying in the middle of a fertile plain of which the land is uniform in quality and which is cut off from the rest of the world by an impenetrable wilderness, and where perfect competition prevails throughout. Thünen is not portraying any real state of affairs with his isolated state, but he obtains it from the study of the real world. He extracted one aspect of the real economic world and worked out from it this ideal type, which helps him to reveal the relationships between actual events. In the same way we have discovered the different forms of economic systems, the types of centrally directed economy, the forms of market, and the monetary systems. In fact, we have discovered our whole morphological system in the facts of the real economic world. That is where they are and where the scientist has to discover them. These different systems do not exist in their pure form, but are often mixed with one another. In so far as we extract their significant characteristics we isolate them from their particular combination in the real world and give them a pure form. Thus we arrive at our types, which do not portray by themselves the real economic world, but are really "ideal" in the logical sense. The contrast between "real" and "ideal" types is a logical one. Neither "ideal" nor "real" is meant normatively; the "ideal" type is not an ideal of perfection, and is in no way an ethical concept (see also p. 69 and Note 13 and the references given there).

The question has arisen of how the ideal types are related with what are called "models". The pure forms which are abstracted from the real economic world are used as models from which theoretical deductions follow. For example, "monopoly" has been and is usually combined with other forms, but we isolate it and use it as a model or ideal type, that is, a precise set of conditions on the basis of which the theory of monopoly explains how prices are formed and what quantities are supplied. Models when correctly worked out are not "constructed". Quite the opposite.

If models are simply constructed *a priori*, as has often been the case with the different forms of market (see examples in Note 34), then naturally one can make as many different models as one wishes, but their value will be small for understanding economic life, and so will that of the theories which are built on them. Such models serve only as an intellectual game, like chess. Certain conditions are fixed and then deductive reasoning has a full field to play in. Nobody holds that the game of chess resembles anything in the real world, or is applicable for understanding its problems, nor is an intellectual game such as that played with arbitrarily constructed models. The theory of types and the analysis of the different forms of economic life is still full of difficulties. This is comprehensible, for the abstraction of significant characteristics, and the discovery of pure forms in the real economic world, is something quite different from the massing together of unanalysed facts in "stages" or "styles" of economic development, as carried on by the Historical School. The working out of the different forms of markets, and of all other types, can only be achieved by economists working on the phenomena of the real world, that is firms and households, studying them morphologically, and refraining from being led away from their field of study by outside discussions.

Note 67. On the logical character of economic theory see p. 230 and Note 25. Goethe said very relevantly (*Maxims and Reflections*, Jubiläum Edition, IV, p. 231): "Theory by itself is only useful in so far as it makes us see the relations between different phenomena". Schiller too, whose work on scientific method should not be overlooked, distinguishes very significantly between three levels of understanding. At the common empirical level, "which does not go beyond the mere empirical phenomenon itself", perceptions are always "single and accidental". Common empiricism has only a single empirical element and nothing beyond. Rationalism looks for "the causes behind phenomena". "The use of the understanding in my opinion is a necessary condition *sine qua non* of all science, but it is in danger of separating what in nature is connected". At the third level, that of "rational empiricism", as Schiller calls it, common empiricism and rationalism are combined into scientific understanding. "So we find that only a full and free working of our intellectual powers combined with the purest and widest use of our sense perceptions makes for scientific understanding" (letter to Goethe of 19 January, 1798). Schiller has certainly described the decisive step. Further see Lotze: *Logic*, 1874, pp. 92 ff., 175 ff., 378 ff.

Note 68. On definitions, their value, their role, and their misuse, see pp. 25, 50, 95, 133, 298, and Notes 1, 9, and 23.

Note 69. Husserl: *Logische Untersuchungen*, I, 15; see also above, pp. 37 ff.

Note 70. The discussion of the Historical School and its methods in *Schmollers Jahrbuch* for 1937 and 1938 gives a description of how the idea of truth was undermined and destroyed during the nineteenth and the beginning of the twentieth century by the "historicising" of all branches of thought and of values, and particularly of economics. This discussion suffered somewhat from the fact that the personality of Schmoller himself was too much in the forefront. In reality "Historismus" with its notion of the relativity of truth was a movement which affected the whole intellectual life of the time.

But it involved itself in contradictions. Schumpeter writes: "The purpose and value of this intellectual approach are clear. As far as practical scientific work is concerned we are operating not with "truths" but with *methods*; that is, simply working on the data in such a way as to arrive at results which correspond with our observations (preface to the 4th Ed., *Theory of Economic Development*, 1935). In criticism of this we must add that every relativist, including Schumpeter himself, claims that his relativist principles are true absolutely, and in spite of disclaimers to the contrary works with a concept of truth which is thus in contradiction with his own principles. Similarly Pareto, with his great influence, who was constantly concerned to prove that the notion of truth can be dispensed with, nevertheless regarded this "truth" as true. "Spengler's work", said Ortega, "contradicts itself in that he does not notice that his proof of the relativity of cultures, that is of men's actions, has itself an absolute form. In so far as the historian discovers the relativity of human history he is concerned with knowledge which is no longer merely relative" (*Die Aufgabe unserer Zeit*, pp. 228 f.). "Everything is relative only my relativist opinion is absolute". This is surely a position which it is difficult to believe and maintain.

Note 71. For the treatment of economic problems from the standpoint of general history see pp. 91, 223, 247, 256, 295.

Note 72. On the contrast between our concept of economic systems on the one hand and the "stages" and "styles" of economic development on the other see pp. 90, 109, 223.

On the impossibility of creating a special theory for each economic system see pp. 99, 235, 236, and Note 26.

Note 73. The separation of economic theory from the theory of business administration results simply from a misunderstanding of their problems. On the attitude of recent writings on business administration see M. Lohmann in *Weltw. Archiv.*, 1936, Vol. 44. Of recent work on business administration in which its relations with economic theory are maintained we would mention M. R. Lehmann: *Allgemeine Betriebswirtschaftslehre*, 1928; W. Prion: *Die Lehre vom Wirtschaftsbetrieb*, 1935, especially Book I; M. Lohmann: *Betriebswirtschaftslehre*, 1936.

Note 74. On contemporary problems of economic constitutional policy and their solution see the works mentioned in Note 19.

Note 75. On the relation between law and economics see F. Böhm: *Wettbewerb und Monopolkampf*, 1933, and *Die Ordnung der Wirtschaft*, 1937; H. Grossmann-Doerth in *Der Hanseat. Rechts-Zeitschr.*, 20. Jahrg., 1937, pp. 282 ff.; G. Schmölders in *Zeitschrift für die gesamte Staatswissenschaft*, Vol. 101, 1940, pp. 64 ff. The theory of the different forms of market ought to be particularly fruitful for legal thinking and legal policy. For example, property rights for someone who is a monopolist are entirely different in content from those of someone who is in competition with others. The monopolist owner of a mineral spring who supplies a village with water is in an entirely different position from the owner of a spring who is in competition with other suppliers. In the case of the monopolist, his power is much larger and the inhabitants of the village are dependent on the owner of the spring, unless fresh competition in the supply of water emerges. The problems of limiting property rights, and of the legal force of contracts, have an entirely different significance according to the form of market. They have to be treated differently both from the point of view of policy and from that of scientific study, according to the different forms of market obtaining in each case.

I wish to acknowledge a debt of thanks to various colleagues and others for many valuable suggestions. Paul Hensel and Hans Otto Lenel of Freiburg were kind enough to read the proofs. Once more I owe a very special debt of thanks to my wife.

INDEX OF NAMES

INDEX OF SUBJECTS

MIX
Papier aus verantwortungsvollen Quellen
Paper from responsible sources
FSC® C105338

If you have any concerns about our products,
you can contact us on
ProductSafety@springernature.com

In case Publisher is established outside the EU,
the EU authorized representative is:
Springer Nature Customer Service Center GmbH
Europaplatz 3, 69115 Heidelberg, Germany

Printed by Libri Plureos GmbH
in Hamburg, Germany